Beer Lover's Texas

Mike Cortez

Globe
Pequot

Guilford, Connecticut

Globe Pequot

An imprint of Rowman & Littlefield

Distributed by NATIONAL BOOK NETWORK

Copyright © 2015 by Rowman & Littlefield

All photography by the author
Maps: Alena Joy Pearce © Rowman & Littlefield

British Library Cataloguing in Publication Information Available

Library of Congress Cataloging-in-Publication Data is available
ISBN 978-1-4930-0654-0 (pbk. : alk. paper)
ISBN 978-1-4930-1721-8 (electronic)

∞™ The paper used in this publication meets the minimum requirements of American National Standard for Information Sciences—Permanence of Paper for Printed Library Materials, ANSI/NISO Z39.48-1992.

All the information in this guidebook is subject to change. We recommend that you call ahead to obtain current information before traveling.

Contents

About the Author

Mike Cortez was born and raised in Houston, Texas, and currently resides in Austin. He has worked as a writer and photographer for many different publications and websites ranging from the *Houston Chronicle* to the Thrillist. With a deep appreciation for writing about the art of food and drinks, Mike runs the blogs *Bite Me Austin* and *Texas Beer Guide*. One of his biggest passions aside from craft beer is supporting local businesses and organizing events that benefit charitable organizations and those in need. Mike continues to learn about the art of homebrewing and hopes to one day open a brewpub of his own.

Acknowledgments

Writing this book has been an exciting experience for me. I got to meet some great people on the road while visiting the breweries, brewpubs, and craft beer bars in the state. I enjoyed many amazing beers, feasted on delicious Texas barbecue, and saw some beautiful natural scenery. I spent nearly every weekend for seven months traveling Texas to make this book, and I would like to thank all of the brewers that took the time to talk with me, especially during holiday weekends.

A big thank you goes out to Jessica Torres, who kept me motivated and joined me on most of the trips. I can't thank you enough for all of the moral support and keeping me going. I would also like to thank my friends Joshua Govea and Nathan Jefferson, who got me into homebrewing. To my parents, Louis and Rosalind Cortez, thank you for all of the support y'all have given me and always encouraging me to go big. To all of my friends and family who have been there for me and were so understanding about my absence from so many events while writing this book, I am sorry and thank you. Lastly, thank you to the person who helped me with my very first blog and got me started in writing.

I raise a pint to all of the great people I have met on this journey and to all of the hardworking men and women brewing beer in this great state. I apologize to all of the great breweries that opened after I started this project and could not be included in the book. I am so excited to see the continued growth and success of all Texas breweries. Thank you all for all you do!

Introduction

Welcome to Texas. It is the second largest state in the country and over the last 5 years has become a booming craft beer destination. Texas breweries have helped add jobs and boost the state's economy. Beer drinkers' palates have started to evolve in search of something new and more refined, which is where craft brewers have stepped up. Craft beer has become an art form; brewers use only the best ingredients to create amazing ales and lagers that have won numerous medals and accolades. In a state where everything is big, the brewers in Texas have worked hard to make beers that turn heads and keep the taste buds delighted.

For as long as beer has been brewed in the state, Lone Star, Pearl, and Shiner have been the best known beers, but today there are many different beers to choose from. Austin and the surrounding Hill Country have long been the epicenter for the craft beer explosion in the state, but Dallas, Houston, and San Antonio are quickly growing and adding more great beers to the market. Until recently, much of the state west of Austin was considered commercial beer territory, but thanks to a growing number of craft beer bars and gastropubs, west Texas residents are getting a taste of craft beer. With so many breweries popping up in the state, some have chosen to establish themselves in smaller rural towns to reach a different audience, but it can sometimes be a challenge to make beer that will be appreciated both by commercial beer drinkers and those with refined craft beer palates.

As a native Texan, I am excited to see the growth of the craft beer industry in the state, and it is great to see so many hardworking brewers win awards for their wonderful beers. It makes me proud to have traveled this state to visit the breweries, brewpubs, and craft beer bars of Texas. I hope that this guide helps you as you travel through the state on your journey to find your next favorite beer. I invite you all to drink local. Cheers!

How to Use This Guide

This guide is meant to be as comprehensive as possible in this time of craft beer's quickly growing popularity. There will more than likely be places in this book that close before publication and more that pop up too late to be included. I aim to give recommendations and a taste of what each place has to offer. Not every place will be for everyone, but I feel that every place has at least one if not more beers, food items, or positive points that can be appreciated by any reader/taster.

Each brewery listing is broken into three parts: general information at the top, brewery description in the middle, and a Beer Lover's Pick at the bottom. I consider myself a beer enthusiast, but I am far from a beer snob because I appreciate all beers for what they are. The Beer Lover's Pick is the beer you should try if you can only try one, but there are far more on each tap list and I encourage you to order tasters, flights, and growlers/bottles to go. Have fun, enjoy the vibe, talk to the owners/brewers, and revel in the fact that Texas is a state with great craft beer.

Brewery vs. Brewpub: Not every brewery, brewpub, and beer bar is created equal. It's difficult to pigeonhole many of these places into one of these categories. The most difficult is the brewpub. Today bars and restaurants are getting into brewing their own beers, but even breweries are switching from a brewery license to a brewpub license, which allows them to sell to distributors for resale as well as sell growlers and bombers of beer to go. I encourage you to read the full description of every brewery and brewpub location to decide if you want to visit.

Beer Lover's Pick: Each Beer Lover's Pick is a highlight beer. These beers are chosen in a variety of ways; some are my personal favorites, while others are considered the brewery's crowning achievement. In some cases, it's their flagship beer or the brewer's favorite. Everyone's tastes are different, so order a taster of the Beer Lover's Pick first and decide if you want to go back for a full pint.

Pub Crawls: If you're visiting a city or want to experience multiple places at once, a pub crawl is the way to go. These sections cover pub crawls for the larger Texas beer cities that have great establishments within close proximity of each other.

After the brewery, brewpub, and beer bar listings, you'll find chapters on:

Beer Festivals: A look at a few of the larger annual beer festivals in Texas.

BYOB: Brew Your Own Beer: In this chapter there are some great clone recipes of the region's beers you can brew at home as well as some other great beers that are worth brewing.

In the Kitchen: Did you know that beer is the perfect ingredient for a lot of foods? This chapter is all about recipes you can cook at home using Texas beers.

Glossary of Terms

AAU: Alpha acid units—measurement of potential bitterness in hops.

ABV: Alcohol by volume—the percentage of alcohol in a beer. A typical domestic beer is a little less than 5% ABV.

Ale: Beer brewed with top-fermenting yeast. Quicker to brew than lagers, most every craft beer is a style of ale. Popular styles of ales include pale ales, amber ales, stouts, and porters.

Altbier: A German style of ale, typically brown in color, smooth, and fruity.

Barley wine: Not a wine at all but a high-ABV ale that originated in England and is typically sweet. American versions often have large amounts of hops.

Barrel: Production of beer is measured in barrels, also referred to as a BBL. A barrel equals 31 gallons.

Beer: An alcoholic beverage brewed with malt, water, hops, and yeast.

Beer bar: A bar that focuses on carrying craft or fine imported beers.

Bitter: An English bitter is an English-style ale, more hoppy than an English mild but less hoppy than an IPA.

Bock: A German-style lager, typically stronger than the typical lager.

Bomber: Most beers are packaged in 12-ounce bottles. Bombers are 22-ounce bottles.

Brewpub: Typically a restaurant, but sometimes a bar, that brews its own beers on the premises.

Clone beer: A homebrew recipe based on a commercial beer.

Contract brewery: A company that does not have its own brewery and pays someone else to brew and bottle its beer.

Craft beer: High-quality, flavorful beer made by small breweries.

DIPA: A Double India Pale Ale is a strong version of the classic style India Pale Ale (IPA). These usually include higher hopping rates, a thicker body, and more alcohol.

Double: Most often means a higher-alcohol version of a beer, most typically used in reference to a double, or imperial, IPA. Can also be used as an American translation of a Belgian dubbel, a style of Belgian ale.

ESB: Extra-special bitter. A traditional malt-heavy English pub ale with low bitterness, usually served on cask.

Ester: An ester is a chemical compound created by yeast during fermentation. It often takes on the fruity notes in the aroma and flavor ranging from banana, to bubble gum, to dark raisins.

FG: Final gravity—the density of the beer after fermentation.

Flagship beer: Flagship beers are traditionally the beer that put the brewery on the map. These are beers that each brewery is most well known for. This is a classic brewery term, but today the term flagship is less common with newer breweries. Flagship can mean best-selling beer that month or year. Many breweries in today's climate specifically opt out of the term flagship. For the purposes of this book "flagship" means best-selling beer or most widely known beer.

Gastropub: A beer-centric bar or pub that exhibits the same amount of care selecting its foods as it does its beers.

Growler: A half-gallon jug of beer. Many brewpubs sell growlers of their beers to go.

Hard cider: An alcoholic drink made from fermented fruit juice, traditionally apples.

Hops: Flowers used in beers to produce aroma, bitterness, and flavor. Nearly every beer in the world has hops.

IBU: International bitterness units—measurement of a beer's hop bitterness.

Imperial: A higher-alcohol version of a regular-strength beer.

IPA: India Pale Ale. A popular style of ale created in England that has taken a decidedly American twist over the years. Often bitter, thanks to more hops used than in other styles of beer.

Kölsch: A light, refreshing German-style ale.

Lager: Beer brewed with bottom-fermenting yeast. Takes longer and is harder to brew than ales. Popular styles of lagers include black lagers, Doppelbocks, pilsners, and Vienna lagers.

Lambic: A Belgian style of brewing in which the beers are produced by spontaneous fermentation by means of natural exposure to wild yeast and bacteria.

Malt: Typically barley malt, but sometimes wheat malt. Malt provides the fermentable sugar in beers. The more fermentable sugar, the higher the ABV in a beer. Without malt, a beer would be too bitter from the hops.

Microbrewery: A brewery that brews less than 15,000 barrels of beer a year.

Nanobrewery: A brewery that brews 4 barrels of beer per batch or less.

Nitro draft: Most beers that are served on draft use kegs pressurized with carbon dioxide. Occasionally, particularly with stouts, nitrogen is used, which helps create a creamier body.

OG: Original gravity—the density of the liquid before fermentation.

Pilsner: A style of German or Czech lager, usually light in color. Most mass-produced beers are based on this style.

Porter: A dark ale, similar to stout but with fewer roasted characters.

Quad: A strong Belgian-style ale, typically sweet and high in alcohol.

Regional brewery: A brewery that brews up to six million barrels of beer a year.

Russian imperial stout: A stout is a dark, heavy beer. A Russian imperial stout is a higher-alcohol, thicker-bodied version of regular stouts.

Saison: Also known as a Belgian or French farmhouse ale. It can be fruity and can also be peppery, and is usually refreshing.

Seasonal: A beer that is brewed only at a certain time of year to coincide with the seasons.

Session beer: A low-alcohol beer, one you can have several of in one long drinking "session."

SRM: Method in which brewers specify beer color.

Stout: A dark beer brewed with roasted malts.

Strong ale: A style of ale that is typically both hoppy and malty and can be aged for years.

Tap takeover: An event where a bar or pub hosts a brewery and has several of its beers on tap.

Triple (Tripel): A Belgian-style ale, typically lighter in color than a dubbel but higher in alcohol.

Wheat beer: Beers, such as hefeweizens and witbiers, that are brewed using wheat malt along with barley malt.

Yeast: The living organism in beer that causes the sugars to ferment and become alcohol.

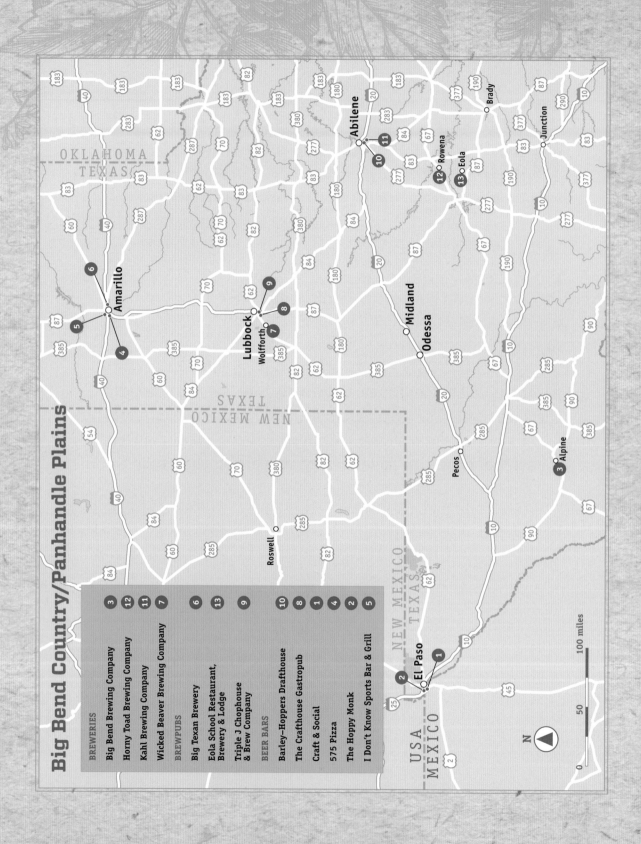

Big Bend Country/Panhandle Plains

BREWERIES

- 3 Big Bend Brewing Company
- 12 Horny Toad Brewing Company
- 11 Kahl Brewing Company
- 7 Wicked Beaver Brewing Company

BREWPUBS

- 6 Big Texan Brewery
- 13 Eola School Restaurant, Brewery & Lodge
- 9 Triple J Chophouse & Brew Company

BEER BARS

- 10 Barley–Hoppers Drafthouse
- 8 The Crafthouse Gastropub
- 1 Craft & Social
- 4 575 Pizza
- 2 The Hoppy Monk
- 5 I Don't Know Sports Bar & Grill

Big Bend Country & the Panhandle Plains

In the Wild West, Texas is a new frontier for craft beer. For the longest time people stayed true to the beer that they knew. Over the years, breweries, brewpubs, and craft beer bars have popped up across the Panhandle and Big Bend region, helping to both educate and welcome the locals to a new vision of good beer. This vast and rather desolate land is quickly becoming a booming area thanks to the rich oil beneath the Texas soil. The areas around Odessa and Midland have quickly become populated, growing towns, and many of the west Texas breweries have focused on getting their beer to the restaurants and bars in the region. From full-scale large breweries like Big Bend Brewing Company to small brewers like Wicked Beaver, they are all working on the same goal of providing the state with great craft beer that Texans can all be proud to stand behind.

Breweries

BIG BEND BREWING COMPANY

3401 W. Hwy. 90, Alpine, TX 79830; (432) 837-3700; bigbendbrewing.com; @FortBend Brewing

Founded: 2012 **Founders:** Matt Kruger & Steve Anderson **Brewer:** Steve Anderson **Flagship Beer:** Tejas Lager **Year-Round Beers:** Big Bend Hefeweizen, La Frontera IPA, No. 22 Porter, Terlingua Gold Ale, Tejas Lager **Seasonals/Special Releases:** Oktoberfest, El Corazon, Marfa Light **Tours:** Tues through Sat 2 to 4 p.m. **Taproom:** Yes

Big Bend Brewing Company is located in the quiet west Texas town of Alpine and was founded by Matt Kruger and Steve Anderson. Before landing in the Big Bend region, Matt was an entrepreneur from Chicago who discovered Marfa on a trip with his wife. They were so captivated by the art and natural beauty of the area that they ended up eventually purchasing a vacation home in Marfa. Steve was a veteran brewer who got his start in 1993 brewing with Waterloo Brewing Company in Austin, which was the first brewpub in Texas. After Waterloo went out of business in 2001, he took a position as the brewmaster for Live Oak Brewing where he remained until partnering with Matt to build a brewery of their own. With so many breweries popping up around the Texas Hill Country, they saw that west Texas was new territory for craft beer and decided to take the risk and try something different. The partners built a brewery with an "If you build it, they will come" attitude, and they established Big Bend Brewing Company in the winter of 2012.

From the start, Big Bend knew they faced many challenges. West Texas was not known for being a craft beer region, so they had to brew beers that would appeal to the locals and would be light enough to enjoy throughout the scorching hot summer. The partners were surprised when the beer hit the market and almost instantly sold out. Their local demand for beer was so high that it forced the brewery to expand to a 30-barrel brewhouse in the summer of 2014. While they eventually plan to expand their distribution to the big cities such as Austin, Dallas, and Houston, Big Bend wants to keep their focus on west Texas and supplying the region where craft beer is starting to take off. As of the end of 2014, El Paso was their largest market with a focus on their hometown of Alpine and their neighbors a mere 2 hours away in Midland and Odessa. Sixpacks of their beer can even be found in the convenience stores in Big Bend National Park.

Big Bend Brewing Company has found great success with their year-round releases, but their biggest seller is their **Tejas Lager**. It is a sessionable 4.7% ABV pilsner that pours clear and golden with a frothy white head. It is a great introductory beer that you can ease into with a crisp refreshing balanced mouth of malt and hops with a clean dry finish. It cools you off on a hot day and seems to quench your thirst, yet beckons you for another sip. For some, hoppy beers can be too heavy in the summer, but Big Bend has created their **La Frontera IPA**. La Frontera is a 7.8% ABV IPA that has a wonderful bouquet of malt and aromatic hops that follows onto the mouth. The beer has an approachable grapefruit bite, but it remains subtly smooth. There isn't a very bitter back end that you will find with most IPAs; instead you get a dry finish from this medium-bodied beer. While the beer has a higher alcohol content, it remains light and easy to enjoy in the Texas heat.

If you are heading out to see the Marfa lights or planning to spend a weekend hiking in Big Bend National Park, I suggest making a stop in Alpine to visit the fine folks at Big Bend Brewing Company. They offer tours twice daily from Tuesday through Saturday. Their beers are available in cans and on draft, but you will have to head west to get a taste. If you are looking for a beer that will keep you cool during the dog days of summer, Big Bend has you covered.

Big Bend Hefeweizen
Style: Hefeweizen
ABV: 5.6%
Availability: Year-Round
If there is one thing owner and brewer Steve Anderson picked up from his days at Austin-based Live Oak Brewing, it was how to make a great hefeweizen. The beer has a delightful bouquet of clove and banana esters that makes your mouth water. It has a light body that feels invigorating on the mouth with hints of wheat and citrus, with just a slight indication of white pepper that gives the beer a clean finish.

HORNY TOAD BREWING COMPANY

313 Edward St., Rowena, TX 76875; (325) 212-1177; hornytoadbrewery.com
Founded: 2012 **Founder:** Mike McNeill **Brewer:** Mike McNeill **Flagship Beer:**
Angelo Amber Ale **Year-Round Beers:** Kickapoo IPA, Angelo Amber, Concho Cream Ale
Seasonals/Special Releases: Pump Jack Porter, Peach Wit, Mesquite Bean Brown Ale,
Rowena Radler **Tours:** Occasionally **Taproom:** Yes

Horny Toad Brewing Company is located in a tiny west Texas town with a population of fewer than 800 residents. Rowena is the birthplace of infamous outlaw Bonnie Parker. The brewery was founded by Mike McNeill, who settled with his wife in her hometown. Mike is an Army veteran who served his country during Desert Storm and up until 1998 when he went inactive. In 2004 he was called back into service and sent to fight in Iraq. When he returned home from Iraq in 2006, he was motivated to change his career field and decided to turn his hobby of homebrewing into a new venture. He purchased an old service station along the main drag on Edward Street and established Horny Toad Brewing in 2012.

Mike got his start in brewing in 2000 when he received a Mr. Beer kit as a Father's Day present. He enjoyed brewing as a hobby and was inspired to eventually

move on to more advanced brewing techniques. The plastic Mr. Beer kit fermenter that started his passion now sits on the bar at the brewery as a tip jar. Today Horny Toad is brewing on a 7-barrel brewhouse that is constructed out of repurposed dairy equipment. Mike takes pride in the fact that everything in the brewery is done manually without any automated processes, giving him full control over each batch. Since Horny Toad is based in such a small town where there isn't much of a scene for craft beer, Mike has to create beers that are light and balanced without being too heavy or hoppy. The **Angelo Amber Ale** is the signature beer for the brewery; it is a 5.7% ABV amber-style beer that many will find inviting and easy to drink. It has a malty brew with a light hoppy finish that is not over the top and is a great introductory beer for someone starting their journey into craft beer. While Angelo Amber Ale is the flagship beer for the brewery, the **Concho Cream Ale** has really taken the spotlight and received the most praise. It is a 4.6% ABV cream ale that is perfect as a session beer and goes down smooth in warm weather. The beer pours a lightly hazy yellow with a thin head and soft carbonation. It has a citrus and yeasty nose that somewhat follows onto the palate with a malty base and a slightly sour finish that makes me think of a saison more than a cream ale. The beer finishes dry and doesn't leave behind any harsh aftertastes, making it a great go-to beer for basking in the Texas sun.

Beer Lover's Pick

Kickapoo IPA
Style: IPA
ABV: 6.5%
Availability: Year-Round

Brewing craft beer in a town where locals usually stay true to their favorite commercial brews can be a big risk. It can be an even bigger risk when you are brewing a beer like an IPA that is loaded with deliciously citrus and bitter hops. Horny Toad has decided to brew an IPA for its fans that want something with more of a kick. The Kickapoo IPA is a great balanced IPA that is brewed with loads of Columbus, Cascade, and Centennial hops, giving the beer a very aromatic bouquet of citrus and pine. The beer has a medium body with a light head and a deep copper color. On the mouth the beer is a balanced blend of malts and hops with a clean citrus finish. The Kickapoo IPA isn't quite as heavy as a West Coast–style IPA, but it is a great beer of the style nonetheless.

Horny Toad Brewing was built with passion by a man who has proudly served his country. Now Mike McNeill is working to serve his community and share great beer. Oddly enough the brewery sits across the street from a memorial to Prohibition. Before Prohibition had even passed, the residents of Runnels County where Rowena is located voted themselves to be a dry county. On April 28, 1911, they buried a bottle of whiskey and a bottle of beer, and they marked the spot with a headstone that reads "Here Lies Our Liberty." Today beer flows through Runnels County thanks to Mike and Horny Toad Brewing Company.

KAHL BREWING COMPANY

757 S. Treadaway Blvd., Abilene, TX 79602; (325) 518-9395; http://kahlbrewingco.com; @sixguntxale
Founded: 2013 **Founders:** Jeremy & Audra Kahl **Brewer:** Jeremy Kahl **Flagship Beer:** Hollow Point Pale Ale **Year-Round Beers:** Hollow Point Pale Ale, Buckshot Weissbier, Incendiary Blonde **Seasonals/Special Releases:** Outlaw Double IPA, Powder Burn Jalapeno Porter **Tours:** Second Sat of the month **Taproom:** No

In the west Texas city of Abilene, Kahl Brewing started out as a story of passion for craft beer. Owners Jeremy and Audra Kahl were bankers before Jeremy decided to turn his love of beer into a career. After over 15 years of homebrewing, Jeremy left behind the corporate life and broke ground on the future site of Kahl Brewing.

Jeremy got to work building the 4-barrel brewhouse all by hand. The steel was fabricated and welded by Jeremy himself along with the bar, which he repurposed from the floor of his sister's old house.

Jeremy has come a long way since then. Kahl brews beers that keep that Texas spirit while drawing on their German heritage in developing beers that are lighter and easily approachable. The **Powder Burn Jalapeno Porter** is a step out of the norm. As of late, chile beers have quickly come on to the scene, but there don't seem to be many brewing it in the style of a porter. The roasted notes of the malt give the jalapeno a subtle roasted chile pepper flavor without the kick from the spice. **Hollow Point Pale Ale** is a very approachable 7.3% ABV pale that gives a great bouquet

WICKED BEAVER BREWING COMPANY
10611 P.R. 1320, Unit No. 1, Wolfforth, TX 79382; (806) 833-6969; wickedbeaverbrewing .com; @WickedBeaver
Founded: 2011 **Founders:** Michael Adams & Che Shadle **Brewer:** Michael Adams
Flagship Beer: Midnight Ale **Year-Round Beers:** Midnight Ale, Cream Weaver, Hoperation IPA, Timber Ale, Blood Eagle **Tours:** Check Website **Taproom:** No

Wicked Beaver Brewing Company was founded by childhood friends Michael Adams and Che Shadle. Michael went to Texas A&M to study civil engineering, and while in college he checked out a local homebrewing store and realized that brewing your own beer was both more fun and cheaper than buying beer off the shelf. Che attended Texas Tech, also for civil engineering. As the two friends grew up, they realized Lubbock didn't have a craft beer scene. They kept their day jobs and decided to go forward with starting their own brewery. Michael handled the brewing while Che worked on the business and sales side of things. They have worked to bring craft beer to west Texas as the first full production brewery near Lubbock. In the beginning Wicked Beaver had an issue with bad bottles hitting shelves, but the partners strived to correct the errors and focused on changing the packaging from bombers to cans, as well as pushing for getting kegs of their beers into bars and restaurants.

The name Wicked Beaver almost came as a joke as the partners were trying to decide on a name. They found that consumers usually went for something unique and a name that would catch their attention, so they decided to go with Wicked Beaver because beavers in west Texas are ironic because of the dry, desert climate. Much like the name of the brewery, Michael and Che have come up with unique names for their beers as well. They have also gone against the norm with their beer styles, because none of their beers exactly follow the specific style guidelines.

Michael says that their focus is to brew beer that they enjoy and they feel proud to stand behind.

Wicked Beaver currently brews five beers, which are all available year-round. The black lager–style **Midnight Ale** is their flagship, with notes of toffee and chocolate. It is mild and smooth with a clean light finish. It will not overpower food and is still great to drink during the hot summer. **Blood Eagle** is what Wicked Beaver is calling a Viking ale. This 6.36% ABV ale takes on some unusual characteristics because it is brewed with juniper berries and set to age in red wine barrels from neighboring Llano Estacado Vineyards. Wicked Beaver has some interesting beers that are definitely worth checking out. They have future plans to expand their space as they continue to grow. I can only hope that they continue their goal of bringing more craft beer to west Texas.

Beer Lover's Pick

Timber Ale
Style: Amber
ABV: 8%
Availability: Year-Round

Wicked Beaver is always looking for ways to be different and set themselves apart from the herd. Their big amber-style Timber Ale is quite different from many of the typical amber beers on the market. As if the 8% ABV wasn't enough to spark your interest, they aggressively hop. It pours with a beautiful copper color and has a strong citrus nose of grapefruit, caramel, and pine. On the mouth the beer quickly grabs your taste buds with a hop bitterness that turns to a malty sweetness as it swirls across the palate and eventually finishes dry and piney. It is quite peculiar the first time you try it because most wouldn't expect such complexity from an amber-style beer. This is definitely a beer I suggest you explore, especially if you are not usually a fan of ambers. It pairs nicely with spicy Indian dishes or hot wings. It is worth picking up a bomber to see what your palate thinks of this brew from Wicked Beaver.

Brewpubs

BIG TEXAN BREWERY

7701 I-40, Amarillo, TX 79118; (806) 372-6000; http://bigtexan.com/brewery;
@TheBigTexan
Founded: 2011 **Founders:** Danny Lee, Bobby Lee & Tom Money **Brewer:** Tom Money
Flagship Beer: Pecan Porter **Year-Round Beers:** Honey Blonde Ale, Palo Duro Pale Ale,
Texas Red Amber Ale, Pecan Porter, Rattle Snake IPA, Whoop Your Donkey IPA, Whiskey
Barrel Stout, Bomb City Bock, Jack Rabbit Red, Marshall Marzen **Seasonals/Special
Releases:** Summer Wheat, Raspberry Wheat, Hefeweizen, Smokey & The Bacon, Oak Ale,
1836 Chocolate Bock Lager

The Big Texan Steak Ranch has to be one of the most iconic and well-known steakhouses in the world. It is safe to say that the steakhouse is the crown jewel of the city and draws in the majority of tourists visiting Amarillo or just passing through. The establishment has been featured on countless TV shows and in numerous articles for their 72-ounce steak challenge, but what people may not know is that there is a brewery within the doors of the restaurant. Big Texan Brewery was launched in 2011 by a homebrewer with a big dream. Brewer Tom Money approached Big Texan Steak Ranch owners Bobby and Danny Lee with the idea of brewing beer inside of the steakhouse. After a series of meetings and countless taste testings, the

Lee brothers agreed that converting the steakhouse into a brewpub would be a great idea and jumped on Tom's dream.

Due to a lack of funds and space, Tom ran into many obstacles when it came to setting up the brewery. Instead of having an area dedicated to brewing, Tom had to share space with the cramped and very busy kitchen, but it hasn't stopped him from cranking out a large number of beer recipes. The setup is quite unusual because Tom brews using a kitchen tilt skillet as a mash tun along with a small boil kettle.

Tom worked to design beers that would represent Texas and pair well with steaks. Many of the beers are lower in alcohol content like the popular **Pecan Porter,** which comes in at 4.5% ABV. The beer is malty and rich with a very forward flavor of pecans with hints of molasses and burnt caramel and has a very great finish. It is light on the mouth so it can be enjoyed no matter how warm it is outside. The **Palo Duro Pale Ale** is a lighter ABV pale coming in around 4.75%, but it comes with a full flavor finish thanks to the Amarillo and Hallertauer hops.

No trip to Amarillo is complete without a stop at the Big Texan, so if you are feeling hungry then step up to the table and take on the 72-ounce steak challenge or grab a beer and watch the action. Big Texan does sell beers to go, with options from a liter up to a mini keg. The beer makes for a great souvenir to go with your leftovers and helps cool you down after your meat sweats.

EOLA SCHOOL RESTAURANT, BREWERY & LODGE
12119 FM 381, Eola, TX 76937; (325) 469-3314; eolaschool.com; @EolaBrewery
Founded: 2006 **Founder:** Mark Cannon **Brewer:** Mark Cannon **Flagship Beer:** Farm Ale
Year-Round Beers: Farm Ale, Stout, Windmill Pale Ale, XXXX Extra Quad, Big Prick IPA

Eola is a tiny town just east of San Angelo. In the epicenter of the town sits Eola School Restaurant, Brewery & Lodge where owner/brewer Mark Cannon has been brewing beer and cooking up food since 2006. Eola School was originally the only school for the town until it shut its doors in 1983. Over the years the building suffered fire damage and was starting to show signs of decay when Mark showed up and purchased the property. With his skills, Mark has rebuilt the school and the most damaged portions of the building by hand. The Portland native moved to Texas to be closer to his family and with him came his craving for craft beer. Due to the lack of funding and resources, Mark has managed to teach himself to brew and even take over the kitchen duties. In a town so small, Mark is the one-man show of the place as he handles all aspects of the business.

Upon your arrival, Eola School looks like something out of a horror movie, but once you step inside you are greeted personally by Mark and you see the hard work

and dedication he has for the craft. Beers are served in Styrofoam cups, so if you are particular about beers being in their proper glassware then Eola isn't the place for you. The beers at Eola are simple and straightforward. The **Farm Ale** is a light smooth beer that has a delicate lemony citrus mouth that you can pick up on the nose. It is a very light-bodied 4.8% ABV beer that you can spend all day drinking. Texas's sweltering high temperatures can make drinking big heavy stouts a challenge all year round. Mark's **Chocolate Stout** is a medium-bodied stout with light carbonation. It flows lightly on the palate with notes of roasted coffee and chocolate. The nose is simply roasted malt with dark chocolate. The beer's medium body makes it great for drinking no matter the temperature outside. It is not sweet or overpowering and I find the flavor to be very mild for food pairing.

There isn't much in the town of Eola; it is the stereotypical small town that you can blink and miss. But I would recommend not missing a trip out to visit Mark and check out the beers he is brewing at the Eola School Restaurant, Brewery & Lodge. The beer and food are there, but the lodging still has some ways to go. You will be impressed to see the work Mark has done to the old school and how much passion he has for what he is doing. I respect how he has rebuilt the building and has taken on all the roles of brewing, cooking, and hosting. If you want to get a slice of the friendly and inviting charm of Texans, then make sure to add Eola to your map of beer destinations in Texas.

TRIPLE J CHOPHOUSE & BREW COMPANY

1807 Buddy Holly Ave., Lubbock, TX 79401; (806) 771-6555; triplejchophouseandbrewco. com; @TripleJFoodBrew

Founded: 2006 **Founders:** Joyce Bigham, Joe & LaTisha Keller **Brewer:** Justin Zimmerman **Flagship Beer:** Raider Red **Year-Round Beers:** Raider Red, Whynot Wheat, Black Cat Stout, Big Bad Leroy Brown, American Pale Ale, Burning Kilt Scot's Ale, IPA, **Seasonals/Special Releases:** Oktoberfest, Winterfest, Vienna Spring, Dos Czechies, Give 'Em Helles

Lubbock is known for a few things: the Texas Tech Red Raiders, being the hometown of music legend Buddy Holly, and Triple J Chophouse & Brew Co. Okay, so maybe Triple J's isn't exactly a tourist destination, but it should be if you are looking for delicious food and great beer. Triple J's is located just a block away from the Buddy Holly museum and many of the popular nightlife destinations in town.

Triple J Chophouse is a family partnership between barbecue restaurateur Joyce Bigham, her son Joe, and his wife LaTisha Keller. When the Hub City Brewery closed down in 2006, the family took action and purchased the building with its brewing equipment still standing. It didn't take long before Triple J's Chophouse opened for business and started cooking great food at an affordable price in a casual yet unique atmosphere. Their motto has always been "Well Crafted Beer and Damn Good Food, That's What We Do," and they have done a great job at it.

Head brewer Justin Zimmerman learned the brewing trade while working under Triple J's original brewer Mike Sipowicz. Once Mike left to start his business in wine,

Justin took over the brewing duties and remains there today.

The beers being brewed at Triple J all seem to harmonize with the style of foods coming out of the kitchen. The **Raider Red** is a tribute to the local Texas Tech Red Raiders. The 6.2% ABV American amber ale is a smooth drinking beer that is unfiltered and lighter in color and has a very light hop characteristic. The **Windmill Wheat** is a low 4.5% ABV very light brew with a floral bouquet and hints of honey and coriander.

Beer Bars

BARLEY-HOPPERS DRAFTHOUSE

721 S. 1st St., Abilene, TX 79602; (325) 788-0357; facebook.com/pages/Barley-Hoppers
-Drafthouse/535980339819277; @CraftandSocial
Draft Beers: 45 **Bottled/Canned Beers:** 125

Barley-Hoppers is pretty new to the quiet town of Abilene, but they have worked hard to bring craft beer to west Texas. The bar is owned by Tobias and Priscilla Gonzales, who have taken their love for craft beer and are making it their mission to promote good beer. Before the couple opened the bar, Tobias worked for Ben E. Keith Distributors in El Paso. Tobias really found his passion for beer during his time

working for the distributor and felt the need to return home to Abilene to spread the gospel of craft beer. Abilene might be a small and quiet town, but Barley-Hoppers has seen considerable support from the community ever since they opened their doors. Barley-Hoppers features firkins every quarter from a different brewery, and they even host quarterly beer dinners, which have become a big hit. Every Tuesday at the drafthouse is Pint Night, when patrons can buy a beer and keep the glass, and Barley-Hoppers is really making it worth it for the brewers because the customers are selling out of the glassware almost weekly.

The bar is quite large on the inside with the bar on one side of the building and a smaller seating area for more intimate gatherings on the other, as well as a large outdoor patio where you can grab a bite from whatever local food truck is parked there for the evening. The building is actually an old bank that has been converted many times over the years. The original safe is still standing, but they have converted the area into a beer storage room.

If you are out in Abilene, this is without a doubt the best place to grab a beer. While many bars say that their employees are very knowledgeable about the beers that they carry, Barley-Hoppers goes the extra mile because all of their bartenders are Cicerone certified, so they are always more than happy to help find you a beer you will like.

THE CRAFTHOUSE GASTROPUB
3131 34th St., Lubbock, TX 79410; (806) 687-1466; crafthousepub.com; @crafthousepub
Draft Beers: 18 **Bottled/Canned Beers:** 20

Owned by husband and wife Jason and Kate Diehl, The Crafthouse Gastropub was one of the first bars in Lubbock to push craft beer and gastropub-style food. All of the food is made from scratch daily, and they strive to use mostly local ingredients. From the condiments and breads to the sausages, Crafthouse makes everything fresh in house. Jason is a big soccer fan, so they take pride in opening up early to give local soccer fans a place to enjoy games with great food and craft beer. The establishment is small and quaint with an intimate feeling and is a good location for small gatherings or even a date night.

Chalkboards announce the beers they keep on tap, which are usually a great spread of national favorites and Texas beer from breweries such as Saint Arnold, Live Oak, and Wicked Beaver. To complement the ever-rotating taps of beer, Crafthouse cooks some great dishes like Chicken Fried Pork, Craft Ramen, and Cauliflower Risotto. They even offer a great brunch menu that will cap off a big

breakfast stout nicely. The Crafthouse Gastropub is a wonderful little place that you wouldn't expect to see in west Texas and makes for a fine beer oasis in the town of Lubbock. For a good meal and a great selection of craft beer, look no further than the Crafthouse.

CRAFT & SOCIAL
305 E. Franklin Ave., El Paso, TX 79901; (915) 219-7141; craftandsocial.com;
@CraftandSocial
Draft Beers: 20 **Bottled/Canned Beers:** 40

Craft & Social is in downtown El Paso and is owned by Rafael Terrazas and his brother-in-law Eric Nunez. Rafael found his obsession with beer while living in Europe. He found love with the Trappist ales and Belgian-style beers that piqued his curiosity to continue his search for new beers. When he moved back to the States, he found a successful career in New York, but on a visit back home to El Paso he realized that the city was seriously lacking craft beer. It was at this point he knew that he wanted to bring beer to El Paso and worked on plans to open his own brewery.

Unfortunately, the plans for the brewery fell through, but this didn't stop Rafael from pursuing his passion for spreading craft beer, and with the help of his brother-in-law Eric, they broke ground on what is now Craft & Social.

Craft & Social was the first place in El Paso to fill growlers, giving patrons the opportunity to sample new beers to find one they like and buy a growler to take home. They have taken on a variety of respectable beers that they offer both on the wall and in bottles, which they also sell to go. They have certainly helped the El Paso craft beer scene flourish with such an inviting establishment where you can stop in and ask questions without feeling intimidated. Craft & Social is very laid back and their focus is to educate and provide the city with great beer. The inside decor is minimalistic with pieces of local art, so the focus is on the beer. The white honeycomb tiled tap wall is encased by dark wood panels, bringing your attention to the beers currently on tap. Craft & Social is the kind of place where you can spend all day enjoying a tour of their beers on tap. I recommend this place as a must when stopping in El Paso and don't forget to grab a growler for the road.

575 PIZZERIA
2803 Civic Circle, Amarillo, TX 79109; (806) 331-3627; 575pizzeria.com; @575Pizzeria
Draft Beers: 13 **Bottled/Canned Beers:** 85+

Amarillo sits almost isolated in the Panhandle of Texas, but it is a city with an up and coming craft beer scene. Brian and Amanda Kelleher, owners of 575 Pizzeria, decided to do their part to bring craft beer to the city and since 2006 they have been baking some of the best pizza and serving some of the best craft beer that can be found for miles. Brian was an Amarillo native who went to Denver, where he found his affection for craft beer. He realized Amarillo was lacking anything close to the beer scene of Denver, so he decided to return home and become the first craft beer destination in the city.

575 Pizzeria, named after the temperature of their oven, has received a lot of attention for their pizzas. Both the dough and sauce are made in house, and the pizzas are topped with only the freshest ingredients. For the longest time, wine was the usual pairing with fresh pizza, but as of late, craft beer has taken the lead when perfectly complementing a good pie. 575 features 13 taps of constantly rotating beer and around 85 bottles and cans on hand. They carry the usual commercial brands, but if you try to order a "light" beer, they will gladly suggest a craft alternative. 575 has recently opened a second location in town boasting more beers on tap and a larger dining space, but the original location off Civic Circle remains their flagship that the original patrons frequent. It is also the home base for their yearly charity

event People Pints & Pedals. 575 is a place to check out in Amarillo on your way out west to visit the Cadillac Ranch or a great place to recover after a long day hiking in Palo Duro Canyon.

THE HOPPY MONK
4141 N. Mesa St., El Paso, TX 79902; (915) 307-3263; thehoppymonk.com;
@TheHoppyMonk
Draft Beers: 70 **Bottled/Canned Beers:** 150+

The Hoppy Monk is an El Paso institution dedicated to bringing craft beer to the city. They strive to live by their motto "Good people drink good beer," which they adopted from famed writer and eccentric legend, Hunter S. Thompson. They have done a great job of supplying good beer to the good people of El Paso and have expanded their operation to the south Texas plains in San Antonio. Mixing a vibrant locale with craft beer and great food, the Hoppy Monk is setting the bar high for others even thinking about opening a gastropub in El Paso. While the menu has many options, their burgers are highly recommended. Options include their Blue Fox Burger, topped with cider-poached pears, blue cheese sauce, and a walnut aioli coupled romantically with a Belgian triple, or the Farouk Burger that they smother with Duchesse de Bourgogne onion jam, gooey aged cheddar, and aioli. If you are a leaf eater, they have you covered as well with a great selection of salads and a surprisingly delicious veggie burger consisting of a black bean and pumpkin patty.

El Paso is an up and coming craft beer location, and the Hoppy Monk is doing a great job continuing the craft beer growth in the region. The bar is wide and space is plenty, but the outdoor patio is the place to be while enjoying your beers. The large wooden patio offers a great place to view the surrounding mountain ranges, but the attention goes to their stone wall featuring a neat water wall of flowing taps. No trip to El Paso is complete without a stop at the Hoppy Monk—and if El Paso is too far, stop in at their central Texas location in San Antonio.

I DON'T KNOW SPORTS BAR & GRILL
1301 S.W. 6th Ave., Amarillo, TX 79101; (806) 331-7985;idontknowsportsbarandgrill.com
Draft Beers: 220

I Don't Know Sports Bar in Amarillo may have set the record for the most beers on tap in Texas, if not the world. Owner Dennis Paetzold was a busy man around Amarillo running a successful asbestos removal company and 6th Street Automotive

Repair. It was at the auto shop that he thought to himself how nice it would be to have a place where you could have a bite and a beer while you wait for your car: So that is exactly what Dennis decided to do. One side of the building was the auto shop and on the other side was a bar and grill. Living up to the fact that everything is bigger in Texas, Dennis decided it was either go big or go home, so as soon as he opened I Don't Know Sports Bar, his tap wall started to grow. There was no need for bottles or cans when he reached the point of 220 beers on tap. Even with that many beers on tap, he plans to install even more. It is not clear if he is going for a world record or he just has a fascination for beer, but I Don't Know Sports Bar is a beer lover's paradise. While the craft beer scene is slowly starting to catch on in Amarillo, this is the place to learn everything you need to know about the different styles out there.

I Don't Know not only has a notable list of beers, but they are making some delectable food too. Go with any burger or sandwich on the menu and you will be satisfied, but add their jalapeno bacon to it and take your meal to the next level.

The area around I Don't Know is rather industrial, but this hidden gem is a diamond in the rough. They have TVs and projection screens around the building, so it is great for watching sports. They also have a stage and dance floor that was repurposed from the old Pampa Junior High, used on Friday and Saturday nights when they feature live music. Since Amarillo is such a small town, you have a great mix of locals from old to young. I would certainly keep my eye on this place as they continue to install more taps. Overall this is a fun and friendly place to grab a bite and have a beer. You might as well take your car next door for a detailing while you're having fun.

Gulf Coast/Piney Woods

BREWERIES

B-52 Brewing Company	4
8th Wonder Brewery	19
Galactic Coast Brewing	26
Karbach Brewing Company	8
Long Pint Brewery	5
No Label Brewing Company	7
Saint Arnold Brewing Company	15
Southern Star Brewing	3
Texas Beer Refinery	25
Texas BIG BEER Brewery	2
Texian Brewing Company	22

BREWPUBS

Beerfoot Beach Bar	28
Moon Tower Inn– Moon Tower Sudworks	20
Padre Island Brewing Company	29

BEER BARS

BRC Gastropub	12
Brewery Tap	14
Brews Brothers	27
Cedar Creek Bar & Grill	11
Cottonwood	10
The Ginger Man	21
Hay Merchant	16
Juls Restaurant, Lounge & Cafe	1
Liberty Station	13
Lucky's Pub	18
Mongoose Versus Cobra	17
Nobi Public House	23
Petrol Station	9
Rockwell Tavern and Grill	6
Skallywag Suds N' Grub	24

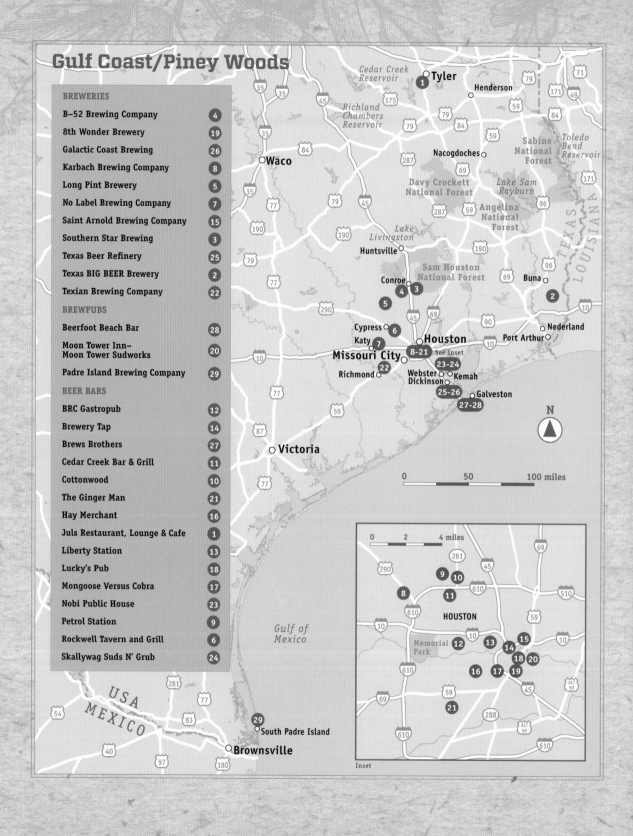

Gulf Coast/
Piney Woods

The Texas Gulf Coast and Piney Woods region are like one big hug across the state. The Gulf Coast stretches along the coast from the border of Mexico to the border of Louisiana, while the Piney Woods region fills out the far east Texas area along the Louisiana border up to Oklahoma. A majority of the beer is found in the Gulf Coast region in and around Houston with popular breweries like Saint Arnold and Karbach. The farther south you go you will find that craft beer is a slow-moving concept and many people tend to stick to their usual commercial brands, but that is not to say that there aren't establishments working to change the status quo. The Piney Woods region is another region that is slowly coming into the craft beer realm, but Texas BIG BEER Brewery out in the small town of Buna is working hard to bring big beers to the market with bold flavors. Throughout these two regions there is a wave of new breweries and craft beer bars opening up in smaller towns to give their local residents new options and to educate them about craft beer. If you are on the hunt for great craft beer, start your journey in Houston and work your way out. These are vast regions, so it is going to take you some time.

Breweries

B-52 BREWING COMPANY

12470 Milroy Ln., Conroe, TX 77304; (936) 447-4677; b52brewing.com; @B52brewing
Founded: 2014 **Founders:** Brent & Chad Daniel **Brewer:** Chad Daniel **Flagship Beer:**
Payload Pils **Year-Round Beers:** Payload Pilsner, Wingman Wheat IPA, B-52 Double IPA,
Schwarzbier, Rye Saison **Seasonals/Special Releases:** Fest Beer **Tours:** Sat 12 to 4
p.m. **Taproom:** Yes

B-52 Brewing Company is located less than an hour north of Houston in the woods of Conroe. It was founded by brothers Brent and Chad Daniel, who used old family property to break ground on their brewing oasis in the woods. The brothers were both professional gamblers who made a career out of online poker and decided to play their hand at opening their own brewery. Chad found his love for brewing in college where he learned the craft of brewing. He would brew beer and give it away to friends who were really impressed with his beer, and he uses some of those recipes at the brewery to this day. The brothers were able to start the brewery with their own money and some help from their family They erected a large steel

building for the brewhouse and a couple shipping containers for an office, and the taproom was used as a storage container during the Persian Gulf War.

The name B-52 didn't have much of a meaning behind it for the brothers, but they wanted a "bad ass" name that would represent America and the B-52 bomber was a force to be reckoned with. While neither of the brothers have military backgrounds, the name is a nod to their grandfather, who served in World War II.

B-52 Brewing beers are authentic and true to style, but they want to focus on adding a positive light to lagering. The brothers feel like lagers get a bad rap, so they are working to brew beers that can be appreciated by all. They are also in the process of experimenting with wild fermentation and barrel aging beers. The current lineup is still in development, but the **Payload Pils** is a light enjoyable 5.1% ABV pilsner that has a light citrus flavor with a lightly bitter bite. It is crisp on the mouth with a dry finish. It is ideal for the spring and summer months and a great beer to pair with seafood or burgers.

Since B-52 holds a brewpub license, you can stop by the brewery for a couple pints and pick up a growler of beer to go. They are considering featuring beers from other local breweries in their taproom, but due to Texas Alcoholic Beverage Commission (TABC) laws it would hinder them from self-distributing their beer. B-52 is still a very new brewery, but they have their legs on stable ground and are going to be a brewery to follow as they taxi down the runway.

Beer Lover's Pick

Wingman Wheat IPA
Style: Wheat IPA
ABV: 5.7%
Availability: Year-Round
The Wingman Wheat IPA from B-52 Brewing is a unique beer concept. It is a blend of a wheat beer recipe with the hop profile of an IPA, fermented using English ale yeast. The final product is a very smooth, easy-drinking beer that has a light hazy appearance of gold with a medium white head. The beer is light on the palate with a lightly sweet flavor of malt and yeast followed by a mild hop bite that is enjoyable and leaves a dry finish. It is a great beer to enjoy over an afternoon at a barbecue or just a casual beer to change up the palate. With such a light flavor and body, I think it has great appeal for those who prefer a lighter beer.

8TH WONDER BREWERY

2202 Dallas St., Houston, TX 77003; (713) 229-0868; 8thwonderbrew.com; @8thWonderBrew

Founded: 2011 **Founders:** Ryan Soroka, Alex Vassilakidis & Aaron Corsi **Brewer:** Aaron Corsi **Flagship Beer:** Alternate Universe **Year-Round Beers:** Alternate Universe Altbier, Hopston TXIPA, Intellectuale Witty Blonde, Dome Faux'm Throwback Cream Ale, Rocket Fuel Vietnamese Coffee Porter **Seasonals/Special Releases:** BrewGK Candy Apple Ale, Brewston Dry Hopped Pale Ale, Milagro Organic Agave Ale, Haterade **Tours:** Sat 6 to 9 p.m. **Taproom:** Coming Soon

8th Wonder Brewery was a dream that started in a food truck. Partners Ryan Soroka and Alex Vassilakidis originally started their business as the food truck Eatsie Boys with chef Matt Marcus. As the popularity of food trucks exploded in Houston, the partners found a big success in the market and eventually opened a brick and mortar restaurant. It was at this time the partners decided to make plans for their brewery with their co-founder and brewer Aaron Corsi.

8th Wonder Brewing is located just outside the realms of downtown in the historic warehouse district "EaDo" (East Downtown) that was once the original Chinatown of Houston. Over the last 10 years the area has come alive with bars, restaurants, and the new BBVA Compass Stadium that is home to the MLS soccer team, the Houston Dynamo. 8th Wonder is very close to many of the other professional

sports stadiums such as Minute Maid Park, Toyota Center, and NRG Stadium. One step inside of the 8th Wonder Brewery and you will see that they definitely have a love for the hometown teams. The name 8th Wonder is a salute to the historic Astrodome, which was dubbed the 8th Wonder of the World as it was the first air-conditioned, domed stadium, the original home for the Colt .45s (who became the Astros).

8th Wonder's passion for both Houston and its people is shown in the beers that they brew. Houston is home to the largest Vietnamese community in the state and **Rocket Fuel Vietnamese Coffee Porter** is a beer with rich coffee-forward notes that is made with lactose and cold-brewed coffee from Houston roasters Greenway Coffee Company. **BrewGK Candy Apple Ale** was a collaboration brew with legendary Houston rapper Bun B of the group UGK. Bun B was originally looking for a cider-style beer, but after working with 8th Wonder they came up with a candy apple ale brewed with green apples and homemade caramel syrup. **Hopston TXIPA** is a nod to the great city they live in. They wanted to make their own version of a West Coast IPA, but since everything is bigger in Texas they decided to make their own style. With a moderate 88 IBUs, this Texas IPA is a very inviting IPA that would be a great tiptoe into bigger beers. The 6.2% ABV makes this an easy-drinking beer, but it will definitely catch up to you in the Texas heat. Many of the beers brewed at 8th Wonder are lower in alcohol and are balanced and approachable with big flavor profiles. They currently only self-distribute in Houston, with future plans to branch out in the state and possibly can a few of their beers.

Beer Lover's Pick

Rocket Fuel Vietnamese Coffee Porter
Style: Coffee Porter
ABV: 4.6%
Availability: Year-Round
8th Wonder wanted to make a beer to honor the Vietnamese culture of Houston. They were looking to make a beer in the style of Cafe Sua Da, which is a very popular Vietnamese specialty consisting of dark roast brewed coffee and sweetened condensed milk. The porter is light on the palate with heavy roasted coffee notes and a subtle sweetness from the lactose. It is rich in flavor and makes for a great dessert beer without being too sweet. Though I am not usually one to pair sweeter porters or heavy stouts with food, I would recommend pairing this with a rich chocolaty dessert. The roasted coffee notes will help reduce the sweetness of the dessert and clear your palate.

GALACTIC COAST BREWING COMPANY

1675 Dickinson Ave., Dickinson, TX 77539; (832) 738-1960; galacticcoastbrewing.com; @GalacticCoast
Founded: 2012 **Founders:** John Ennis & Mike Taylor **Brewer:** Mike Taylor **Flagship Beer:** Sneaky Blonde **Year-Round Beers:** Sneaky Blonde, Rocket Ride, Goblin Hunter **Tours:** No Public Tours **Taproom:** No

Houston, we have beer. Galactic Coast Brewing Company is an out of this world brewery started by John Ennis and Mike Taylor in Dickinson. The brewery pays homage to both the local space program at the nearby Space Center Houston and the Gulf Coast region they call home. Brewing on a 7-barrel brewhouse, the partners are creating beers that are approachable yet full flavored. John Ennis had worked in the Houston bay area as the publisher and founder of *The Scene* magazine while his partner Mike was a third-generation electrician for over 30 years.

John and Mike realized they had an obsession with beer, and they were always looking to try something new. Mike was a homebrewer and a member of the Bay Area Mashtronauts. He quickly taught himself how to brew and started to create recipes of his own. After nights of drinking and chewing the fat, John and Mike fantasized about opening a brewery. It wasn't long before the partners decide to take the brewing out of the garage and start up a business of their own.

Today John and Mike have worked to bring beer to the local scene and give drinkers a galactic experience. You would expect all the beers to be named after space themes, but the partners decided to keep the space theme mostly within the brewery itself and named their fermenters after shuttle missions and space vehicles. Due to lack of space the brewery has found it challenging to keep up with demand, but they are currently working on expanding the brewery and experimenting with adding a few beers to their lineup. The **Sneaky Blonde** is the flagship and one of the biggest sellers for Galactic Coast. The beer is semisweet with a citrus finish and a perfume-like bouquet that makes for a pleasant summer drinking beer, but they don't call her sneaky for nothing—the beer has a 7% ABV, but you will never be able to tell from this smooth deceptive blonde. The **Rocket Ride** is a malt-forward brown ale that is more of a dark amberish color. It doesn't quite follow the rules of your average brown ale, but that is what Mike wanted. Sometimes breaking the rules is a good thing, and in this case it worked in their favor.

Unfortunately, due to the tight space and the expansion underway, Galactic Coast is not open to the public nor do they host tours. To get your hands on this great beer, you will have to hit one of the local bay area watering holes. Galactic Coast is on draft only and currently self-distributes to the small cities between Clear Lake and Galveston.

Beer Lover's Pick

Goblin Hunter
Style: Year-Round Halloween Seasonal
ABV: 6.52%
Availability: Year-Round

So I know you might be asking yourself what a year-round Halloween seasonal is. It is hard to pinpoint exactly what Goblin Hunter is. It is a semisweet mellow beer that can be compared to your average Oktoberfest or fall seasonal, except the Goblin Hunter isn't a lager. The beer's name is a double entendre for both the Halloween season and the American XF-85 Goblin prototype parasite jet fighter aircraft.

The beer is smooth and malty with notes of toffee and caramel. The hops are low and the beer is light on the palate. It goes great with burgers or mild cheese and can even calm the burn from spicy delicacies. Goblin Hunter is only sold on draft, and you will have to head down to the bay area of Houston to find this luscious treat. Happy hunting!

KARBACH BREWING COMPANY

2032 Karbach St., Houston, TX 77092; (713) 680-2739; karbachbrewing.com;
@karbachbrewing
Founded: 2011 **Founders:** Chuck Robertson, Ken Goodman, David Greenwood & Brad
Batson **Brewer:** Eric Warner **Flagship Beer:** Hopadillo IPA **Year-Round Beers:**
Hopadillo IPA, Weisse Versa Wheat, Weekend Warrior Pale Ale, Symphony for the Lager,
Rodeo Clown Double IPA **Seasonals/Special Releases:** Barn Burner Saison, Love
Street Summer Seasonal, Karbachtoberfest, Mother in Lager, Hell-Fighter Imperial Porter,
Pontificator Smoked Doppelbock, Hop Delusional Imperial IPA, Krunkin Pumpkin, Yuel
Shoot Your Eye Out **Tours:** Mon 4:30 to 7:30 p.m., Thurs 4:30 to 8:30 p.m., Fri 4:30 to
7:30 p.m., Sat 12 to 3 p.m. **Taproom:** Coming Soon

Karbach Brewing Company is located on the edge of the Spring Branch neighborhood in Houston. Founders Chuck Robertson, Ken Goodman, David Greenwood, and Brad Batson used their background of experience to build the brewery. Chuck and Ken were the founders of the C.R. Goodman Distribution Company that was founded in 1982 in College Station and was one of the original craft beer distributors in Texas. The distribution company was bought out by Dallas-based Ben E. Keith Distributors in 2008. After Chuck and Ken sold their company they saw an opportunity to bring a new brewery to Houston, so they went in with their partners David and Brad to get the project started. To complete the team, the partners brought on brewmaster Eric Warner with his extensive background in the brewing industry, and in 2011 Karbach Brewing Company came to life. Coincidently, Karbach is brewing in the same warehouse that was once the C.R. Goodman Distribution Company on Karbach Street, which the brewery is named after.

Brewmaster Eric Warner is both well known and highly respected in the craft beer industry. He graduated from Lewis & Clark College in Portland, Oregon, with a degree in German studies. After graduating he moved to Germany to attend the Technical University of Munich at Weihenstephan, where he received his Diplom-Braumeister in 1990. Before making his way to Houston to work with Karbach he was the CEO for Maryland-based Flying Dog Brewing Company. He was the co-founder of Denver-based Tabernash Brewing Company, which eventually merged with Left Hand Brewing in 1998. Eric has helped Karbach become one of the fastest-growing breweries in the country. After just 2 years in business, Karbach announced a $15 million purchase of a 19,000-square-foot, 2-story facility adjacent to the current brewery, which would house a new 120-barrel German-designed brewhouse that would put the brewery on track for producing 60,000 barrels annually and would give them the room for expansion in the future.

In 2013 Karbach made national news when the *New Yorker* listed them as the second-fastest-growing brewery in the nation. They produced nearly 19,000 barrels of beer in 2013 with a projected total of 29,000 by the end of 2014. Originally Karbach was only distributed in Houston, but as of 2014 they have extended to Austin and San Antonio with plans for further reach into other Texas markets soon. Since their opening in 2011, Karbach's beers have been in high demand. A majority of their beers are hop forward, which put them on the list for the hopheads in the state. Their flagship is the 6.6% ABV **Hopadillo IPA.** It has a mild bitter-forward flavor that mellows out with a malt finish. The beer is copper in color with a heavy citrus and grass nose from being dry-hopped before packaging. Since the beer is dry-hopped, you get a large hop bouquet without being overly strong or bitter on the palate, which makes this beer approachable and easy to drink.

If there is one thing that Eric knows about it is German beer; he even wrote the book *German Wheat Beer*. Eric had a spirited debate with brewery founder David Greenwood on German hefeweizen versus Belgian whites, which inspired their **Weisse Versa Wheat.** It is a 5.3% ABV wheat hybrid that uses German hefeweizen yeasts with Belgian white spices. Weisse Versa pours a rich hazy orange with a full white head. The nose brings the typical notes of clove and coriander with just a slight hint of banana esters. On the mouth you get a refreshing burst of citrus and malt that has a very light body. The beer finishes clean with just a slight bitterness on the back end. It is a great approachable beer that is perfect for session drinking and pairing with most dishes.

Karbach is a definite must for any craft beer seeker. The beers are all well balanced and full flavored with great occasional specialties including barrel-aged beers. Tours are held on Monday, Thursday, Friday, and Saturday, so there are plenty of opportunities to stop in. Parking is limited to the street, so observe parking signs and dress for the weather because their current event space is located outside in the back of the brewery. Once the new brewery is finished, they will have a dedicated taproom, kitchen, and events space and the tours and tastings will be indoors.

Beer Lover's Pick

Love Street Summer Seasonal
Style: Kölsch
ABV: 4.9%
Availability: Summer

Love Street is a kölsch-style summer release from Karbach Brewing Company that is named after the infamous '60s nightclub that was located in downtown Houston along the historic Allen's Landing site. The beer is a perfect complement to the sweltering Texas heat and a great easy-drinking sessionable beer. With its lower 4.9% ABV the beer is perfect for a long afternoon on a patio or floating down the river. The beer pours a deep yellow in color with a grassy and grain nose. It is light bodied with a clean refreshing flavor that has hints of straw, malt, and an ever so slight touch of citrus. This is one of my favorites for Texas summer seasonals because it is easy to drink and doesn't leave you feeling full. Since it is a summer release, I find this beer pairs great with a backyard barbecue or a fat juicy burger. In Texas, because of the heat we usually can't wait for the summer to end, but the fact that this beer is available in summer only makes me wish it was summer all year round.

LONE PINT BREWERY

507 Commerce St., Magnolia, TX 77355; (713) 304-5069; lonepint.com; @LonePint
Founded: 2012 **Founders:** Heather Niederhofer & Trevor Brown **Brewer:** Blake
Niederhofer **Flagship Beer:** 667 Neighbor of the Beast **Year-Round Beers:** Yellow
Rose, 667 Neighbor of the Beast, Gentleman's Relish, The Jabberwocky, Tornado Shark
Seasonals/Special Releases: Zythophile Series, Knecht Ruprecht, Po-Cha-Na-Quar-Hip
Tours: Sat 12 to 4 p.m. **Taproom:** No

Lone Pint Brewery is in Magnolia and was founded by siblings Heather Niederhofer and Trevor Brown. They shared a love for craft beer and bonded over homebrewing in Trevor's garage, where they first started talking about brewing professionally. Trevor had a background in engineering while Heather worked in sales and account management, a good combination for taking that leap into starting a brewery. Since both Heather and Trevor had secure careers, they decided to keep their day jobs until the brewery was stable and bringing in a stable profit. They leased out an old auto body shop in downtown Magnolia, installed a 30-barrel brewhouse, and in the fall of 2012, Lone Pint was open for business. Lone Pint is still a side project for siblings Heather and Trevor, who still have their full-time jobs. They host the tours and tastings on Saturday and spend Sunday brewing and attending to the brewery's maintenance.

Lone Pint really hit the market strong when their beers were released. They focus on using only the best grains and raw whole cone hops to create memorable Texas ales that are hoppy and delicious. **Yellow Rose** was one of the first big releases for Lone Pint. It is a 6.8% ABV IPA that uses a single malt and is brewed with infamous Mosaic hops. Yellow Rose is a citrus bomb of a beer. The nose resonates aromas of grapefruit and tropical fruits. It has a complex citrus-forward mouth that perfectly balances the malt and clean bitterness from the Mosaic hops. It is a great go-to IPA that can go with most dishes, but I find it to be amazing with pizza or a greasy burger. A majority of Lone Pint's beers are heavily hopped, but the **Gentleman's Relish** focuses more on the malt side. It is a 6.2% ABV brown ale that is named after an old English snack consisting of anchovy paste spread on toast. Rest assured, there are no anchovies used in this beer. Instead it is a medium-bodied ale that pours a rich deep mahogany color. It has a nose of roasted malts and dried fruits and a coffee presence on the mouth along with molasses and nuts followed by a faint bitter finish. I am not usually a fan of brown ales, but Lone Pint did a great job on this beer that seems like it is on the borderline between an ale and a porter.

Lone Pint offers tours on Saturday from noon to 4 p.m. The brewery is on track to be a big hit once they extend their distribution farther into the state. Their beers

Tornado Shark
Style: American Strong Ale
ABV: 7.6%
Availability: Year-Round

Tornado Shark might be one of my favorite beers. It is named after two of Heather's biggest fears, but there is nothing to fear about Tornado Shark unless you are afraid of great beer. It is brewed with American two-row malted barley and aggressively hopped with four different American whole cone hop varietals. The beer pours a rusty brown with a caramel piney bouquet on the nose. The beer really opens up on the palate with a perfect balance of hops and malts. Tornado Shark has a medium body that is almost creamy with a light sweetness, making for a great beer that leaves you wanting more. It is a great beer to pair with sharp cheese like an Asiago or robust dishes with lots of spice such as curries. If you find this beer on tap, I highly recommend grabbing a pint and enjoying it slowly. It opens up with different flavors as it warms up.

are in high demand in the Houston and Austin areas, and bottles are available in select areas, so we can only hope the siblings will soon quit their day jobs and focus solely on the growth of the brewery.

NO LABEL BREWING COMPANY

5351 1st St., Building A, Katy, TX 77493; (281) 693-7545; nolabelbrew.com; @NoLabelBrewCo
Founded: 2010 **Founders:** Brian & Jennifer Royo, Gilberto & Melanie Royo **Brewer:** James Wolfe **Flagship Beer:** El Hefe Weizen **Year-Round Beers:** Eleven Amp IPA, 1st Street Ale, El Hefe Weizen, Pale Horse, Ridgeback **Seasonals/Special Releases:** Mint IPA, Elda M. Milk Stout, Black Wit-O, Don Jalapeno **Tours:** Fri 4 to 7 p.m., Sat 12 to 3 p.m. **Taproom:** Yes

Located in Katy, No Label Brewing Company is a family-run business founded by husband and wife team Brian and Jennifer Royo along with Brian's parents Gilberto and Melanie Royo. Brian and Jennifer met as students at the University of Houston. After graduation Brian picked up homebrewing after some friends bought him a kit. He quickly became fascinated with brewing and would spend his free time brewing in his garage with his father Gilberto. Brian's first passion had always been construction, but he started to realize he had more interest in beer. One evening while sharing his homebrewed beers with his parents, Brian disclosed his idea of starting a brewery, and as supportive parents they not only backed his dream but decided to go in with him. Brain quit his construction job to focus on the brewery, and at the end of 2010 No Label Brewing Company was officially established and the brewery was settled in an old rice silo in Old Town Katy. The name No Label represented both the different personalities of the partners as well as the direction they aimed for with their beers, which occasionally go their own route and don't fit neatly into any particular style.

James Wolfe was a big fan of No Label, so he came on as a volunteer. He started to work his way up and in due course was hired on as the head brewer. This gave Brian more time to focus on the quickly growing business. They hit the market with three core beers, and their offerings have grown over the years. No Label produces well-balanced beers that are light and approachable and can be appreciated by everyone. **El Hefe Weizen** is a traditional German hefeweizen that Brian brewed for Jennifer. It is a light-drinking floral beer with a strong bouquet of banana and clove. The aroma follows onto the palate with a clean softly sweet profile that is

Elda M. Milk Stout
Style: Milk Stout
ABV: 6.89% ABV
Availability: Winter
This beer was named after a boat Melanie Royo grew up on in Panama. The Elda M. Milk Stout is a delicious and creamy milk stout that is brewed with ten different malts. It is nearly black in color with a brown head on the pour. The bouquet reaches your nostrils with sweet aromas of burnt caramel, roasted malts, coffee, and dark chocolate that extend onto the palate. The beer is a little on the sweeter side but not overbearing or filling. It has a satisfying creamy texture on the mouth that warms you up on a cool winter day. I find it pairs better with desserts than with main courses. I suggest letting this beer warm up to around 60 degrees to really let the flavors open up.

appealing and approachable. The **Pale Horse** was a nod to the Revelations 6:8 quote from one of Brian's favorite Johnny Cash songs, "The Man Comes Around." It is a 5.9% ABV pale ale with a caramel and citrus hop nose, and it pours golden in color with a medium white head. On the palate it has a malt-forward profile that has a sweetness to it followed by the poised hop bitterness. I find the Pale Horse to be a very balanced beer that is easy to drink and would make for a great introductory pale ale for new craft drinkers. The 5.9% ABV still makes this beer light enough for a seasonable afternoon with its light body and refreshing finish.

No Label has come a long way in a short time, but they have many more things in the works, such as their Off Label series of beers, which will give them a much larger variety of styles and specialties throughout the year. No Label also participates in many community events, so follow them on social media to see where they will be next. Brian and Jennifer are football fanatics, so you can occasionally find them hosting tailgating events during University of Houston games. The brewery is open for tours and tastings on Friday and Saturday. No Label is always family and pet friendly, so feel free to bring the whole gang and see why you just can't put a label on No Label Brewing.

SAINT ARNOLD BREWING COMPANY

2000 Lyons Ave., Houston, TX 77020; (713) 686-9494; saintarnold.com; @SaintArnold
Founded: 1994 **Founders:** Brock Wagner & Kevin Bartol **Brewers:** Brock Wagner, Stephen Rawlings, Aaron Inkrott, Dennis Rhee & Casey Motes **Flagship Beer:** Saint Arnold Amber **Year-Round Beers:** Amber, Brown, Weedwacker, Fancy Lawnmower, Elissa IPA, Santo, Endeavour, Boiler Room Berliner Weisse **Seasonals/Special Releases:** Spring Bock, Oktoberfest, Summer Pils, Christmas Ale, Winter Stout, Pumpkinator, Sailing Santa, Divine Reserve, Bishop's Barrel, Icon, Homefront IPA **Tours:** Mon through Fri 2 to 4 p.m., Sat 11 to 2 p.m. **Taproom:** Yes

Saint Arnold Brewing Company is in Houston just outside of downtown and was founded in 1994 by Brock Wagner and business partner Kevin Bartol. Kevin eventually parted ways with the brewery, but the business continued to grow and has become one of the most iconic breweries in Houston. With a beautiful large brick brewery and a grand taproom, Saint Arnold has become a hot spot for their Saturday morning tours. Large windows look out onto the Houston skyline as patrons pack in along the rows of tables and scatter along the floor to drink beer and spend time with friends.

Saint Arnold Brewing Company is the oldest craft brewery in Texas and owner Brock Wagner has become a leading voice in appealing the strict Texas Alcoholic Beverage Commission's outdated laws, which both restricted and limited breweries' growth. Brock was originally an investment banker and avid homebrewer before the

idea came to start a brewery of his own. He grew tired of the banking industry, quit his job, and decided to focus on his passion. Brock used his investment industry knowledge and started to research the financials for starting a brewery. Eventually Brock and his college buddy Kevin Bartol put all of their funds on the table to launch the brewery. Starting out was rather rough; many locals weren't drinking craft beer yet and did not even know what the term "craft beer" meant. With guerrilla marketing and word of mouth, Saint Arnold began to grow and by 2007 they had reached max capacity at their original location. They opened the location of their present brewery in 2009, which gave the company plenty of room for future expansion.

Saint Arnold has always focused on brewing world-class beers that are true to style, approachable, yet still full flavored. A great example of their well-rounded beers is the **Fancy Lawnmower,** a 4.9% ABV German-style kölsch and a light-bodied, sessionable beer. It has a nose of grain and malt with a mouth of grass and citrus hops with a clean sweet malty finish. **Santo** is another great beer from Saint Arnold. It breaks the style and goes dark. The beer uses the **Fancy Lawnmower** recipe but is altered using Munich and black malts for a clean smooth-drinking beer that has quickly become a go-to favorite. Santo is another light and easy-drinking beer coming in at only 4.7% ABV.

Saint Arnold Endeavour
Style: Double IPA
ABV: 8.9%
Availability: Year-Round
Endeavour originally was brewed as a special release in the Divine Reserve series. The beer was so popular that Saint Arnold had no other choice than to add the beer to the year-round rotation. The beer has a citrus grassy nose and a medium-bodied mouth with a complex blend of sweet malts and bold flavorful hops thanks to the blend of Columbus, Simcoe, and Centennial hops. It was a completely different animal for Saint Arnold, as they had not tried to brew a big hoppy beer with the exception of the Elissa IPA. They recommend serving the beer at 45 degrees or warmer to let the beer open up its hop characteristics. This is a big bold beer with 76 IBUs that you should enjoy slowly and savor.

Many of Saint Arnold's beers are sessionable, with the exception of their Divine Reserve and Bishop's Barrel specialties. No stop in Houston is complete without a visit to Saint Arnold; but beware, Saturday morning tours can get busy so plan accordingly. Luckily, they welcome outside food, board games, and cards to make your visit even more fun.

SOUTHERN STAR BREWING
1207 N. FM 3083 Rd. East, Conroe, TX 77303; (936) 441-2739; southernstarbrewing.com; @SouthernStarBC
Founded: 2007 **Founders:** Dave Fougeron & Brian Hutchens **Brewer:** Sam Wright
Flagship Beer: Pine Belt Pale Ale **Year-Round Beers:** Bombshell Blonde Ale, Pine Belt Pale Ale, Buried Hatchet Stout, Valkyrie **Seasonals/Special Releases:** Walloon, LeMort Vivant, Red Cockaded Ale, Black Crack **Tours:** Fri 4 to 10 p.m., Sat 1 to 10 p.m.
Taproom: Yes

Southern Star Brewing is 45 minutes north of Houston in Conroe. It was founded by Dave Fougeron and Brian Hutchens. Southern Star was noted as the first brewery in the state to package all of their beers in cans, which triggered many local breweries to follow suit. Dave and Brian met while playing disc golf and quickly became friends when they realized their similar tastes in beer and their common interest in the hobby of homebrewing. Dave was originally the head brewer for Saint Arnold before he decided to strike out on his own and open his own brewery with Brian. The partners broke ground on the brewery in a business park in Conroe. Brian's previous career in construction allowed the partners to do a majority of the labor themselves. The name came to the partners while playing disc golf and from there the rest fell into place. Southern Star opened their brewery in 2008 and brought on Sam Wright as the head brewer.

With Sam manning the brewing, Southern Star has created a great lineup of beers. While **Pine Belt Pale Ale** might be the signature beer for the brewery, **Bombshell Blonde Ale** is what they spend the most time brewing. It is a light easy-drinking 5.25% ABV blonde ale that is brewed with American pale and Vienna malt, which combined give the beer a smooth texture on the mouth and a clean profile of sweet malt and yeast that is also present on the nose. Bombshell is a great everyday drinking beer that is sessionable and delightful. If you are looking for something with a little more kick, **Valkyrie** might be more your style. The 9.5% ABV Double IPA is a force to be reckoned with. It is Southern Star's take on the West Coast–style IPAs and is loaded with Simcoe, Centennial, and Columbus hops. Coming in with 100 IBUs, this beer is not for the faint of heart. It has a sweet citrus nose that lulls you

in, but on the mouth it is a bitter medium-bodied beer with hints of grapefruit, caramel, and pine. The malt base gives Valkyrie a sweet overtone and a complex experience that makes a big hit.

Southern Star hosts tours every Friday and Saturday until 10 p.m., so this gives you more than enough time to stop by. The taproom and brewhouse are in two different buildings, but they are not climate controlled, so if you are planning a visit be sure to dress accordingly. They occasionally host live music and food trucks during their taproom hours and you are always welcome to bring your own food. The brewery is a family-friendly place that welcomes kids and even your four-legged friends. Southern Star's beer can be found across Texas as well as in Alabama, Florida, Indiana, Louisiana, South Carolina, Kentucky, Ohio, Tennessee and a few random locations in between. While I highly suggest picking up a "sixer" of Southern Star beers, I can't stress enough heading to the brewery to check out their Taproom Series of beers that are only available at the brewery. This is where they experiment with different styles and recipes and create one-off brews without having to make large batches. Southern Star has come a long way in their time, and they have big plans to continue to grow. By late 2015 Southern Star will be expanding into their new brewery, which Dave says will help the company put out more beer and give fans a bigger space to enjoy while visiting the brewery.

Buried Hatchet Stout
Style: Stout
ABV: 8.25%
Availability: Year-Round
The Buried Hatchet Stout is a beautifully bold stout with a medium body that is perfect for year-round drinking. It pours a dark brown with a tan head and has a rich nutty coffee nose. The mouth is creamy with notes of coffee and chocolate and just a little bitterness from the hops on the back end for a dry finish. It leaves a lingering roasted taste in your mouth that is enjoyable for fans of dark roast coffees. If the beer summons your sweet tooth, Buried Hatchet makes for a great beer float over vanilla ice cream. Thanks to the creaminess of this stout, it makes for a delicious and intoxicating treat.

TEXAS BEER REFINERY

1825 Dickinson Ave., Dickinson, TX 77539; (832) 722-4627; texasbeerrefinery.com; @TxBeerRefinery

Founded: 2013 **Founders:** Ryan Rhodes & John Hearn **Brewer:** John Hearn **Flagship Beer:** Mexican IPA **Year-Round Beers:** Mexican IPA, American Dream Pale Ale, Tex's Blonde, Bayou City Brown **Seasonals/Special Releases:** Crawfish Porter, Imperial IPA, Gulf Coast Gose, Double Lime Mexican IPA **Tours:** Sat 2 to 5 p.m. **Taproom:** Yes

Texas Beer Refinery is located in a business park in Dickinson, less than 45 minutes south of downtown Houston. It was founded by Ryan Rhodes and John Hearn, who met at a local bar conversing about their appreciation for craft beer. John had been a long time homebrewer, and he eventually taught Ryan the trade. Between homebrewing and enjoying the fruits of their labor, John and Ryan began to talk about starting a brewery of their own. Eventually the partners were tired of talking about "what if" and decided to move forward. In 2013 they officially opened Texas Beer Refinery, which was named after their careers in engineering in the oil and gas industry and as a nod to the refineries that surround Dickinson.

Right from the start John and Ryan worked hard to get their name out by participating in as many beer festivals as possible. They wanted to take their brewing concept to a different level by offering their beers on draft and in growlers only.

The growlers hit the stores and captivated their customers, because they were the first brewery in Texas to package their beer in 64-ounce growlers for retail sale. Unfortunately, due to their size, Texas Beer Refinery beers can only be found in and around the bay areas south of Houston.

Texas Beer Refinery beers have all been created by John, who has a long background in homebrewing and has even won awards for some of his creations. He has created some interesting concepts by exploring different styles and ingredients. The **Mexican IPA** is a unique beer that is a standard American IPA recipe but adds fresh Mexican key limes in the boil to give the beer a semisweet citrus finish. The beer is light bodied and pours light golden in color. The key limes are present in the nose with a soft grass characteristic. On the palate you get the great flavor of the malt that is sweetened by the key limes and gives the beer a soft bitter bite that is stimulating and enjoyable. **Tex's Blonde** is a very sessionable blonde ale at 5.3% ABV. It pours a hazy yellow color with a malty citrus bouquet. A light-bodied beer that is approachable and inviting, it has indications of banana and clove with a slight bitter finish. Much of their lineup follows this formula: simple and balanced with lower alcohol contents and welcoming profiles.

Crawfish Porter
Style: Porter
ABV: 5.8%
Availability: Crawfish Season (Mid-Spring)
Texas has adopted the Louisiana love for crawfish boils, and Texas Beer Refinery has taken that affection to another level. I know what you are thinking, and no, there's no crawfish in the beer, but it is brewed with 30 pounds of fresh crawfish in the boil. We are assured that no crawfish died in vain as they were eaten after the beer was brewed. The Crawfish Porter is a take on the popular oyster stouts, except this is a little more subtle. It pours a medium-bodied dark brown with a roasted malty nose. On the mouth the beer is surprisingly smooth and has hints of coffee with an earthy and lightly salted briny finish on the palate. The beer is quite clean and I was rather impressed with how much I liked it. It took a couple sips for me to really grasp the beer, but now I look forward to spring for some mudbugs and a pint of Crawfish Porter.

Texas Beer Refinery has open house tours every Saturday from 2 to 5 p.m. Due to their limited size, their beers can be a little hard to find, but growlers are sold in area stores as well as at the brewery. They have an expansion in the works and are moving to a location 5 miles up the road in Kemah. They are also exploring new ideas such as creating custom beers for clients, so I am interested to see the future of the brewery as they continue to grow.

TEXAS BIG BEER BREWERY

400 County Rd. 3136, Buna, TX 77612; (409) 926-2638; texasbigbeer.com; @TEXASBIGBEER
Founded: 2012 **Founders:** John & Tammy McKissack **Brewer:** John McKissack **Flagship Beer:** Big Texas Blonde **Year-Round Beers:** Renaissance Cowboy, Big Texas Blonde, Texas Crude, Working Stiff Ale, Beeriac IPA, 2nd Base Cream Ale **Seasonals/Special Releases:** Big Experimental Brew, Queen's Limited Release, Wheat Wine, White Chocolate Porter, Irish Cream Stout, Czar of Texas **Tours:** Third Fri of the month 5 to 9 p.m. **Taproom:** Yes

Texas BIG BEER Brewery is located near the Texas/Louisiana border in the small town of Buna, and it was founded by John and Tammy McKissack. John was a civil engineer who ran a podcast called "BrewCrAzY" with his wife Tammy. The podcast would interview local breweries on getting a start in the business, building a brewery, and other insider news for beer fans. John was a longtime beer fan and homebrewer who was inspired by his father, also a homebrewer since the '60s. With the success of the podcast, John started to find most of his free time revolving around beer and testing new brewing techniques. He decided to leave behind his career in engineering and take the risk of starting a brewery of his own.

Using their own funds, the McKissacks broke ground on their brewery, but when it came to their name "Texas BIG BEER Brewery," they were met with opposition from the Texas Alcoholic Beverage Commission. Due to Texas laws, breweries were prohibited from promoting their beer for having high alcohol contents with terms like "strong" or "big." Also, if a product was under 4% ABV, it could only be labeled as "beer" and anything over had to be labeled as an "ale" or "malt liquor." In the fall of 2011, Jester King Brewing Company from Austin sued the TABC, stating that their laws violated their rights under the Equal Protection Clause of the Fourteenth Amendment. Jester King won their case, and the lawsuit helped breweries such as Texas BIG BEER Brewing to accurately label their beers no matter the ABV. In 2012, the McKissacks officially opened and released their big beers to the public.

From the beginning John knew he had to set himself apart from the rest of the state, especially being located in such an isolated area. He wanted to make beers that were not only big by alcohol content, but big on flavor as well. Their first release and flagship beer is the **Big Texas Blonde,** which is a 10.5% ABV Belgian-style blonde ale that pours a deep golden yellow with a frothy white head. The beer is a heavily malt-forward beer that you can pick up on the nose along with notes of sweet citrus. On the mouth it is almost impossible to tell that this is such a massive beer. It has a sweetness thanks to the Belgian Candi syrup that gives this blonde an almost triple flair. It is a sweet yet enjoyable beer that will sneak up on you if you are not careful. Another notable brew from Texas BIG BEER Brewing is a collaboration with well-known and award-winning homebrewer Mike "Beeriac" Heniff, the **Beeriac IPA.** It is a heavily hopped 8.95% ABV mammoth that pours a rich amber with a seductive bouquet of citrus, pine, and malts. On the mouth you are instantly greeted with the bite of the hops that lights up your senses with delight as it mellows out, and notes of sweet caramel malts finish out the experience. It is a well-balanced IPA that is big and bold but still approachable, but I must warn you that the ABV will catch up to you before you know it.

Renaissance Cowboy
Style: Scotch Ale
ABV: 8.2%
Availability: Year-Round

Everything in Texas is bigger, including our beer. The folks at Texas BIG BEER Brewery have developed big beers that are big on flavor as well as alcohol content, but their focus is on the profile itself. The Renaissance Cowboy is a work of art that John McKissack has put much time into perfecting. To ensure the beer would perfectly mimic the Scottish style, he has replicated the water profile that is found in Edinburgh. Blending the water profile along with English ale yeast, malts, and barley gives this beer a sweet malty flavor that has the kind of faint smoky finish that you would normally find in scotch. It is a very mellow easy-drinking beer that becomes even more complex and delicious as the beer warms to room temperature. The nose is malty with notes of toffee and caramel that follow onto the palate with a slight alcohol warmth. It is a year-round beer, but I really enjoy it during the colder seasons.

Texas BIG BEER Brewery had a goal from day one to brew the best beers possible with big flavors and profile, with the alcohol content as just a byproduct. John is his own worst critic, ensuring that each batch is brewed to perfection, and if it isn't to his standards he is not afraid to dump the batch. They are definitely making a name for themselves in making well-rounded big beers and their dedication to the craft is quite clear. John and Tammy along with their daughter make up the crew at the brewery, and they are putting in 18 hours practically 7 days a week. They are in the process of bringing back tours on the third Friday of each month, but be sure to check their website for updates. The beers are only available in limited areas, so I recommend picking up a bottle or two at the brewery—but be sure to drink responsibly.

TEXIAN BREWING COMPANY

1125 Farm to Market 359, Richmond, TX 77406; (281) 762-2604; texianbrewing.com; @TexianBrewing
Founded: 2012 **Founders:** Joshua & Lindsey Haley **Brewer:** Caleb Wilson **Flagship Beer:** Battle Line **Year-Round Beers:** Battle Line, First Stand, Broken Bridge, Brutus, Charlie Foxtrot **Seasonals/Special Releases:** 1824, Summer Sandia, Liberty, Fireside **Tours:** Check Website **Taproom:** Yes

Texian Brewing Company is in Richmond, Texas, which is just west of Houston, and was founded by husband and wife Joshua & Lindsey Haley. Joshua found his love of craft beer when on a trip through Fredericksburg, Texas, he stopped at Fredericksburg Brewing Company. He ordered a Helles Keller and he was hooked. He picked up homebrewing in college from friends and dreamed of one day opening a brewery of his own. After Joshua graduated he worked in the banking industry, but when his company started to restructure, he decided to bail and focus on his plans to start a brewery. With the help of his family, Joshua and Lindsey were able to break ground on the site where Texian Brewing lies today. Texian Brewing is named after the Texian Army, who fought against the Mexican army during the Texas Revolution.

Joshua had a love for Texas history and wanted to add it to both the brewery and the beer. Inside the brewery are replicas of artifacts from Texas history and flags that have flown over the state. The beers are all named after events in Texas history and even tell the story on the cans. The **Battle Line** is named after the legend of Lt. Colonel William B. Travis. He knew his army was outnumbered at the battle of the Alamo, so he drew a line in the sand and offered any of his soldiers a chance to leave. Sadly, Travis and all of his soldiers lost their lives, and this 6.5% ABV brown ale is named in his honor. The beer is dark brown in color with a tan frothy head.

It has a medium body with rich chocolate and coffee notes on the mouth. It is a very enjoyable brown that draws a line in the sand to separate itself from many of the bland boring browns produced by others. It is a very enjoyable beer that is both sweet and mellow with a clean finish. The **Brutus** is a mighty English-style IPA that has a prominent malt profile with a bitter hoppy finish. It has notes of earth and wood with a minor citrus finish. It is named after a ship in the Texian Navy that battled against Mexican forces and halted Mexican ships from delivering supplies to Santa Ana.

Texian Brewing is a great place to check out in west Houston. It is a family-friendly brewery that often has a Friday movie night along with food trucks to make the evening complete. Pets are also welcomed at the brewery, so you don't have to leave your four-legged friends behind. At the time of publication no tours were scheduled, so check their website for upcoming tours and news.

Broken Bridge
Style: Dunkelweizen
ABV: 5.3%
Availability: Year-Round

Broken Bridge is named after General Sam Houston, who ordered a bridge to be destroyed to trap Mexican soldiers from escaping and allowed Texans to ambush the Mexican army. The beer is a great well-balanced dark beer that pours heavy but has a mellow medium body. It has notes of clove and banana, but it is not overly sweet or overpowering. The beer is very enjoyable for everyone from craft aficionados to novice commercial drinkers. It is a great introductory beer that is very easy to approach and is a great choice no matter the time of year. The mouth is rich and malty with roast coffee notes and even a little dark chocolate. The Broken Bridge is a great beer to pair with barbecue or burgers, which will complement the meat without overpowering it, and the beer doesn't leave behind a lingering aftertaste so it works great as a palate cleanser.

Brewpubs

BEERFOOT BEACH BAR

2816 Avenue R ½, Galveston, TX 77550; (409) 762-2337; yagaspresents.com/beerfoot;
@BeerfootIsland
Founded: 2012 **Founders:** Mike Dean & S.C. Inman, III **Brewer:** Charlie Taboada

Beach Bar is located just along the historic seawall on Galveston Island. The bar features a remarkable array of craft beers with a spotlight on locally brewed beers, but the beers that are brewed in-house are what really make this place great, thanks to their brewmaster Charlie Taboada. Every month they feature a guest brewer who comes in and makes a recipe of his own. Unfortunately, once the beer from the guest brewer is gone, it is gone for good. This makes for an interesting concept that has drawn local brewers from places like Karbach and No Label, which have brewed a special beer just for Beerfoot.

The building itself comes with a sense of history and charm. It was the original home to Club D'Elegance, the first African-American nightclub on the island. Now

Want to Brew?

Every month Beerfoot Beach Bar selects a homebrewer and gives them the opportunity to brew their recipes on their equipment and sell it at their bar. Beers are rated and scores are tallied at the end of the year to see who has the Best BODY (Beer of da Year) for cash and prizes. Many of the past guest brewers have been brewers from local breweries, but you can sign up for the chance to be selected to brew on their system. This is a great opportunity for a homebrewer who is looking to go pro to see if their beers have what it takes to make it. For more information be sure to check out Barefoot Beach Bar's website, and best of luck to all you avid homebrewers.

the building has a new life that is brewing up the attention of craft beer fans on vacation. The bar faces toward the beach across the street with roll-up glass doors that let the salty air in. The crowd is a mix of younger locals, and it gets really busy during the high tourist seasons from spring break till the end of summer. Drinking on Galveston beaches is prohibited, but you can get a growler filled and take it back to your room to enjoy during your vacation, or take one to go and keep the memory of your Galveston trip alive with every sip.

MOON TOWER INN—MOON TOWER SUDWORKS

3004 Canal St., Houston, TX 77003; (832) 969-1934; http://damngoodfoodcoldassbeer .com; @daddymeatstacks
Founded: 2013 **Founders:** Evan Shannon & Brandon Young **Brewer:** Matt Greer
Flagship Beer: East Brown & Down **Year-Round Beers:** East Brown & Down, Porter, Pale Ale, IPA **Seasonals/Special Releases:** Dome Faux'm Throwback Cream Ale

Moon Tower Inn is far from fancy. It is in an old industrial neighborhood just outside of downtown Houston and would be easy to miss if not for the lines of cars parked along the street. Built out of a couple of shipping containers, Moon Tower is doing things their own way and they follow their own rules. If you head over to their website, you are just told to "get off the damn internet" and "get your ass to 3004 Canal St. HTX."

Moon Tower is Houston's only full-scale brewpub with a kitchen grilling up wild game hot dogs, mouthwatering burgers, and specialty sandwiches. There isn't much atmosphere, just a large yard scattered with picnic tables, but don't let the lack of

scenery fool you. Moon Tower is a very popular destination for both beer and food.

While the food and 66 taps of craft beer are big hits, the beer that Moon Tower is brewing on their 3-barrel brewhouse has really caught my attention. Moon Tower Sudworks is still rather new, but that isn't stopping them from cranking out impressive and interestingly named beers. They collaborated with fellow Houston brewers at 8th Wonder Brewery to create **Dome Faux'm Throwback Cream Ale,** which is a tribute to the historic Astrodome and the light easy-drinking beers once sold there.

If you are in town for an Astros game, this is a great place to hit before heading to Minute Maid Park. You are just a couple miles away from the best wild game hot dogs in the city and an extraordinary lineup of beers. They plan to continue brewing new recipes along with collaborations with local brewers, so it will be exciting to see what the future will hold for Moon Tower Sudworks.

PADRE ISLAND BREWING COMPANY

3400 Padre Blvd., South Padre Island, TX 78597; (956) 761-9585; pibrewingcompany.com
Founded: 1995 **Founder:** Markkus Haggenmiller **Brewer:** Markkus Haggenmiller
Flagship Beer: South Padre Blonde **Year-Round Beers:** Texas Longboard Lager, Pelagic
Porter, South Padre Blonde, Speckled Trout Stout, Tidal Wave Wheat, Padre Pale Ale
Seasonals/Special Releases: La Nortena Winter Ale, Cinco de Mai Bock, Oktoberfest

South Padre Island is known for its wild spring break parties and the busy flood of summer tourists, but just a few blocks away from the madness on the beach, Padre Island Brewing Company is serving up wonderful food and brewing great beers. Padre Island has focused on offering a wide variety of dishes, from burgers and sandwiches to surf and turf options as well as pizzas. The beers are created by third-generation brewer and owner Markkus Haggenmiller, who moved to South Padre from Minnesota. His father was a brewer for Hamm's Brewing Company and Markkus wanted to keep the tradition of brewing alive in his family. He has focused on ensuring that both the food and beer are made using only top-quality ingredients for an experience that customers will enjoy. The best part about Padre Island Brewing Company is that though it is located in a tourist area, you will not find the usual high tourist prices. Both the beer and the food are reasonably priced to keep both locals and tourists coming back.

The beers at Padre Island are easy-drinking sessionable beers that are not over the top. The beers might follow the standard styles commonly found in other brewpubs, but Markkus has done a great job brewing true to style beers with full flavors. The **Padre Pale Ale** is a great beginner beer to start your palate off with a lighter style yet with full flavor. The beer pours a rich golden color with a light white head. The bouquet is rather light but you can smell the aromas of caramel, grains, and pine. On the mouth the beer has a light easy body with just a light bitterness from the hops. It is a great day-drinking pale ale that pairs perfectly with their selection of burgers and sandwiches.

There is nothing better than a nice beer on a hot day near the beach. Whether you are in Padre for spring break or just touring the state for good beer, Padre Island Brewing is a great destination to check out. The food is solid and reasonably priced and the beers are definitely great. This is my go-to spot when I need craft beer in south Texas.

Beer Bars

BRC GASTROPUB

519 Shepherd Dr., Houston, TX 77007; (713) 861-2233; brcgastropub.com; @BRCgastropub

Draft Beers: 28 **Bottled/Canned Beers:** 30

BRC GastroPub opened its doors in 2010, giving patrons a southern take on the classic European gastropub. Restaurateurs Lance Fegen, Lee Ellis, Carl Eaves, and Will Davis wanted to bring a rather new concept at the time to Houston: mingling upscale new American cuisine with craft beer. Chef Timothy Andrews works hard to ensure that only the best-quality foods leave the kitchen. From the perfectly fried chicken to the succulent prime rib slab, BRC isn't cutting any corners when it comes to their culinary selections to pair with their ever-rotating wall of beers.

BRC hosts a beer dinner with a different brewery on the middle Wednesday of every month. For each dinner Chef Andrews prepares a custom menu to accentuate the style of the featured beers. Since everything is made fresh in house, you can

expect a night of beer and food pairing that's hard to beat. Aside from the special beer dinners, BRC offers daily food specials that are usually big hits.

If you are looking for a great happy hour, BRC offers $2 off drafts from 2:30 to 7 p.m. Monday through Friday and $10 carafes of mimosas on the weekends during brunch. BRC has a small yet great bar and a shaded outdoor patio for small get-togethers. They will gladly fill your growlers so you can enjoy one of their great beer selections at home.

BREWERY TAP

717 Franklin St., Houston, TX 77002; (713) 237-1537; brewerytaphouston.com
Draft Beers: 32 **Bottled/Canned Beers:** 12

The Brewery Tap is in downtown Houston in what was once part of the first and largest brewery in town. The brewery went out of business in 1950, but today it is a historic landmark and a British pub that honors the past. The Brewery Tap has the feel of a classic pub where patrons gather to watch soccer and pass time over pints. The bar's beer list centers on European brews but still carries some trendy regional crafts. Beers are served in 20-ounce British imperial pint glasses that give the patrons more beer for their buck.

The Brewery Tap is a laid back bar that is warm and engaging. It offers an escape from the bustling downtown atmosphere, a relaxed place to unwind. The crowd is a blend of downtown residents and professionals working nearby. The prices here are possibly the cheapest you will find in the area and alcohol isn't the only kind of spirit you will discover here. The Brewery Tap is believed to be an actively haunted spot. Thanks to the ghosts that haunt the pub, when drinking at the Brewery Tap, you're never drinking alone.

BREWS BROTHERS

2404 Strand St., Galveston, TX 77550; (409) 763-2739; facebook.com/brewsbrothersgalveston; @BrewsBrothersTX
Draft Beers: 25 **Bottled/Canned Beers:** 30+

Among the shops and restaurants in the historic Strand district of Galveston sits Brews Brothers, which features an assortment of craft beers from Texas and beyond. Brews Brothers is also admired for having one of the best burgers on the island. Inside is long and narrow with an old bar that practically runs the length of the building, and outside tables are spread along the sidewalk to enjoy the tropic air and people-watch as you kick back with your favorite brew.

Brews Brothers saw a shaky start when the business partners couldn't see eye to eye on how to grow the business. Owner Justin Strait was adamant about turning the bar into a brewpub so he could pursue his passion for brewing and share it with the world, while his partner was set on keeping the business as a bar.

James Cunningham was a sales rep for Houston-based Saint Arnold Brewing when he met Justin. James instantly understood Justin's vision of bringing a brewpub to Galveston, so when the opportunity arose he offered to buy out Justin's partner and help bring craft beer to the island. After temporarily shutting down to file new paperwork and licensing, Brews Brothers reopened in the spring of 2013 with plans to add a brewery and kitchen. Once the kitchen was ready, they brought on former Petrol Station chef Troy Witherspoon from Houston to create the menu and design the best burger in Galveston as well as unique one-off specialty dishes weekly. In the late spring of 2014, Brews Brothers started work on adding the brewhouse with Nate Decker as their head brewer. Nate has plans to brew some very diverse beers that you won't find at your average brewpub. He is working on some interesting sours and has plans for barrel aging some of his beers once the brewhouse is fully up and running. For now Brews Brothers continues to bring in some of the best beer available on Galveston Island, and even when the tourist seasons have passed, they want to keep the locals coming in for a great meal and a welcoming place to try new beer.

CEDAR CREEK BAR & GRILL
1034 W. 20th St., Houston, TX 77008; (713) 808-9623; cedarcreekcafe.com
Draft Beers: 37 **Bottled/Canned Beers:** 60+

Located in the Heights neighborhood of Houston, Cedar Creek is a cozy bar and grill that gives you that Hill Country vibe even though it is in the middle of a big city. The outdoor lawn lets guests sprawl about with tables, chairs, and even a fire pit for the colder seasons. Inside the place is lined with tables and a large wraparound bar. Cedar Creek serves breakfast, lunch, and dinner, but my recommendation will always be the burgers. They have many great options for pub grub, but their burgers will leave you feeling like you have never had a real burger before. Their Laredo Burger always goes down easy with a crisp IPA, or try their Cowboy with a clean dry lager. No matter what your choice, Cedar Creek keeps a wide selection of the best craft beers available in the city. Every week they feature Texas Tuesdays when they drop the prices of their Texas beers and liquors. Cedar Creek has become a very popular place not only for their beer but for the laid back good times to be had.

Cedar Creek is only one of many businesses for the Creek Group, who also own the Dry Creek, Canyon Creek, and Onion Creek locations relatively close by. They all carry that laid back feel so no need to get all dressed to impress; at Creek establishments, you can show up in flip-flops and shorts without feeling underdressed. Grab your friends and head on down to Cedar Creek for burgers and beer next time you are in the Heights neighborhood in Houston.

COTTONWOOD

3422 N. Shepherd Dr., Houston, TX 77018; (713) 802-0410; cottonwoodhouston.com; @cottonwoodbar
Draft Beers: 42 **Bottled/Canned Beers:** 10

Cottonwood is a partnership born out of experience. Rob and Sarah Cromie, who co-own another Houston craft beer destination, Liberty Station, with Charles Bishop, teamed up with chef Daniel Ajtai and Houston developer Harres Exezidis to reform an abandoned building in the Garden Oaks neighborhood into a beautiful and spacious establishment with a focus on craft beer, bourbon, and Texas pub fare.

The original side of the building was roughly shaped like the historic Alamo in San Antonio, so the partners decided to call the bar Cottonwood, which is the English translation of Alamo. The spacious patio sprawls out from the tin roof cover into an outdoor oasis of picnic tables and umbrellas. Under the covered patio Cottonwood features live music and is host to many special events.

The Cromies have brought the focus on great craft beers that made Liberty Station a success to Cottonwood and persistently keep the taps rotating. It is unusual to see

something more than once, which is great for those always looking for something new but a disappointment to those who like to stick with what they know. Cottonwood also hosts mini tap takeovers from breweries and even hosts occasional beer dinners. While the beers are from across the country, the main focus is on local Texas beer. Luckily for Cottonwood, there seem to be more and more local breweries popping up every year.

Be sure to check out Cottonwood for a great drink on the patio when the weather is nice. They can accommodate gatherings of any size. They feature $1 off drafts from 4 to 7 p.m. daily, so relax with a cold beer and a game of beanbags.

THE GINGER MAN

5607 Morningside Dr., Houston, TX 77005; (713) 526-2770; houston.gingermanpub.com; @Gman_Houston
Draft Beers: 69 **Bottled/Canned Beers:** 140+

The Ginger Man was the original craft beer destination in Houston when it opened in 1985. The bar is in the upscale neighborhood Rice Village, which is surrounded by Rice University and the Texas Medical Center. Houston was the original location, but the bar has multiplied and opened locations across Texas as well as non-franchised but sister establishments in New York and Connecticut. Ginger Man was named after the 1952 novel of the same name by J. P. Donleavy. Original owner Bob Precious moved to the Northeast and sold off the Texas locations, so the bars up north no longer have business ties but merely share the common goal of serving good beer with good service.

The crowd is diverse with craft beer fans and local college students, and you can sometimes find a patron wearing his hospital scrubs after a long day in the operating room sharing beers with a suit-and-tie professional. The warm wooden interior spills out into a patio out back that is lined with picnic tables like a traditional German biergarten. Famed beer writer Michael Jackson once claimed the Ginger Man was one of his favorite bars in the US, and it undeniably has set the bar high for newcomers to the scene. This is a bar that truly focuses on giving their patrons the best.

HAY MERCHANT

1100 Westheimer Rd., Houston, TX 77006; (713) 528-9805; haymerchant.com; @HayMerchant
Draft Beers: 80 **Bottled/Canned Beers:** 60

Located in the trendy Montrose area of Houston, Hay Merchant is one of the many admired businesses owned by Houston mixologists Bobby Heugel and Kevin Floyd. The bar's name comes from the occupation of German immigrant Mitchell (Michael) Louis Westheimer, who Westheimer Road is named after.

Hay Merchant quickly exploded as a craft beer destination in the active nightlife area of Houston. The brick building echoes that of an old speakeasy but with a trendy sense of industrial design. The bar beckons your attention to the red brick wall with framed chalkboard slabs listing the current beers on tap. In the kitchen their chef creates culinary concoctions that flatter their selection of ever-rotating taps.

Hay Merchant has an upscale vibe without the price gouging. The food is delicious and the crowd is young and fun. This isn't the kind of place for a quiet conversation over beers; it's more of a fun and vibrant bar. Owner and beverage director Kevin Floyd is constantly looking to stay on top of the craft beer game, frequently trying new beers to put on the wall, and has even developed a barreling program in his house including having special firkins designed just for the bar. Hay Merchant is a must-see in Houston if you are looking for a place with good food and impressive beer.

JULS RESTAURANT, LOUNGE & CAFE
7212 Old Jacksonville Hwy., Tyler, TX 75703; (903) 581-5857; juls903.com; @juls903
Draft Beers: 20 **Bottled/Canned Beers:** 30

Juls is a concept that you would expect to see in a trendy section of a big city like Dallas or Houston, but owner Matt Shulz brought his dream to the small town of Tyler. An architectural beauty, the 10,000-square-foot, 2-story establishment features a cafe, restaurant, lounge, and a peaceful shaded patio that sits above the water.

Inside, Juls has an upscale atmosphere thanks to chef and Las Vegas native Phil Norsetter, who commands the kitchen with an array of Asian fusion dishes including a very exciting compilation of sushi. The food may be the focal point, but the craft beer selection is guest of honor. General manager Jarrod Manes brings his admiration for beer to Juls with 20 taps of some of the finest beers around. Jarrod likes to keep a strong focus on Texas breweries, but Juls also features beers from across the country.

You will not find any other place in Tyler quite like Juls. You could literally spend your entire day here moving from the cafe, to the patio, to the main dining room and a long evening in the lounge. The level of culinary expertise will impress even the most refined palates, and beer lovers will take pleasure in the variety of beers featured. Since Tyler isn't exactly a big tourist hub, many of the patrons at Juls are locals looking to enjoy some amazing food, great drinks, and fun nightlife. Juls unquestionably left an impression on me. I wish there was a location near me, and I would highly recommend this place to anyone visiting Tyler.

LIBERTY STATION

2101 Washington Ave., Houston, TX 77007; (713) 640-5220; libertystationbar.com; @libertystation

Draft Beers: 14 **Bottled/Canned Beers:** 40

Liberty Station is just outside downtown Houston in the Sixth Ward neighborhood on the popular nightlife strip of Washington Avenue. The building is an old auto repair shop transformed into a laid back environment with cold beer, stiff drinks, and some of Houston's best food trucks.

Liberty Station likes to stick to the slogan "No crap on tap" and features an ever-revolving list of beers, but you will not find the big commercial beers like Bud or Miller here. They pride themselves on serving fine craft beers and providing a laid back place where regulars can enjoy a few drinks without the obnoxious nightlife buzz. Liberty Station often features special events and tappings with breweries, so you never truly know what you will find on their ever-rotating wall of beers. They also host art events featuring works from some of the best up and coming artists in town.

The owners Rob and Sarah Cromie along with Charles Bishop also co-own Cottonwood, another successful establishment in Houston. They keep the same relaxed approach and engage those that just want a casual place to gather with friends. Dress codes are not enforced, there are no cover charges, beer is cheap, and they are dog friendly on the patio. Parking is a little limited at Liberty Station: you

can park along the street but be careful of parking signs. The last thing you want after a fun day is to see your car towed.

LUCKY'S PUB

801 St. Emanuel St., Houston, TX 77003; (713) 522-2010; luckyspub.com/; @luckyspub
Draft Beers: 65 **Bottled/Canned Beers:** 250

Lucky's Pub just outside of downtown Houston is a place for all things sports and beer. It offers over 300 available selections to choose from, boasting a vast selection of taps and a row of glass-door beer coolers. Lucky's Pub is one of the largest sports bars in the city, and they have prime real estate a stone's throw from BBVA Compass Stadium, Minute Maid Park, and the Toyota Center. There are large projection screens in both the front and the back rooms for large sporting events and a bunch of TVs placed throughout the building for adequate sports coverage. Outside is a large deck that looks upon the massive BBVA Compass stadium that for some odd reason makes me think of the Thunderdome from *Mad Max*.

If the beer is not enough reason to go to Lucky's, their award-winning chef bakes some remarkable hand-tossed pizzas and grills some enormous mouthwatering burgers. Lucky's is also home to some very large events such as the annual St.

Patrick's Day Festival, which takes over the surrounding parking lot and side streets for one massive green party. They are also the headquarters for many local sports fans. When the Houston Dynamo are playing, the streets run orange as the fans pre-game at Lucky's before cheering their team on. They return after the game for either a celebration or to drink away their sorrows.

Parking is limited during special events and concerts at a neighboring venue, but on a normal day they have a small but free parking lot out back. With the opening of the BBVA Compass Stadium, the area has become somewhat saturated with bars, so many of the parking lots nearby charge. Next time you are in town to cheer on your favorite sporting franchise stop in to Lucky's Pub or plan around their big St. Patrick's Day Festival. They now have locations in the Heights and Cypress areas of Houston should the downtown location not be an option for you.

MONGOOSE VERSUS COBRA
1011 McGowen St., Houston, TX 77002; (713) 650-6872; mongooseversuscobra.com; @barMVSC
Draft Beers: 44 **Bottled/Canned Beers:** 15

Mongoose Versus Cobra is located in the Midtown district of Houston on McGowen just off of Main Street. The building is a far cry from its former self; it was originally Auditorium Grocery Store when it opened in 1915. After the grocery store closed down, it went through a mix of owners and different businesses

until it went vacant in the mid '80s. It lay dormant until 2012 when its new owners converted the ivy-covered building into a classy bar that has emphasized the architectural aesthetics of the building both inside and out.

Mongoose Versus Cobra comes from the old short story "Rikki-Tikki-Tavi" by Rudyard Kipling. The owners found the struggle between the two animals fascinating and wanted to name the bar after their favorite piece of literature. The mongoose represented the craftiness of the bar while the snake's venom represented the spirits (alcohol).

Mongoose keeps the old charm of a speakeasy alive with their classic cocktails and fine whiskeys, but it is clear that they have a strong dedication to craft beer here as well. As you walk in, three large slates along the original brick wall reveal the current beers on tap. The menu is rather small but features light pub fare to snack on while you enjoy your drinks. Mongoose can be seen as a place for an evening of drinks with friends while still holding that sophisticated charm that makes for a great date spot as well.

NOBI PUBLIC HOUSE
241 E. NASA Pkwy., Webster, TX 77598; (832) 932-5111; facebook.com/pages/
Nobi-Public-House/350740171688975; @nobipub
Draft Beers: 40 **Bottled/Canned Beers:** 225+

Nobi Public House is in the city of Webster, just a couple miles from the NASA Johnson Space Center. With over 200 beers available and delicious Vietnamese food, Nobi has become a very popular place for craft beer fans. Nobi is owned by brothers Andy and Charles Nguyen, and it was a creation born out of the brothers' two businesses. The brothers shared space in a shopping strip with Charles running a Shell gas station and Andy running Nobi Asian Grill. Charlie has an appreciation for craft beer and constantly kept his store stocked with it, and patrons would often stop in to grab a couple bottles to dine next door at his brother's restaurant. The two brothers saw the increasing demand for craft beer and the success of the restaurant, so they decided to combine forces. In 2012 Nobi Public House opened and was quickly recognized in the craft beer community for both their selection of beers and their delightful Vietnamese food. For the craft beer fans, it not only offers them over 200 beers to select from, but they also feature cask selections, nitro taps, and growler fills. Nobi is a laid back bar with a simple yet modern design. It is the perfect place to gather for a few pints and a bite. They often team up with local breweries for special events and keg tapping events, so keep up with them on their social media outlets for upcoming events.

PETROL STATION

985 Wakefield Dr., Houston, TX 77018; (713) 957-2875; facebook.com/PetrolStation; @Petrol_Station

Draft Beers: 36 **Bottled/Canned Beers:** 10

Petrol Station is in the Oak Forest neighborhood of Houston. This small converted gas station has won Stone Brewing Company's Most Bitter Bar contest 3 years in a row, and bitter is meant in a good way. The immense assortment of craft beers and colossal burgers keeps both beer snobs and the average Joe coming in.

Owner Ben Fullelove found a huge success with Petrol Station but had plans to open a brewery of his own. Texas's laws did not allow Ben to own his bar and run a brewery as well, so Ben packed up and began contract brewing his brand Brash Brewing through Clown Shoe Brewing in Massachusetts. In the summer of 2013 Texas brewers successfully battled politicians in the state capital and changed the laws so Ben can now hold a brewpub license and keep his interest with Petrol Station. Brash is expected to be running in full gear by the start of 2014, but Petrol Station will continue to be a craft beer destination in Houston.

Petrol Station is a very chill place to grab a beer. The interior is rather small with a handful of tables, but the large outdoor beer garden sprawls outward and wraps around the front of the building. Houston is known for its hot and humid

summers so be sure to dress accordingly. Parking is free but be mindful of the neighboring houses. The food is excellent but the burgers are big, so you'd better bring your appetite. If you need help picking out a beer, their bartenders are quite knowledgeable and will help you find something you'll like.

ROCKWELL TAVERN AND GRILL

12640 Telge Rd., Cypress, TX 77429; (281) 256-9223; rockwelltavernandgrill.com; @RockwellTavern
Draft Beers: 40 **Bottled/Canned Beers:** 100+

Rockwell Tavern and Grill—located in the northwest suburbs of Houston in Cypress—is the definition of a hidden gem. They feature over 140 beers and classy American dishes with a Texas twist. The burgers are a personal favorite and owner Tiffany Richie's enthusiasm for local craft beer makes for a great experience every visit.

Rockwell Tavern passed through a few proprietors until it was finally taken over by current owners Tiffany Richie and Melinda Mayes. They have worked hard to keep the small business alive and have received great support from local breweries. Rockwell frequently hosts special events and beer dinners. The menu is rather large and offers patrons a mixture of options, most of which are under $10. The portions are huge and everything is made fresh daily.

Rockwell Tavern has been known to get the first releases from local breweries, so this is a great place to visit and try something new. They constantly post their latest tappings, special events, and upcoming beer dinners on their Facebook page. I would highly suggest keeping tabs on Rockwell. The restaurant is family friendly and casual. There isn't much in the way of atmosphere as the focus is on the beer and its enjoyable offerings.

SKALLYWAG SUDS N' GRUB

600 6th St., Kemah, TX 77565; (281) 538-8877
Draft Beers: 43 **Bottled/Canned Beers:** 50

Skallywag Suds N' Grub is an oasis located in the popular Kemah Lighthouse District, home to the Kemah Boardwalk. Owner Demetrios Kouloumoundras and his family decided it was time for a craft beer establishment in the popular tourist destination. The Kouloumoundras family has had a long success with their authentic Greek restaurant Bakkhus Taverna Greek Restaurant & Bar, which happens to be just across the street from Skallywag's.

Demetrios wanted a craft beer bar that would be inviting for all with casual food and great drinks. Skallywag's is a great place to escape the tourist rush during the summer but still be within walking distance of the Kemah Boardwalk. There is a hodgepodge of items decorating the interior along with beer signs, but the handwritten chalkboard that lists the beers on tap grabs your attention. Seating is rather limited with a majority of patrons bellying up to the bar or the wooden ledge that runs along the windows to eat. Barrels stand in as makeshift tables or a place to rest your drinks. The kitchen cooks up food truck–style food with interesting flavors and ingredients. The burgers here are nothing to play with. The brisket ground patties make for a juicy and unforgettable experience, or you can go for one of their wild game burgers such as buffalo or elk. The chicken wings are quite unusual, but in a good way; unlike many places that choose to bake or fry their wings, Skallywag's chooses to smoke their wings, which leaves them plump and juicy. The chicken seems to slide off the bone while the amazing flavors send your taste buds into sensory overload.

Skallywag's features many local beers from bay area purveyors such as Galactic Coast Brewing and Texas Beer Refinery, as well as many other beers from across Texas and beyond. The bartenders are knowledgeable about the beers they tap and are a great help when it comes to deciding what to eat. I highly recommend Skallywag Suds N' Grub if you are visiting the Kemah Boardwalk. The prices are cheaper than many of the surrounding tourist traps, and it is probably the only craft beer bar for miles around. You will leave Skallywag's with a full belly and a craft beer experience that you won't soon forget.

Houston Area—Pub Crawls

Houston is a rather spread out city. While there is public transportation, a car is the best method of getting around. Since you are on a pub crawl, it is advised that you look for a designated driver. A great solution to getting around town is the Houston Wave, which is a small-bus company that takes passengers around the city's nightlife destinations. Now you just have to decide which area of Houston you want to start your craft beer excursion in. Load up on food because this is going to be a long day.

Houston—Montrose/Museum District

Rudyard's British Pub, 2010 Waugh Dr., Houston, TX 77006; (713) 521-0521; rudyards pub.com; @Rudyards. Rudyard's is a Houston institution. It has been since 1978 and it's still going strong. They are known for live music, darts, burgers, and of course beer. With almost 100 beers to choose from, Rudyard's is a great place to visit for good beer. Start your trip here with a juicy burger to coat your stomach for the long afternoon followed by a few rounds of the darts game cricket before heading down the road.

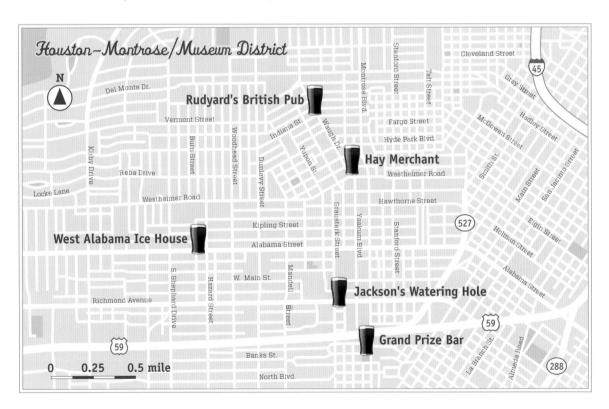

Hay Merchant, 1100 Westheimer Rd., Houston, TX 77006; (713) 528-9805; hay merchant.com; @HayMerchant. Hay Merchant is quickly becoming one of the best craft beer bars in Houston. It is connected with the notable restaurant Underbelly. With 80 beers on draft and a bunch more in bottles, Hay Merchant is a lively spot to watch sports, grab a bite, and enjoy some of the best craft beer available. I'm sure you are probably stuffed from the burger at Rudyard's, but the food at Hay Merchant is too good to miss. Trust me when I say there is always room for their Warm Pretzels, Nacho Fries, or Sweet & Spicy Pig Ears.

Grand Prize Bar, 1010 Banks St., Houston, TX 77006; (713) 526-4565; facebook .com/pages/Grand-Prize-Bar/139353646088917; @GrandPrizeBar. Grand Prize Bar has a dive bar mentality but doesn't quite fit the vibe. The bar has a strong hipster following, but what is important is the beer. The bar is dimly lit and low key with loud music. This is a great place to gather with friends and offers many places throughout the building to congregate including their outside areas. Belly up to the bar and order a round. Don't let the beards and fully tattooed patrons scare you; they are there for the good beer selection too. This could be a great chance to challenge someone to billiards for rounds of beers.

Jackson's Watering Hole, 1205 Richmond Ave., Houston, TX 77006; (713) 528-2988; jacksonsbarhouston.com; @JacksonsHouston. New Orleans off-Bourbon hospitality meets Texas dive bar charm: That's the idea behind Jackson's Watering Hole. It is a laid back icehouse-style bar that has a welcoming atmosphere with a great selection of beers. Thursday nights are specifically great because they feature $2 pints from locals like Karbach and 8th Wonder, including Louisiana's own Abita. By this time on the pub crawl, I can only imagine you are feeling pretty comfortable in your own skin, so let the liquid courage persuade you onto the stage to belt your heart out with a karaoke rendition of "Sweet Caroline" or "Maggie May."

West Alabama Ice House, 1919 W. Alabama St., Houston, TX 77098; (713) 528-6874. The West Alabama Ice House is another Houston staple and has been around since 1928. It is an open-air building where patrons spread out across picnic tables around the building. This is a true dive bar with no real frills other than great people and a great selection of craft beer. You can spend all day here talking with folks or playing rounds of horseshoes. You get a very mixed crowd of people, from old-timers sipping on their commercial beers that they have stayed loyal to for years to the college crowd looking to get a real sense of what drinking in Houston is about. The West Alabama Ice House is a must when visiting Houston and is a perfect way to end a pub crawl through the surrounding Montrose neighborhood of Houston.

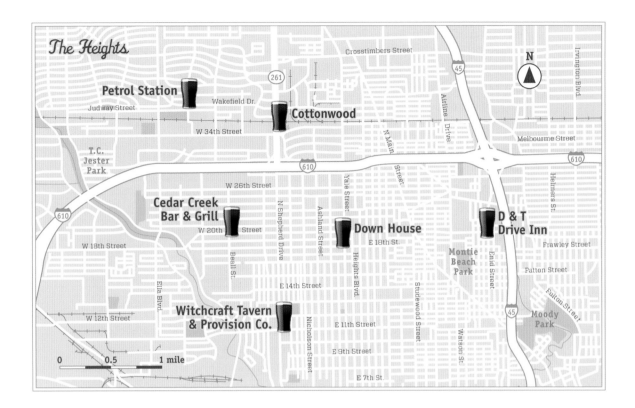

Houston—The Heights

Petrol Station, 985 Wakefield Dr., Houston, TX 77018; (713) 957-2875; @Petrol _Station. If you were to visit Houston and had time for only one bar, Petrol Station would be that bar. An old gas station turned craft beer mecca, the Petrol Station is a must for any craft beer fan or hophead. They have been voted the Most Bitter Bar in the nation numerous times in Stone Brewing Company's Most Bitter Bar Challenge. Not only does Petrol Station have an amazing selection of the finest craft beer available in Texas, they also have an amazing selection of food. It is only fitting to start the crawl here, so you can stuff your face with their Rancor Burger and a big IPA to get the day started.

Cottonwood, 3422 N. Shepherd Dr., Houston, TX 77018; (713) 802-0410; cotton woodhouston.com; @CottonwoodBar. Cottonwood looks like the Alamo from the side, but don't be confused—you are not in San Antonio. This is an open concept bar that spills out onto a large patio with plenty of picnic tables and seating. They focus on craft beer, whiskey, and good food, so this is a great place to spend all afternoon playing beanbags and hanging out with friends. This is personally one of my favorite bars in town because of their atmosphere and the fact that they support the community by hosting many different events for local nonprofits and causes. They have a great outdoor stage that features live music most nights of the week, so bring your dancing shoes for this stop along the pub crawl.

Cedar Creek Bar & Grill, 1034 W. 20th St., Houston, TX 77008; (713) 808-9623; cedarcreekcafe.com; @CedarCreekCafe. Cedar Creek makes you think you stepped into the Hill Country with their laid back vibe and great outdoor spread including fire pits. Nestled along the trees, Cedar Creek serves up some great burgers and craft beer. Time passes by quickly here because it is such a relaxing place to hang out. By this point it might be time to refuel, but if you're not up for another burger, they have some great appetizers to share. I always recommend their Pig Fries or their Frickles to go with a nice crisp lager. If you need a little pick-me-up, Cedar Creek also makes some great coffee. If you are starting to feel a little sluggish, their Cuban Breve will definitely put a pep in your step to keep you from literally crawling to the next pub.

Down House, 1801 Yale St., Houston, TX 77008; (713) 864-3696; treadsack.com/downhouse; @DownHouseHTX. The Down House is quite interesting as it sits in a "dry" area of the Heights neighborhood where selling alcohol is forbidden. That is of course unless you are part of a secret club. Not a Skull & Bones kind of club or any type of illegal bootlegging operation, Down House simply scans your ID and provides the information to the Texas Alcoholic Beverage Commission, which registers you as a member of the club. Now that you have access, you can enjoy all of their great craft beer and cocktail selections. Down House is really popular for their brunch, but people often spend their days here drinking beer and hanging out on the outdoor patio. While their tap list is somewhat small, they tend to bring on big beers along with specialties and rare one-offs. In case you skipped the coffee at Cedar Creek, this will be another great chance to wake up a little.

D & T Drive Inn, 1307 Enid St., Houston, TX 77009; (713) 868-6165; treadsack .com/dtdriveinn; @DandTIceHouse. D & T Drive Inn is the definition of a dive bar, at least from the outside. Inside you will find 50 taps of delicious craft beer and a very surprising menu from their kitchen. The patio out back is the place to be to relax with friends over beers or play washers until your arm goes numb. D & T is a laid back place that is unpretentious and inviting, which makes for a great casual neighborhood bar. Their beer selection is constantly rotating, but you can always guarantee they will have a great selection. While the bar might be out of the way on the itinerary, you will find it to be a great spot in the Heights.

Witchcraft Tavern & Provision Co., 1221 W. 11th St., Houston, TX 77008; (832) 649-3601; witchcrafttavern.com; @WitchcraftTav. On the final stop of the crawl, you'll find Witchcraft Tavern & Provision. It is a small neighborhood bar with a focus on upscale pub grub and craft beer. They keep the taps constantly rotating with a spectacular selection of craft beers that focus on the local breweries. The food is a serious contender for best gastropub grub in town. If you are not burgered out by now, I would suggest their Andouille Burger, but if you want something a little classier I would suggest their Tenderloin Champignon or Lamb Pop Chops. Top the day off with a great beer from one of the local Houston breweries and start planning for your next trip back to town.

Hill Country

The Texas Hill Country has long been the epicenter for the craft beer movement in the state. In 1993, a law was passed making brewpubs legal in Texas and the first one was Waterloo Brewing Company, which was established in Austin just three months after the bill was passed. Austin was home to other popular brewpubs such as the Copper Tank, Bitter End Bistro & Brewery, Lovejoys Tap Room & Brewery, and Draught House Pub & Brewery. The early Austin brewpubs are where many brewers got their start before going on to working with or forming their own breweries. Unfortunately, out of the original brewpubs that started the movement in the state, Draught House Pub & Brewery is the only remaining original in the city. Austin was even home to the legendary Celis Brewery, which was eventually bought out by Miller Brewing. The Hill Country is also one of the most popular destinations in the state for the best barbecue as well as the center for Texas's wine industry. The rolling hills, flowing water, and natural beauty make the Texas Hill Country one of the most beloved regions in the state. The Hill Country is home to some of the most famous breweries in the state such as Real Ale, Live Oak, and Jester King, as well as up and coming breweries like Austin Beerworks, Hops & Grain, and Rogness Brewing. Some may say the market is becoming oversaturated, but it isn't stopping the growth of new breweries and brewpubs in the region.

ADELBERT'S BREWERY

2314 Ritland Dr. #100, Austin, TX, 78758; (512) 662-1462; adelbertsbeer.com;
@AdelbertsBeer
Founded: 2011 **Founders:** Scott & Ramona Hovey **Brewers:** Scott Hovey, Taylor
Ziebarth **Flagship Beer:** Dancin' Monks **Year-Round Beers:** Naked Nun, Philosophizer,
The Traveler, Scratchin' Hippo, Dancin' Monks, Black Rhino, Tripel B, Flyin' Monks
Seasonals/Special Releases: Vintage Monks, Barrel of Love, Barrel Aged Naked Nun,
Oaked Triple B, Contemplating Waterloo, Triple Treat, Sundowner **Tours:** Fri 5 to 8 p.m.,
Sat 1 to 4 p.m. **Taproom:** Yes

Adelbert's Brewery was born out of love. It was founded by Scott and Ramona
Hovey and named after Scott's brother George Adelbert Hovey (known as Del),
who passed away in 2000. Scott worked in semiconductors, but often thought of
starting his own business in a completely different field. He got into homebrewing

and started to do research on how to start a brewery. After a while, Scott felt that he fit in perfectly with the craft beer culture and began working on the business plan for the brewery which officially opened in 2011.

Adelbert's year-round beers are all named after stories about Scott's brother Del's life experiences. When a popular beer company launched their "Most Interesting Man" spokesman, Scott realized that his brother was the real "Most Interesting Man" and that his stories should be shared with all in the hope that others could connect with the stories of Del's life.

Adelbert's is committed to brewing Belgian-style, bottle-conditioned ales. The beers are meant to be shared with friends and family while gathering to tell old stories of good times. The beers are corked and caged for those who are looking for a beer to appreciate and not exactly for floating the river or tailgating. It is beer that is to be enjoyed over time and while taking in the experience and the story behind the beer. Each bottle includes a food pairing on the label to help make the dining experience complete.

Two of the beers that are named for great stories in Del's life are the **Naked Nun** and the **Scratchin' Hippo.** The **Naked Nun** is a 58% ABV wit ale that is crisp and gratifying. The bouquet brings scents of citrus and clove with a delicate spice. It has a flavor of straw, citrus, and coriander with a dry clean finish. It is a great

Beer Lover's Pick

Black Rhino
Style: Dark Ale
ABV: 5.6%
Availability: Year-Round
Adelbert's Black Rhino is a clean dark ale that pours heavy and black but is surprisingly light and refreshing. It has hints of cocoa and coffee but an overall earthy complexity. It has a nose of sweet roasted malts and chocolate. It is named after a story about Del hunting the indigenous rare black rhinos during photography safaris in Kenya to get the perfect shot. This story represents both the color and the rarity of the beer and it can be enjoyed just about any time. Scott suggests pairing this beer with salty appetizers or bold musky cheeses, and he did a great job with this suggestion, as the beer leaves a clean finish and gives your palate the cleaning it needs so that it can welcome a new flavor after each sip.

year-round beer that is light in flavor and perfect for most dishes. The backstory on this beer is not about some wayward frisky nuns but instead was about when Del was living in Colombia and was robbed while hiking down the Cerro de Monserrate. The bandits took everything from Del including his clothes, leaving him naked. While hiding from the public, he was able to get the attention of some nuns that were walking by who helped Del by giving him a blanket and bus fare to get home. **Scratchin' Hippo** is a 6.9% ABV *bière de garde*, which is a French-style farmhouse ale. It is a dark lightly roasted malt-forward beer with notes of caramel and light cocoa. It is a very complex beer with a soft creaminess on the mouth. It is an illustrious beer to take your time with and savor. The story behind the beer is about Del's time in Kenya, when he was rudely awoken from his slumber to his house violently shaking. Del thought it was some sort of earthquake, but as he ran outside he was shocked to see that the rumbling was from a massive hippo from nearby Lake Naivasha, scratching itself against the house.

Adelbert's Brewery is doing some great things when it comes to brewing beer and celebrating life. They have done a great job in bringing traditional Belgian-style beers to central Texas, and their beers can be found across Texas and also in California, New Mexico, South Florida, and Long Island. I have yet to come across a beer from Adelbert's that I didn't enjoy, and I look forward to their future releases.

AUSTIN BEERWORKS

3009 Industrial Ter., Austin, TX 78758; (512) 821-2494; austinbeerworks.com; @AustinBeerworks
Founded: 2011 **Founders:** Will Golden, Mike McGovern, Michael Graham & Adam DeBower **Brewer:** Will Golden **Flagship Beer:** Peacemaker **Year-Round Beers:** Fire Eagle, Black Thunder, Pearl-Snap, Peacemaker **Seasonals/Special Releases:** Heavy Machinery, Sputnik **Tours:** Thurs 5 to 9 p.m., Fri 5 to 10 p.m., Sat 1 to 7 p.m., and Sunday 1 to 6 p.m. **Taproom:** Yes

Austin Beerworks is Austin's answer to craft beer. They do things the way they want and brew the beer that they like. The brewery is located in an industrial business park in north Austin. While they have been listed as one of the fastest-growing breweries in the nation, most people know them for their 99-pack of beer. The package is a 7-foot-long heavy duty box including a whopping 85 pounds of beer. When the word got out that the brewery was doing a 99-pack of beer, it grabbed national attention. There is more to the brewery than what some called a gimmick, because Austin Beerworks is brewing serious beers. Austin Beerworks was the first Austin brewery to package all of their beers in cans, which keeps the beer fresh and away from light contaminants, but it also lets drinkers take the beer on the go with ease whether they are tailgating or floating the river.

Austin Beerworks was founded by Will Golden, Adam DeBower, Michael Graham, and Mike McGovern. Brewer and co-founder Will Golden got his taste for craft beer while traveling through Europe and tried Duvel for the first time. It set him off on a beer journey that inspired him to try a new style of beers. Will learned the art of craft brewing, and his hobby landed him a job in the industry eventually working for Flying Dog in Maryland. Adam DeBower also comes from a professional brewing background with Real Ale. Together, the partners have developed bold hop-forward beers that represent the "badassness" of Austin.

Austin Beerworks currently has four core year-round beers: the **Fire Eagle, Black Thunder, Pearl-Snap,** and **Peacemaker.** The **Peacemaker** has become the most popular beer in the bunch thanks to their 99-pack release of the beer. It is a 5% ABV extra pale ale that is sessionable and easily approachable, but still has a balanced malty hop-forward profile and a bready nose. They have labeled this as everyday ale and that is exactly what it is. **Pearl-Snap** is a 5.3% ABV German pilsner that is crisp and finishes dry. It has a noticeable amount of hop profile but is not overbearing or bitter, and only has 45 IBUs. The Pearl-Snap is another great sessionable beer from Austin Beerworks that keeps the beer light but big on flavor and overall profile.

Fire Eagle
Style: IPA
ABV: 6.4%
Availability: Year-Round

Fire Eagle is a slap you in the face and keep walking kind of beer. It has a strong hop profile that is brewed with Summit, Columbus, Centennial, and Amarillo hops. A great beer that demands your respect and attention to detail, it pours a rich golden body with a small white head. It has a nose of grapefruit and bready malt. The beer almost has a fruity flavor profile thanks to being aggressively hopped. The Fire Eagle is a great go-to IPA that is well balanced and easy to drink. I try to always have this beer on hand as a go-to daily drinking IPA. The 6.4% ABV makes the beer just light enough to enjoy with ease, and the light body will keep you from feeling full. Grab a Fire Eagle and see how this will become one of your favorite new IPAs.

I highly commend Austin Beerworks for the great beers that they are brewing. The beer is brewed in Austin for Austinites, so you can only find the beer in and around the capital of Texas. Their taproom is open from Thursday through Sunday, giving visitors a great chance to see the brewery up close and try the beers in their freshest state.

BOERNE BREWERY
9 Hill View Ln., Boerne, TX 78006; (830) 331-8798; boernebrewery.com
Founded: 2011 **Founders:** Fred & Jennifer Hernandez **Brewer:** Fred Hernandez
Flagship Beer: Denim-Hosen **Year-Round Beers:** Denim-Hosen, Willy's ESB, Old Courthouse Ale, Hopstrasse **Tours:** Fri 2 to 5 p.m. **Taproom:** No

Boerne Brewery is a small company located just 30 minutes outside of San Antonio in the small German town of Boerne. It is a rather quiet town where everyone knows each other, and it is often an escape for San Antonians and Austinites on a Saturday afternoon. Boerne is a small brewery that takes pride in its small town and focuses on making beer that the locals can appreciate. They are not trying to be the next big hit or make beers that are over the top, with loads of hops, or big heavy stouts. Instead, they have kept the mold rather simple and decided to go with beers that were different yet approachable for people who usually stick with the usual commercial beers.

Boerne Brewing Company was founded by Fred and Jennifer Hernandez. Fred got his start in homebrewing when Jennifer bought him a Mr. Beer homebrewing kit. Fred admits that the beer was terrible, but it inspired him to continue to learn the art and science of brewing. He eventually became obsessed and started to tinker with new recipes and ideas. He really admired the beer Old Peculier from Theakston Legendary Ales. Fred tried repeatedly to create a clone recipe but was never successful, but through trial and error he coincidently created the recipe that is used today for their **Old Courthouse Ale,** named after the old historic courthouse in Boerne. It is a light balanced English old ale beer that pours dark in color and has hints of roast malts and coffee that follow onto the palate. It is a rather light beer that is easy to drink without being too heavy. Another great beer from Boerne is **Willy's ESB.** It was named after William George "Willy" Hughes, who was an immigrant from Kensington in London, England. He was a very successful prominent rancher and the founder of Hastings, Texas. The beer is dedicated to Willy and is an English-style ESB that pours a rich amber color. It has notes of sweet malt and hay on the nose and has a malt-forward profile with hints of toffee and caramel, giving the beer more of a sweet finish than bitter. It is an approachable beer that is more geared toward a beginner's palate.

Boerne Brewery is proud to make beer from locals, for locals and continues to explore new beers to bring to the market. The beer can mainly be found in and around Boerne, so you will have to head into the Hill Country to get a taste. If you want the best experience, then head to the brewery from 2 to 5 p.m. on Friday for a tour and sample their great beers.

CIRCLE BREWING COMPANY

2340 W. Braker Ln., Austin, TX 78758; (512) 814-7599; circlebrewing.com; @CircleBrew
Founded: 2010 **Founders:** Ben Sabel and Judson Mulherin **Brewers:** Ben Sabel and Judson Mulherin **Flagship Beer:** Envy Amber **Year-Round Beers:** Envy Amber, Blur, Alibi Blonde, Hop Overboard **Seasonals/Special Releases:** Nightlight, Tuxedo Tshirt, Smokin' Beech, Epic, WRYteous **Tours:** Fri 5 to 8 p.m. and Sat 1 to 4 p.m. **Taproom:** Yes

Circle Brewing Company was founded in 2010 by childhood friends Ben Sabel and Judson Mulherin who had been home brewing since they were teens. The guys were originally from Nashville, Tennessee, but after high school, the friends went their own way. Judson moved to Indiana to attend Perdue and went on to become an aviation mechanic and contractor. Ben went on to attend the University of Miami to study finance and economics. While Ben and Judson found great success in their respective careers after college, they were lacking passion for their work. They realized that they

Hop Overboard
Style: Pale Ale
ABV: 4.7%
Availability: Year Round

Sometimes you can tell a lot about a person from their name, and usually the same can be said for what breweries name their beers. The name "Hop Overboard," however, doesn't seem to give you very much at first. But the reason behind the name reveals an interesting story of the one that got away—not a girl, but rather the brewing kettles that Circle Brewing ordered that somehow disappeared. Somewhere in transit over the Pacific Ocean, the shipping container holding the 90-barrel system simply went overboard and it is now lying on the bottom of the ocean floor. Luckily, the guys at Circle Brewing were able to get a new system, which helped them expand their operation and keep up with the demand from their new bottling line. Hop Overboard is a light sessionable pale ale at 4.7% ABV. The beer has a medium body and a very floral aroma of malt and hops. It has a very balanced flavor of sweetness from the caramel malts and the citrus from the hops, which give the beer a dry piney finish. Hop Overboard is a great beer to ease your way into heavier IPA's since it has such a balanced profile. It is a beer that goes great with Texas smoked barbeque, flame grilled burgers, or massive slices of cheesy pizza.

each had an entrepreneurial spirit that made them look for something more in life. Brewing beer had always been something the friends enjoyed doing and one day the thought came to them that they should start a brewery of their own. While looking over possible places to start a brewery Ben and Judson settled on Austin due to the strong support for local businesses from the residents. In 2008 they quit their careers and packed up to move to Austin. Their mission was to start a brewery and make well-rounded beers following the German Purity Law of 1516, meaning they would make beers using only water, malt, hops, and yeast. When the partners decided to move forward with starting the brewery, money was tight. They looked to their friends and family, who helped the guys fund the operation and build out their brewery in March of 2010. It took seven months to complete the project and on December 9, 2010, they opened Circle Brewing with their first beer: **Envy Amber.**

Envy Amber is a medium bodied ale that has a pale golden color. The aroma is malty with hints of dried fruit. On the palate, the beer is a balance between malt and hops with a slightly sweet finish. It is a great beer that you can enjoy a few of and not have that full feeling. At only 4.8% ABV, Envy Amber is a great session beer that you can stick with as an everyday beer. Their **Alibi Blonde** is a light and refreshing blond ale that comes in at 4.3% ABV. Its light color matches the beer's light body and the aroma is faint but has the characteristics of citrus and malt. On the mouth, the beer has a German hefeweizen-like flavor profile of citrus and wheat but has more of a body and is a very easy drinking beer. With such a soft flavor profile, the Alibi is an excellent beer to pair with nearly any dish. Alibi is a great beer for those that are new to craft beer, but it can still be appreciated by the most refined palates, which is why Circle Brewing took home a silver medal for Alibi at the 2014 World Beer Cup.

Currently, Circle Brewing's beer can only be found throughout Austin and San Antonio but as they continue to bottle their beers they are hoping to reach Houston and Dallas by the end of 2015.

512 BREWING COMPANY
407 Radam Ln., Austin, TX 78745; (512) 707-2337; 512brewing.com; @512Brewing
Founded: 2008 **Founder:** Kevin Brand **Brewer:** Nate Seale **Flagship Beer:** Pecan Porter **Year-Round Beers:** Wit, Pale, IPA, Pecan Porter **Seasonals/Special Releases:** Cascabel Cream Stout, Black IPA, ALT, Bruin, ONE—Belgian Style Strong, TWO—Double IPA, THREE—Belgian Style Tripel, FOUR—English Strong Ale, Whiskey Barrel Double Pecan Porter, Wild Bear, FIVE—Imperial Stout, White IPA, Peach Sour **Tours:** Sat **Taproom:** No

5 12 Brewing is located in south Austin and is named after the city's area code. The brewery was founded by Kevin Brand, who found his first interest in craft beer while working at a local beer store. Kevin was fascinated with the local beers at the time, and as the craft beer movement started to rise he decided he wanted to learn how to brew. Kevin became infatuated with brewing with different ingredients and trying different styles of beer. Kevin graduated from the University of Texas with a degree in engineering and after graduation, he and his wife moved to California where he was exposed to even more beer and different hops varieties. The

couple eventually moved back to Austin, and Kevin started to make his move to form his own brewery. With help from head brewer Nate Seale, 512 Brewing has become one of the most popular and recognizable breweries in Austin.

Visitors are amazed to see how small 512 is, but it hasn't halted the brewery from putting out their beers across the state. Overall the beers are very approachable and true to style. 512's goal was to make beer that anyone could appreciate and beers that Austinites would enjoy. They brew four year-round beers along with a handful of seasonals that are released throughout the year. The two most popular beers for 512 are their **(512) IPA** that comes in at 7.2% ABV. It is aggressively hopped but still comes in as a smooth and malty balanced beer that is not overly bitter. The 65 IBUs make this beer a great well-versed beer for its style. The next would be the **(512) Pecan Porter,** which was inspired by the large pecan tree in front of the brewery. The beer was originally brewed as a fall seasonal, but after it hit the bars they realized the beer was such a big hit that it needed to be a year-round release. The beer pours a heavy black in color but is actually quite light on the mouth with a medium body. The mouth is rich in chocolate malt and a hint of bitterness from the pecans. The beer is very enjoyable and creamy with a soft sweetness that makes it such a big hit. When 512 decided to make the Pecan Porter a year-round release, it definitely opened the public's eye to the beers that they are

Beer Lover's Pick

Cascabel Cream Stout
Style: Stout
ABV: 6%
Availability: Winter Seasonal
The Cascabel Cream Stout is a great winter warming beer, not only because of its heavy body but because over 20 pounds of Guajillo chiles are added to each batch, which give this beer a slight warmth that you can detect on the back end on your palate. As the beer warms in temperature, the chile flavor becomes more noticeable, but this beer has an amazing overall complexity with rich creamy notes of chocolate and coffee. On the nose you get a mix of nuts and roast malt. Many people say that the chile flavor is overpowered by the sweet roasted malt, and that is why I would suggest letting this beer sit out a little before enjoying. It is a heavy beer with a medium body and leaves a slight sweetness on the palate that I found enjoyable. This beer is a winner for me when it comes to a cream stout.

putting out. They are constantly working on new beers and have a growing barreling project for future releases.

512 Brewing is one of Austin's most iconic breweries and unquestionably a must when trying Texas beers. Tours are held on Saturday, but you will need to reserve your tickets through their website. Tours are kept small due to the space constraints and to make the tours feel intimate. 512's focus is to show their passion for beer using only the finest ingredients. If you want to get a true sense of Texas craft beer, then be sure to try 512 Brewing Company.

GUADALUPE BREWING COMPANY

1580 Wald Rd., New Braunfels, TX, 78132; (512) 878-9214; guadalupebrew.com; @Guadalupe_Brew

Founded: 2012 **Founders:** Anna & Keith Kilker **Brewer:** Ryan Bishop **Flagship Beer:** Texas Honey Ale **Year-Round Beers:** Texas Honey Ale, Americano Wheat Ale, Rye IPA, Scotch Ale, Chocolate Stout **Seasonals/Special Releases:** Big Bend IPA **Tours:** Coming Soon **Taproom:** No

Guadalupe Brewing Company is in New Braunfels, just a mile off of I-35. Back in 2009 when owners Anna and Keith Kilker traveled throughout Europe and the Pacific Northwest for beer, Keith was inspired by many of the beers he experienced on his travels and felt the calling to brew. But Keith had no brewing experience and

his wife Anna laughed it off. Keith was an automation engineer at the time, but the idea of opening a brewery kept coming to him. Keith ended up studying brewing technology at the Siebel Institute of Technology followed by an internship to brew at a Colorado brewpub. All the while, Anna thought Keith was just really passionate about his hobby until he finally approached her to go forth with opening a brewery together. Anna admits she was quite hesitant about the idea as she was enjoying her career in the medical industry. After some convincing, Anna and Keith agreed to go forth and open what is now Guadalupe Brewing Company.

The brewery is named after the Guadalupe River that runs directly through New Braunfels and is a popular destination in Texas during the summer months. With the help of their head brewer Ryan Bishop, Guadalupe Brewing Company has put out a great line of beers that are easy to approach yet come with a higher than usual ABV. They broke into the market with their **Texas Honey Ale,** which is light golden in color and is easy to underestimate. While it goes down smooth with a vibrant yet tolerable citrus honey flavor, the 7.32% ABV will sting you like a bee if not careful. A portion of the proceeds from Texas Honey Ale benefit the Texas A&M Bee Research program. Guadalupe's **Scotch Ale** is a complex malty 8.17% ABV beer with a delicate nose of wood and a faint hint of smoke. The Scotch Ale is a roasty compilation of flavors such as English malts, toffee, burnt caramel, and even dried dark fruit. It is a very enjoyable experience that can go with almost any meal.

The brewery is in the process of expanding and building out a new taproom for guests to enjoy. Once they build out, they plan to have regularly scheduled tours.

Beer Lover's Pick

Guadalupe Big Bend IPA
Style: IPA
ABV: 7.52%
Availability: Summer
The Big Bend IPA is a big IPA that can be appreciated by those who are not fans of big hops. The lower 47 IBUs make this a malt-forward beer that opens up to a floral bouquet of hoppy citrusness as it warms up.

Guadalupe donates a portion of the proceeds from sales to Friends of Big Bend, which supports sustainability and preservation of Big Bend National Park. This is a great beer for the warmer months, which is why it is Guadalupe's summer seasonal beer. Big Bend IPA is great for pairing with multiple dishes including cheese and meats.

Guadalupe Brewing has really caught the attention of the local bars and restaurants surrounding the Hill Country, which is where you will find their beers with ease. They are working to expand distribution throughout the state in the near future, but due to the demand they have to focus on the Austin and San Antonio markets.

HOPS & GRAIN

507 Calles St., Austin, TX 78702; (512) 914-2467; hopsandgrain.com; @HopsandGrain
Founded: 2012 **Founder:** Josh Hare **Brewer:** Josh Hare **Flagship Beer:** Alt-Eration
Year-Round Beers: Alt-Eration, Pale Dog, The One They Call Zoe **Seasonals/Special Releases:** Greenhouse IPA **Tours:** Wed through Fri 2 to 10 p.m., Sat 12 to 8 p.m.
Taproom: Yes

Hops & Grain's brewery is located in east Austin. It was founded by Josh Hare, who also takes the role of head brewer. The focus for Hops & Grain was to grow around an environmentally friendly sustainable brewery. To reduce waste, the spent grains are used to make dog biscuits for your four-legged friends. Hops & Grain also donates 1% of their annual revenue to local environmental nonprofits and supporting local community growers and producers. Their community awareness is part of what makes this brewery fit so well in Austin.

Hops & Grain has two different brewhouses in the brewery. They have their full production 15-barrel brewhouse and their pilot 3-barrel greenhouse system, which they use for special releases and test batches. All of the beers they brew on the greenhouse system are served in the taproom to test them with the public. Well-received beers are perfected to be brewed in bigger batches and hopefully end up in local bars and restaurants.

The brewery has 3 beers that sum up their core. The **Alt-Eration** was the first release and is a 5.1% ABV traditional German-style alebier, which is not a type of beer that you see much in the States. It is a rather time-consuming beer to create because it is brewed as an ale but fermented like a lager, using cold fermentation which takes longer for the yeast to create alcohol. The beer pours a heavy brown but has a light body. It is a malt-forward beer that is followed by a bitter hop bite making this beer a complex and interesting experience on the palate. I find the beer to be light and balanced for an everyday go-to beer; it won Hops & Grain a gold medal at the 2012 World Beer Cup. The **Pale Dog** is the other beer that Hops & Grain launched with. It is a 5.9% ABV pale ale that is another malt-forward beer thanks to the base of two-row malted barley blended with Vienna and Caramel malts, which give this beer a lightly sweet malty taste that is somewhat creamy on the mouth. It has a rich complexity from the malts and it finishes with a citrus bite from the

The One They Call Zoe
Style: Pale Lager
ABV: 5%
Availability: Year-Round
Don't confuse Zoe with a pale ale; this lovely beer is a pale lager. It is brewed in the tradition of German lagers that are dry hopped, but this beer has a complex malty characteristic that makes it mellow with a clean hop bitter finish. It has a bready nose with floral citrus notes and the mouth brings sweet malt notes with pine and citrus bitterness for a creamy mouth feel that is enjoyable. I find Zoe to be one of my favorite regulars from Hops & Grain, and since the beer is canned I find it great to take into the outdoors. It is sessionable and easy to drink and can be paired with mild cheeses or seafood. It is a great everyday drinking kind of beer that I think many will enjoy.

Nugget and Cascade hops. This great beer is unpretentious and well rounded for just about any palate. The beer isn't too bitter and many will find the malt complexity inviting.

Hops & Grain has quickly become a popular brewery in Austin and their beers are in high demand. They have many recipes in the waiting room ready to test out, and the best way to see what they have in the works is to visit their taproom where they have their experimental batches available to try. The taproom is open Wednesday through Friday from 2 to 10 p.m. and Saturday from noon to 8 p.m., so there are plenty of chances to stop in for a few pints.

INDEPENDENCE BREWING COMPANY
3913 Todd Ln., Austin, TX 78744; (512) 707-0099; independencebrewing.com; @IndyBrewing
Founded: 2004 **Founders:** Amy & Rob Cartwright, Giorgio Favia **Brewer:** Brannon Radicke **Flagship Beer:** Stash IPA **Year-Round Beers:** Austin Amber, Stash IPA, Convict Hill Oatmeal Stout, Bootlegger Brown, Independence Pale, Power & Light Pale Ale, White Rabbit **Seasonals/Special Releases:** ESB, Jasperilla Old Ale, Oklahoma Sux **Tours:** First Sat of the month **Taproom:** Yes

Independence Brewing Company was long in the making. Husband and wife Amy and Rob Cartwright both worked in Austin's original brewpubs in the early '90s. Rob learned brewing hands on while working at the former Copper Tank Brewpub, while Amy learned the industry working at the Bitter End Bistro and Brewery. After both businesses closed their doors, Rob felt the need for beer in Austin and he was looking to make a change in the industry. Independence Brewing Company was born in 2004 with the help of their co-founder Giorgio Favia, who helped turn the dream into a reality.

Independence Brewing is a name that is synonymous with Austin and has been brewing strong for the last 10 years. They have worked hard to brew hop-forward beers with diverse styles and big flavors all while being approachable and well balanced. The brewery supports free thinkers who are casual and laid back and that is just who they employ. The beers represent the culture and stories that make Austin such a great city.

The latest beer to come off the line is **Power & Light Pale Ale,** which is in honor of the historic former City of Austin Power Plant that was long an icon of downtown and is currently being converted into luxury lofts. The 5.5% ABV is a crisp pale ale with a great citrus flavor balanced with light citrus hops. **Stash IPA** is a beast when it comes to Texas-brewed IPAs; the beer is 7% ABV with 100 IBUs. This is an aggressively hopped IPA that grabs your senses and almost wrecks your palate in a good way. Stash is one of the few IPAs in Texas that can stand up to the big and bold West Coast IPAs.

Independence Brewing Company makes a wide variety of beers that almost anyone can enjoy. They have started to open their taproom on Friday from 5 to 8 p.m. but still host their first Saturday of the month tours with live music and local food trucks. This is a great time to try their beers fresh and check out the brewery as they expand within their current space.

Beer Lover's Pick

Convict Hill Oatmeal Stout
Style: Imperial Stout
ABV: 9.2%
Availability: Year-Round
Convict Hill is named after the Convict Hill Quarry Park in southwest Austin near where Rob and Amy Cartwright used to live. The park has an interesting past; it produced the limestone to rebuild the state capitol after the original building burned down. Prisoners were used as free labor to mine the quarry and some even lost their lives, which is reportedly why they dubbed the area Convict Hill.

Convict Hill Oatmeal Stout honors those that worked in the quarry and those who lost their lives. The beer is an 8% ABV stout that is rich in roasted toffee and creamy mellow rolled oats. The beer pours heavy and dark but is still medium in body. It finishes clean and leaves you waiting for another sip. Convict Hill has a sweet nose of caramel, malt, and toffee, which is as seductive as it sounds.

This is a great beer to sip on in both warmer and cooler months. The beer is heavy looking but finishes quite nice. It is a little sweet to pair with a main protein dish but makes for a great after dinner treat. I prefer it just below room temperature so that the beer opens up its vast roasted flavors.

INFAMOUS BREWING COMPANY

4602 Weletka Dr. #300, Austin, TX 78734; (512) 487-8786; infamousbrewing.com;
@InfamousBrewing

Founded: 2013 **Founders:** Zach Perry & Josh Horowitz **Brewer:** Matthew Bitsche
Flagship Beer: Hijack Cream Ale **Year-Round Beers:** Hijack Cream Ale, Infamous IPA,
Bugsy's Fire Brush Amber **Seasonals/Special Releases:** Infamy Olde Ale, Sweep the Leg
Peanut Butter Stout, Pumpkin Massacre **Tours:** Fri 4 to 9 p.m., Sat 1 to 5 p.m., Sun 1 to
5 p.m. **Taproom:** Yes

Infamous Brewing Company may have never been if it wasn't for a chance encounter in 2011 at a New York City bar. Zach Perry and Josh Horowitz were regulars at the bar and were introduced to each other by the bartender over a shot of whiskey. As the evening went on the drinks continued and a friendship grew. The bar where Zach and Josh met has closed, but they own the original sign from the bar, which is proudly displayed in the brewery. Matt Bitsche was a homebrewer and welder from Wichita Falls where he built brewing equipment and experimented with designing his own beer recipes. He responded to a Craigslist ad from Zach and Josh, and after some meetings and sampling some of Matthew's beers, the co-founders knew they had found their brewer.

Today Infamous Brewing is located in a business park on Hudson Bend not far from Lake Travis in Austin. The 7-barrel brewhouse is working overtime to keep up with demand for their great beers. They have gained support from both local Austinites and businesses alike. The name Infamous Brewing is the owners' nod to the old days when the criminals were the celebrities and bootleggers and organized crime figures were glorified.

Infamous brews beers named after infamous acts and characters. The flagship beer **Hijack Cream Ale** is named after the Old West train robberies. It is a 5.5% ABV lightly hopped cream ale that is smooth and velvety on the mouth. The hop profile is faint, but it is a crisp-drinking beer that is perfect for Texas heat. **Bugsy's Fire Brush Amber** is named after the infamous mobster Benjamin "Bugsy" Siegel. Though Bugsy was a rough and tough individual, Bugsy's Fire Brush Amber is more subtle and sociable. The 5.5% ABV amber has a minor roasty flavor from the crystal malts and a very light hop characteristic, making for a great introductory beer that is not overly aggressive.

Infamous Brewing is quickly gaining attention around the state for their beers and have become big competitors in the Austin market. If you are planning to visit the brewery, be aware that the brewery is a good 30 minutes northwest of downtown Austin. But trust me when I say this is a brewery that you are going to want to visit.

Hill Country

Pumpkin Massacre
Style: Pumpkin Pecan Porter
ABV: 7.5%
Availability: Fall

In the fall it seems like everyone is out to produce pumpkin-style beers, but the guys over at Infamous Brewing Company are looking to do things a little differently. Implementing Texas pecans with pumpkin puree, the beer gives off the seasonal flavors of a pecan pie. There are hints of nutmeg and cinnamon on the nose, but it greets your mouth with a dry and semisweet complex flavor. You would imagine this to be a much sweeter beer because of the ingredients, but it is given a soft sweetness that opens up a little as it warms. The flavor profile isn't as roasted as a usual porter, but the notes are still there. It is a great beer for fall festivals and to enjoy over Thanksgiving dinner. The 7.5% ABV is almost unnoticeable on the mouth, but it will surely catch up with you on the end.

The Pumpkin Massacre is a great beer to pair with dark chicken or turkey and even rich chocolaty desserts. I prefer to enjoy it just below room temperature so that the pecan and pumpkin flavor profiles can open up. I would even suggest storing a bottle away for a few months to a year to see how the flavors change. This is definitely a beer to check out, even if you are not into pumpkin-style beers.

They have plans to expand their distribution, but at the moment, you will have to head into Austin to pick up their beer. You will be glad you did.

JESTER KING BREWERY
13187 Fitzhugh Rd., Austin, TX 78736; (512) 537-5100; jesterkingbrewery.com; @JesterKingBeer
Founded: 2010 **Founders:** Jeff Stuffings & Michael Stuffings **Brewer:** Garrett Crowell
Flagship Beer: Le Petit Prince "Somewhat" **Year-Round Beers:** Le Petit Prince, Noble King, Wytchmaker, Mad Meg, Ambree, El Cedro, Commercial Suicide and Black Metal **Seasonals/Special Releases:** Bonnie the Rare, Thrash Metal, Gotlandsdricka, La Vie en Rose, Detritivore, Snörkel, Bière de Miel, RU55, Boxers Revenge, Buddha's Brew, Funk Metal, Ol Oi, Viking Metal, Atrial Rubicite, Das Überkind, Das Wunderkind!, Hibernal Dichotomous, 分桃 **Tours:** Fri 4 to 10 p.m., Sat 12 to 10 p.m., and Sun 12 to 6 p.m.
Taproom: Yes

Jester King Brewery is just 20 minutes west of downtown Austin, close to Dripping Springs. It is one of the most recognizable if not most popular breweries in Texas, known for their farmhouse-style beers and the intricate artwork on their bottles. It is nearly impossible to describe Jester King or pin them down to a style because they work to continuously change the game.

Jester King has found inspiration from many of the artisanal farmhouse European breweries, and you get a sense of that in the beers they brew. They are producing around a thousand barrels annually due to their fermenting process. Many of their beers take between 3 to 4 months to ferment, but for their barrel-aged release it can take anywhere from 9 to 12 months if not longer. The fermenting process depends greatly on the environment and weather. Due to the brewery's lack of space and the time it takes for beers to condition, Jester King doesn't have year-round releases. They typically brew **Le Petit Prince, Noble King, Wytchmaker, Mad Meg, Ambree, El Cedro, Commercial Suicide,** and **Black Metal** more often than others because it takes less time for these beers to condition and they don't contain seasonal ingredients that are harder to come by. One of the most common is **Le Petit Prince,** which is a light 2.9% farmhouse table beer. Farmhouse table beers are light-bodied beers developed in Northern Europe that were the drink of choice in regions where the water wasn't safe

to consume. It is a favorite at the brewery and a true definition of a session beer. It has a grassy and citrus floral nose with a dry citrus mouth with a soft sweet finish. **Atrial Rubicite** is very popular in the springtime. It is a 5.8% ABV barrel-aged sour beer re-fermented with raspberries. It pours a soft rose in color with a nose of fresh raspberries. The body is light on the mouth with a tart and invigorating raspberry flavor. The beer has a sour funk that isn't too overpowering, and it has a subtle dry finish. It is a great beer for taking in the outdoors on a pleasant spring afternoon.

Jester King is a must for any beer fan traveling through central Texas. Due to their capacity they release all of their beers at the brewery first. They occasionally release a small limited stock to the retail markets in Dallas and Houston, but if you are in Austin they want you to take the short drive out to visit the brewery in person. Their beers might be priced higher than most other breweries in Texas, but when you factor in the time, the ingredients, and the care that these beers get during the brewing process, it more than makes up for the price of a bottle. The brewery is a converted rustic country machine shop with a brewhouse and taproom. It sits perfectly in the Hill Country with plenty of outdoor seating that makes time just pass by while sipping on their captivating beers. Stanley's Farmhouse Pizza is housed on the

Black Metal
Style: Farmhouse Imperial Stout
ABV: 9.3%
Availability: Occasional
Black Metal was one of the first beers that I tried from Jester King when they first launched. It was one of the most beautiful beers I had ever had. Disclaimer: I enjoyed this beer much more before they changed to the farmhouse style, but the beer is still really impressive. It pours a heavy black body with a foamy brown head. There is a rich nose of chocolate, coffee, and roasted malts. The best I can describe the mouth is that it resembles a chocolate shake. It is not overly sweet but it opens up with a very prominent chocolate flavor that is rich and decadent. The farmhouse yeast give this beer an interesting twist with a faint tartness that reminds me of licorice or a bitter coffee. The beer is a little rich for me to pair with many foods. I find it to be most enjoyable as a dessert beer or with a robust full-bodied cigar. I highly suggest picking up a bottle if you see one on a shelf. This beer also ages great so buy a second for later.

brewery's grounds, serving handcrafted artisanal pizzas using fresh and local ingredients. The pizza is a perfect complement to practically all of the beers that Jester King makes. Since Jester King holds a brewpub permit, they can sell their beers by the pint or sell bottles to go, so they sell not only their beers but they also curate a great list of beers, wines, and sakes from around the world that you can purchase. The tasting room is open Friday from 4 to 10 p.m., Saturday 12 to 10 p.m., and Sunday from 12 to 6 p.m. They change their menu of offerings weekly, so you will need to check their website or social media outlets for the current menu. Be sure to head into the Hill Country and see how Jester King is changing the way beer is brewed in Texas.

LIVE OAK BREWING COMPANY

3301 E. 5th St., Austin, TX 78702; (512) 385-2299; liveoakbrewing.com; @LiveOakBrewing

Founded: 1997 **Founder:** Chip McElroy **Brewer:** Dusan Kwiatkowski **Flagship Beer:** Live Oak Pilz **Year-Round Beers:** Pilz, Hefeweizen, Big Bark Amber Lager, Liberation Ale **Seasonals/Special Releases:** Schwarzbier, Roggenbier, Oaktoberfest, Primus, Dunkleweizen, Liberator Dopplebock, Weisser Rauch Wheat Smoke, Pale Ale, Grodziskie, Helles Rauch Lager, Smoaktoberfest **Tours:** Every Other Sat **Taproom:** No

Live Oak Brewing Company was established in 1997 by Austin native Chip McElroy. Chip got his taste for great beer when he graduated with a PhD in molecular biology in the '80s and hitchhiked across Europe. Chip found an affection for German-style beers and that stayed with him for some time. When he finally returned to the States, he met a friend in San Diego who ended up mentoring him and helped him develop a more advanced approach to homebrewing. After years passed Chip returned to Austin and decided it was time to move forward with starting his brewery.

Live Oak Brewing has always focused on old world–style brewing that not only follows the

Liberation Ale

Style: IPA

ABV: 6.3%

Availability: Year-Round

IPAs might not be the norm when it comes to German-style beers, but brewer Dusan Kwiatkowski created a great beer for the hopheads in Texas. The Liberation Ale is a very bold IPA with a bouquet of grapefruit and citrus. One sip and the 60 IBUs send your taste buds into sensory overload with a semisweet malty complexity and a bitter but positive hop profile. The 6.3% ABV is almost unrecognizable at first, but after a couple pints you will feel its potency. The beer pours cloudy and is light orange in color with a balanced frothy white head. The beer is medium bodied in the mouth and leaves a bitter citrus flavor in your mouth to savor.

Liberation Ale is a great citrus beer to pair with fish and spicy foods. The hops seem to bring down the heat from peppers while cleansing your palate for another bite. The beer grows more intense in citrus flavor while it drops to room temperature as the malty base brings a sweet floral bouquet to the nose. The Liberator is a great Texas-made IPA that almost mimics the popular West Coast IPAs.

German purity laws of brewing but also allows time for slow mashing and fermentation to create the perfect batch. The vast majority of beers brewed by head brewer Dusan Kwiatkowski are German in nature and truly embody the styles they represent. The **Live Oak Pilz** is the flagship for the brewery and the first beer they rolled out, but the **Live Oak Hefeweizen** is their moneymaker. The smooth and lightly cloudy hefeweizen brings expressions of clove and citrus with light but recognizable banana esters. The beer is a medium 5.2% ABV that can definitely cool you off on a warm summer afternoon in Texas. The **Live Oak Big Bark** is a Vienna-style amber lager with a big flavor without the high alcohol content. Coming in at 4.9% ABV, this is a very smooth sessionable beer that is full flavored thanks to the German and Czech malts. It has a mild hop bitterness with a very clean finish. The Big Bark is very inviting for those who are tiptoeing into craft beers but is still appreciated by longtime craft beer fans.

NEW BRAUNFELS BREWING COMPANY

180 W. Mill St., New Braunfels, TX 78130; (830) 626-2739; nbbrewing.com; @NBBrew
Founded: 2011 **Founders:** Kelly & Lindsey Meyer **Brewer:** Kelly Meyer **Flagship Beer:** LuftWeiss **Year-Round Beers:** LuftWeiss, FeuerWeiss, ErdeWeiss, HimmelWeiss, WasserWeiss **Seasonals/Special Releases:** Shiva's Tears, Wicked Fuel, Thunder Kiss, Hot Child **Tours:** Reservations Only **Taproom:** Yes

New Braunfels Brewing Company is a reincarnation of a former brewery of the same name. The original brewery started up sometime during World War I and flew under the radar for a while during Prohibition and continued to brew. Unfortunately, their luck eventually ran out and they were busted for illegally running the brewery.

New owners Kelly and Lindsey Meyer have resurrected the name New Braunfels Brewing Company, and they are making great German-style beers. While the beers have German names, some of the styles tend to veer off a little and are less German than others. Kelly makes sure that his beers use at least 85% local malts and grains to signify the regional characteristics. New Braunfels Brewing Company's goal was to make beer that the locals could appreciate and beer that should be savored and enjoyed by all.

Beer Lover's Pick

Shiva's Tears
Style: Weizenbock
ABV: 8.5%
Availability: Yearly Special Release
The name may teeter on the precipice of cultural taboo, but the beer is a respectful offering to any god. Shiva's Tears is a beautiful weizenbock that pours heavy and dark with a white light head. There are scents of clove and figs with the slightest detection of coffee. On the mouth the body is medium with flavors of roast malts, slight smoke, and even a little earth. It somehow all comes together for a very enjoyable experience. This is another beer I would prefer just below room temperature. This weizenbock is light enough that it can go well with red meats like steak, but be careful of the 8.5% or you will feel the wrath of Shiva.

The beers' names represent the signs of air, fire, earth, sky/heaven, and water. The **LuftWeiss** is the flagship for New Braunfels Brewing Company and rightly named; it is the air that started the brewery. The light 4.7% ABV hefeweizen is a pale hazy yellow with notes of wheat and clove on the nose. The flavor profile is light and crisp with light carbonation. **FeuerWeiss** is an interesting concept that tops 7.2% ABV. It is a category of its own that Kelly is calling a Texas IPA, and while some may complain that 75 IBUs just aren't enough for Texans, the beer has a hop-forward bite that is malty and mellow with characteristics of a hoppy hefeweizen. The beer is an orange brass-like color with an off white head that beckons to be taunted. It is a very drinkable beer that has a medium body and medium carbonation. Does it hold up to being called a Texas IPA? That depends on the drinker. Sometimes it is better to just enjoy a beer than to try to put a label on it.

New Braunfels Brewing is coming along nicely in the market, and they are making a name for themselves by doing something different. With interesting beer styles, they are captivating their audience with beer that stands out in the herd. With New Braunfels being such a small town, it is great to see that the brewery is also becoming a tourist attraction. Their beers can be found along the I-10 corridor between San Antonio and Austin, so be sure to pick up a bottle and see what is brewing in the small German town of New Braunfels.

PEDERNALES BREWING COMPANY

97 Otto Eckhardt Road, Fredericksburg, TX 78624; (830) 998-7486; pedernalesbrewing .com; @PedernalesBrew
Founded: 2012 **Founder:** Lee Hereford **Brewer:** Peter McFarlane **Flagship Beer:** Lobo Lito **Year-Round Beers:** Lobo Lito, Lobo Texas Lager, Lobo Negro, Classic Hefe-Weizen, Classic India Pale Ale **Seasonals/Special Releases:** Classic Dunkel-Weizen, Lobo Oktoberfest, Robert Earl Keen's Honey Pils **Tours:** Fri 3 to 5 p.m. & Sat 1 to 5 p.m. **Taproom:** Yes

Located in the popular German community of Fredericksburg, Pedernales Brewing Company was founded by Texas entrepreneur Lee Hereford, who found success with his endeavors in the Texas wine industry. Lee also owned the publication *TravelHost San Antonio*. Lee had a love for the Hill Country, and with his slew of connections and his knowledge of wine, he decided to go forward with making a brewery of his own.

Pedernales Brewing Company's mission was to make sessionable beers that are light and easy to drink. With head brewer Peter McFarlane manning the brewhouse, Pedernales exploded onto the market with their beers. The price points were low and the beer was easy drinking. Peter's experience as a brewer had taken him from running his own microbrewery to brewing for Leinenkugel's Ballpark Brewery, and even a short stint with Rogue Ales. His long history in the industry has helped Pedernales develop beers that teeter on the line between craft and commercial but are still packed with full flavor.

The **Lobo Texas Lager** is a 5% ABV very approachable lager that is engaging for both craft fanatics and those just looking to step into something new. The beer is golden in color with a sturdy head. The beer is light in aroma with grain and earth but tastes of lightly toasted malts, fruit, and a crisp light hop finish. The **Classic Hefe-Weizen** is an original recipe designed by McFarlane. The beer follows the rules as a classic German hefeweizen with a full bouquet of bananas and clove. The beer is light and refreshing on the mouth with a light body and clean semisweet finish. It is a well-rounded beer that can work on almost any occasion.

REAL ALE BREWING

231 San Saba Ct., Blanco, TX 78606; (830) 833-2534; realalebrewing.com; @RealAleBrewing

Founded: 1996 **Founders:** Philip Conner, Diane Conner & Charles Conner **Brewer:** Erik Ogershok **Flagship Beer:** Firemans #4 Blonde Ale **Year-Round Beers:** Brewhouse Brown Ale, Rio Blanco Pale Ale, Full Moon Pale Rye Ale, Firemans #4 Blonde Ale, Sisyphus Barleywine Ale, Lost Gold IPA, Devil's Backbone, Hans' Pils, 4-Squared **Seasonals/ Special Releases:** Oktoberfest, Shade Grown Coffee Porter, Phoenixx Double Extra Special Bitter, Hefeweizen, Real Heavy, White **Tours:** Fri 2 to 5 p.m. **Taproom:** Yes

Real Ale Brewing Company is in the heart of the Hill Country in Blanco. It is a brand that has seen numerous changes and come a long way from its start in 1996 by Philip and Diane Conner along with their son Charles. They originally opened the brewery in a small basement of an antiques store located in the town square of Blanco. The brewery was small and worked on perfecting the three core beers **Full Moon Pale Rye Ale, Rio Blanco Pale Ale,** and **Brewhouse Brown Ale.** Brad Farbstein was a volunteer who helped out around the brewery practically working for beer. In 1998 Philip was ready to leave the brewing business behind, and that was when Brad spoke up and offered to buy the business. Brad took over in the summer of 1998 and helped keep Real Ale going. Thanks to the craft beer movement of the early 2000s, Real Ale saw a rapid increase of demand. In 2005 the tight space just wasn't cutting it and was hampering the growth of the company. Brad purchased land just outside of the city limits of Blanco and in 2006 the new brewery opened its doors.

Real Ale Brewing has come a long way in its nearly 20 years of existence. They have remained true to Texas, limiting sales to the confines of the state. The beer is all very approachable with full-flavored beers that ride the line of sessionable. The flagship for Real Ale, if not the flagship for all blondes in Texas, is **Firemans #4.** It is a 5.1% ABV blonde ale that is smooth and malty on the mouth with just the faintest citrus zest from the Crystal hops. The nose is that of sweet malt and grains. It is one of the smoothest blonde ales in the Texas market and probably the most popular. Contrary to the popular belief that the beer represents firefighters, the beer is actually named after Firemans Texas Cruzer, which is a local BMX bike company. Another great beer from Real Ale is the classic **Rio Blanco Pale Ale.** It is a 5.3% ABV English-style pale ale that is both smooth and refreshing. The beer has hints of malt, grass, and pine on the nose but the mouth has a lightly sweetened malty flavor with a light spice from the Saaz hops. It finishes bitter but clean on the back end. It is a very enjoyable beer that is a great way to tiptoe into pale ales. Real Ale has successfully continued to brew well-balanced beers that can be respected and appreciated by all.

Devil's Backbone
Style: Belgian-Style Tripel
ABV: 8.1%
Availability: Year-Round

The Devil's Backbone is a Belgian-style tripel that hit the market running when it was released by Real Ale. It was quite different from their original offerings and felt like a beer that would appeal to a more mature palate. It is named after a scenic ridge that runs between Blanco and Wimberley that gives you breathtaking views of the Hill Country, along Farm Road 32 just off US 281.

Devil's Backbone is a well- balanced beer that pours a rich golden color with a thick white head. You can detect notes of yeast, clove, and spice that all follow onto the palate. It has an added sweetness from the candy sugar that is made at the brewery. The beer has a medium to light body that is stimulating on the back end and doesn't leave behind any off-putting aftertastes. This beer makes for a perfect year-round release that pairs great with cheese, pizza, or salty meats. It is a great complement to nearly every experience and is a great beer for just kicking back and enjoying the outdoors in the Texas Hill Country.

Real Ale is a 24-hour production brewery and due to their demand and schedule they only offer tours on Friday from 2 to 5 p.m. Because they are held on a weekday, their tours are often small and intimate so visitors really get the feel of a personal walkthrough. Real Ale beers can be found on draft, and in bottles and cans in most markets throughout the state, so pick up a sixer to see what makes Real Ale so popular in Texas.

ROGNESS BREWING COMPANY

2400 Patterson Industrial Dr., Austin, TX 78660; (512) 670-2537; rognessbrewing.com; @ RognessBrewing

Founded: 2012 **Founders:** Forrest & Diane Rogness **Brewer:** Dan Wheeler **Flagship Beer:** Yogi **Year-Round Beers:** Beardy Guard, Boomslang, Gigantophis, Hefeweizen, Joie d'Ete, Ost, Rook, Titanoboa, Vinton, Yogi **Seasonals/Special Releases:** Belfort, Holiday, Rogtoberfest, Bella, Pro-Am, Tenebrous **Tours:** Check Website **Taproom:** Yes

Rogness Brewing is in Pflugerville, just north of Austin. It was founded in 2012 by husband and wife Forrest and Diane Rogness. Forrest and Diane have designed and perfected all of the recipes at the brewery, but their head brewer Dan Wheeler has taken over the brewing duties. Forrest and Diane met while attending the University of Iowa and working at a camera store. Forrest purchased a home-brewing kit and quickly became involved in learning more about beer. It wasn't long before Forrest had the brewing down and started to teach Diane, and it kickstarted their affection for craft beer.

In 1999 Forrest purchased the Austin Homebrew Supply store, where he quickly became a known and well-respected man in Austin's brewing scene. After having great success with the homebrew store, Forrest felt the urge to continue his brewing professionally. Forrest and Diane decided to move forward with opening Rogness Brewing Company in 2012. Their focus was to brew a wide variety of beer styles and blend unique ingredients to make one-of-a-kind recipes.

Rogness Brewing launched the company with two beers, one being **Yogi,** which was created by Diane. It is a 5.2% ABV chai-spiced amber. The chai grabs your attention, and the mouth brings a zing of sweet spices like clove and cardamom with a light sprinkling of black pepper that gives this beer a distinctive flavor that is both invigorating and pleasant. Forrest wanted his hoppy beers to be known for their bite, and that is why he named **Boomslang, Gigantophis,** and **Titanoboa** after snakes. The **Boomslang** is a smooth 5.5% ABV pale ale with a sneaky 55 IBUs and is named after a highly venomous African tree snake. The **Gigantophis** is an 8% ABV imperial IPA that really gets you with its 80 IBUs. It is named after a massive prehistoric

Holiday
Style: Winter Warmer
ABV: 9.6%
Availability: Winter

Winter warmers are not usually my favorite, but Rogness has won me over with their Holiday. With soothing flavors on the mouth such as cinnamon, brown sugar, and oats, this beer has a complexity that can only make you think of the holidays. It has an intoxicating aroma of fall spices that lure you in. The mouth is a rather light body but is backed up with a bold flavor profile and a whopping 9.6% ABV that will warm just about anyone up. I think Holiday is the perfect beer to unwind and relax with during that hectic holiday season, and it will even help you deal with the usual family arguments over the dinner table. It is a great beer that is not too sweet and well balanced. I would be interested in aging this beer, but it is just too good to hold on to.

snake that could swallow a person whole. This beast is loaded with 2½ pounds of hops to each barrel giving it a great well-rounded hoppy finish. The **Titanoboa i**s a hophead's dream. It is a rarity as a 9.5% ABV 101 IBU triple IPA that practically wrecks your palate with a citrus bomb of hoppy goodness. The well-rounded treat of malt and hops is what makes this beer such a favorite. It is named after the biggest prehistoric snake, believed to be 48 feet long. This beer is hopped with ten varieties at ten different times during the boil, which gives this beer a complexity like no other.

Rogness Brewing is sitting all alone out in Pflugerville, but they are making their name known with their distinct beers. The have their taproom open on Thursday from 6 to 10 p.m. and Friday from 4 to 10 p.m., so this is a great time to check out their beers. If you are not in Austin, you can find their beers across the state and they continue to add new accounts almost daily. Their beers are currently sold in bombers and on draft, but they have future plans to can and bottle their beers in 12-ounce sixpacks. I believe this will certainly help push more Rogness out to the waiting public.

SOUTH AUSTIN BREWING COMPANY

415 E. St. Elmo Rd., Austin, TX 78745; (512) 968-8297; southaustinbrewery.com; @SouthAustinBrew

Founded: 2012 **Founder:** Jordan Weeks **Brewer:** Jordan Weeks **Flagship Beer:** Kolsh **Year-Round Beers:** Kol' Beer, TPA, 6 String Saison, Luckenbock, Coffee Stout **Seasonals/Special Releases:** Belgian Style Golden Ale, Saison D'Austin **Tours:** Check Website **Taproom:** No

South Austin Brewing is, as you imagined, located just south of downtown Austin. It was founded by Jordan Weeks, who also serves as the brewmaster. South Austin Brewing represents the old laid back Austin vibe, and the brewery has been home to many live concerts. Jordan's special events coordinator Chris Oglesby helped to bring that old charm to the brewery with his long history in the Texas music scene. Author of the book *Fire in the Water, Earth in the Air: Legends of West Texas Music,* Oglesby has helped to organize the Groovy Sunday events at the brewery, which draw large crowds who like to listen to local music.

Jordan was born in Bangladesh and spent most of his life living overseas with his parents until he moved to Austin in 1989 after he graduated from the American Embassy School in New Delhi, India. It was in Austin where he found his interest in craft beer. He worked on and off with Austin Homebrew Supply and learned how to brew from the founder Dave Bone. As Jordan grew up he worked in software but

Beer Lover's Pick

TPA
Style: Pale Ale
ABV: 5.5%
Availability: Year-Round

TPA stands for Texas Pale Ale. It is a big statement when you claim your beer represents the state when it comes to pale ales, but they did a great job making a malty pale that is a great light IPA at only 5.5% ABV and has a refreshing citrus zest from the hops. The beer has a well-balanced malt and hop characteristic that is well received in the warm Texas sun. Jordan suggests pairing the beer with local musicians such as Ray Wylie Hubbard or Bob Schneider. I think I found it paired nicely with a little Stevie Ray Vaughan and a spread of Franklin Barbecue.

always had his passion for beer on the side. He reached an age where he felt like the opportunity was right and went about plans to open a brewery of his own. Jordan intended the brewery to be a destination for both locals and visitors alike who could enjoy a great beer and listen to some homegrown local music. The brewery first launched brewing only corked Belgian-style beers. Belgian beers are near and dear to Jordan's heart because that is where his love for beer came from. He used the old world brewing techniques of the monasteries that brewed beer and implemented that into his brewing practices. Now the brewery has made a switch from Belgian-style beers to a set of American-style brews that are packaged in 16-ounce tallboy cans. The **Kol' Beer** is the flagship of the new beers and is a light crisp 4.5% ABV kolsh beer that is very approachable as a session beer and has a great light body that consists of a clean light malt body and a light noble hop bitter finish. The **6 String Saison** is their own special take on Franco-Belgian-style farmhouse ale. This 8% ABV is a malty floral bomb of flavor but is a little different than your traditional saisons. It has a medium body with light banana esters on the nose. This is a beer that will catch up to you with its higher alcohol content, but it is not a heavy beer, so you won't feel so full that you can't have another.

SPOETZL BREWERY

603 E. Brewery St., Shiner, TX 77984; (361) 594-3383; shiner.com; @ShinerBeer
Founded: 1909 **Founder:** Kosmos Spoetzl **Brewer:** Jimmy Mauric **Flagship Beer:** Shiner Bock **Year-Round Beers:** Shiner Bock, White Wing, Wild Hare Pale Ale, Shiner Premium, Shiner Light Blonde, Black Lager **Seasonals/Special Releases:** Oktoberfest, Holiday Cheer, Kolsch, Kosmos, FM 96, Ruby Redbird **Tours:** Mon through Fri 10 a.m. to 3 p.m. **Taproom:** Yes

Spoetzl Brewery is the oldest independent brewery and one of the most recognized beers in the Lone Star State. It is located in the small town of Shiner, which lies about 20 miles south of I-10 between San Antonio and Houston. While the brewery is named Spoetzl, they are most known widely for Shiner beer. The brewery was founded by German immigrant Kosmos Spoetzl. Kosmos was a seasoned brewing veteran who attended a brewmasters' school in Germany, then went on to brew with the Pyramid Brewery in Cairo, Egypt, for 8 years. Kosmos wanted to escape the desert and find a new home with a better climate, so he moved his family to San Antonio. In 1909, Kosmos came across an opportunity with the Shiner Brewing Association, which he leased out with his business partner Oswald Petzold. In 1915, Kosmos purchased the brewery and renamed it the Spoetzl Brewery. Kosmos brought along his Bavarian recipes to create unique beers that appealed to the local German and Czech farmers who wanted a beer that made them reminisce about the old world.

During Prohibition, the Spoetzl Brewery stayed afloat making near beer and selling ice, but some say Kosmos was still brewing and selling beer to local farmers on the low. Spoetzl was one of only five remaining breweries when Prohibition was repealed. Locals celebrated the return of Shiner beer and Kosmos dedicated his time keeping the beer selling within a 70-mile radius from the brewery. After Kosmos passed away in 1950, his daughter Cecilie took over the company and renamed the brewery the K. Spoetzl Brewery after her father. The brewery was eventually sold off in 1969 and passed through different investors over the years before being purchased by Carlos Alvarez of the San Antonio–based Gambrinus Company in 1989. Carlos revived the brand and helped the Spoetzl Brewery to become the fourth largest brewery in the US. What started off as a brewery only selling to local towns is now distributing beer to forty-eight states, with plans to add the two remaining states in the near future. Today brewmaster Jimmy Mauric, who started with the company over 35 years ago when he was only 17, is keeping the brewing traditions of Kosmos alive. The beer is still brewed using the same recipes and is crafted with time and care to ensure each beer is as good as the last.

The Spoetzl Brewery has six year-round core beers along with six other seasonal and special releases. **Shiner Bock** is the most iconic out of the beers brewed at the

Shiner Wild Hare Pale Ale
Style: Pale Ale
ABV: 5.7%
Availability: Year-Round

The Wild Hare Pale Ale was the first ale brewed at the brewery. The line of Shiner beers is now mostly lagers, but back then they wanted to start with something different. It is a pleasant beer brewed with the craft beer drinker in mind, a great beer for the Spoetzl audience that is used to the lighter flavors of their beers such as Shiner Bock. The beer has a malty nose with just a hint of citrus. On the palate the beer is a great blend of malt and hops that finishes with a clean hop bitterness. This is a great introductory pale ale that is not too strong and has an easy-drinking flavor. It is also a great beer to pair with practically any dish. Shiner beers can be found throughout the country but let's be honest; it tastes better when you're drinking it in Texas.

Spoetzl Brewery. While it is the most iconic, it was not released until the '70s. It is an American-style dark larger that comes in at an easy-drinking sessionable 4.4% ABV. It has a deep amber, almost brown-colored body with a full tan head and has notes of caramel and roasted malts. On the palate the beer has a light body with notes of the sweet roasted malt, caramel, and even a little bread on the back end. The beer is low in hops so there isn't much hop bitterness, making this a great entry-level beer for someone that is new to craft beers. **Shiner Premium** beer is a take on the classic recipe, which Kosmos launched back in 1909. It was a beer that was a favorite among the local German and Czech farmers around Shiner who would often find a bottle sitting on their fence post left for them by Kosmos himself. Shiner Premium is a Bohemian-style golden lager with a clean golden body; it is a sessionable 4.4% ABV with a light bouquet of malt and a slight hint of hops. On the palate the beer is rich in malt with a subtle detection of caramel and toffee. It finishes clean with just a light hop bitterness making this an easy beer to enjoy and another stepping stone into the heavier craft beer styles. All of the Shiner beers follow the same easy-drinking style with approachable recipes that are not pretentious or intimidating for newcomers but can still be enjoyed by craft beer veterans.

Today you can step back into the past by visiting the Spoetzl Brewery to get a great history of the brewery and see where they are headed. While the original tin brewery is gone, the current brewery is rich in history. Tours are held on weekdays from 10 a.m. to 3 p.m., but hours change throughout the year so be sure to check their website for up to date information. Thankfully Shiner beer can easily be found across the state, so you shouldn't have a hard time finding some to enjoy. Shiner beer likes to represent the easygoing life of the Texas Hill Country and backyard barbecues, so grab a Shiner and see why they have been one of the most respected beers in the state.

THIRSTY PLANET BREWING

11160 Circle Dr., Austin, TX 78736; (512) 579-0679; thirstyplanet.net; @Thirsty_Planet
Founded: 2010 **Founder:** Brian Smittle **Brewer:** Brian Smittle **Flagship Beer:** Thirsty Goat **Year-Round Beers:** Yellow Armadillo, Thirsty Goat, Bucket Head IPA **Seasonals/ Special Releases:** Wondering Wood, The Doctor, Smittlefest, Double Bucket Head, Silver Back, Black Bucket, Pail Head **Tours:** Sat 12 to 3 p.m. **Taproom:** Yes

Thirsty Planet Brewing Company is just west of Austin on the corridor to the Hill Country. It was founded by Brian Smittle, who also remains the head brewer. Brian learned brewing while attending school in England and was exposed to English-style ales that he came to admire. After he graduated he moved to Colorado and met a brewer at a festival. He was excited to see that there was a brewpub nearby, so he stopped in to check the place out one day and was amazed to see that someone could be paid to brew beer. Brian started volunteering for the brewpub, learning to use the bigger equipment and constantly cleaning things around the brewery. He was eventually offered a full-time job. This set Brian off on a career path as a brewer, and he has now been brewing professionally for over 20 years. Brian ultimately came to the decision that he should start a brewery of his own, and the first slab was poured for Thirsty Planet on his 40th birthday. The first keg rolled out of the brewery in the spring of 2010, and they have seen a large demand for their beers ever since.

Thirsty Planet got its name from an organization that the owner Brian Smittle donated to, Heifer International, which provides livestock and farming skills to impoverished regions around the world. He received a photo of a goat that his donation provided for a family and Brian thought to himself, "That goat sure looks thirsty." Brian admits the Thirsty Planet was originally going to be named Thirsty Goat, but he went with Thirsty Planet because he wanted to brew different beer styles from around the world.

Thirsty Planet has come a long way in the last few years and it shows in the numbers. In 2013 they produced over 10,000 barrels of beer, and that is a lot considering their beer is only available in Austin and the surrounding cities. Unfortunately, if you are in Houston or Dallas, you will need to head into the Hill Country to get a

Wondering Wood
Style: Smoked Porter
ABV: 6.1%
Availability: Late Winter

In Texas, barbecue is king and nothing pairs better with barbecue than a good beer. The Wondering Wood is a seasonal release from Thirsty Planet that features a different local smokehouse each year. The first Wondering Wood featured Franklin Barbecue. They smoked the malt that was used in the beer at Franklin and brewed a beer that was both interesting and delicious. The smoke was present on the nose and even had a hint of meatiness. It had a soft sweetness with a present smokiness to the beer. It was very enjoyable and went perfect with a spread of smoked meats. The next year they featured Stiles Switch BBQ and Brew. This time the beer had more chocolate notes on the mouth than the last time and even a bit of bacon on the back end thanks to the smoke. The smoke was stronger on the nose this time and seemed to be more complex with a heavier body. I am not usually a fan of smoked beers, but I think this concept is interesting and I am excited how the style changes yearly. I highly suggest having barbecue on hand while drinking this smoked porter to get a great experience.

taste. The beer is currently only sold in draft, but they are planning to have sixpacks of bottles available in retail stores by the beginning of 2015. The flagship for Thirsty Planet is **Thirsty Goat,** a 6.5% ABV American amber ale with a light malty sweetness and a balanced hop finish. The beer pours a rich amber color with a thick white head and has a sweet bready nose. It goes down smooth with a medium body. The **Bucket Head IPA** is a personal favorite of mine. The 8.9% ABV American-style IPA is a big beer no doubt and is aggressively hopped. The beer is well rounded with a balance of malt and hop features. The Bucket Head can have you walking funny after a few because of its higher alcohol content, so this beer might not be for a beginner. It has a subtle sweetness quickly followed by a burst of "hoppiness" on the palate. On the nose you can distinctly notice the beautiful citrus and floral scent of the hops. This is a great beer for hopheads who want a beer that is big and bold.

Thirsty Planet opens its taproom on Saturday from 11 a.m. to 7 p.m., with four tours starting at noon. The tours are currently free, but they will start charging soon and all of the funds from the tours will be donated to a local nonprofit organization.

TWISTED X BREWING COMPANY

23455 W. RR 150, Dripping Springs, TX 78620; (512) 829-5323; texmexbeer.com; @TexMexBeer

Founded: 2011 **Founders:** Jim Sampson, Shane Bordeau & Ted Stewart **Brewer:** Jim Sampson **Flagship Beer:** Twisted X **Year-Round Beers:** Twisted X, Cow Creek, Fuego, Chupahopra **Seasonals/Special Releases:** Señor Viejo, Siesta Prickly Pear Lager **Tours:** Mon through Thurs 1 to 8 p.m., Fri & Sat 11 to 8 p.m., Sun 12 to 6 p.m. **Taproom:** Yes

Twisted X Brewing Company is in Dripping Springs, Texas, or as many like to call it, "The Gateway to the Hill Country." It is just 25 miles west of Austin and has become a popular area for craft beer as of late. Twisted X was founded by friends Jim Sampson and Shane Bordeau. Ted Stewart came on board in 2012 to help with the brewery's expansion. The brewery originally started in a small garage in Cedar Park brewing on a 10-gallon system until the team was able to build out their full production brewery in Dripping Springs with a new 30-barrel brewhouse. Twisted X beers are in a league of their own because they fall under the category of Tex Mex Beer, which the brewery has trademarked.

Owners Jim and Shane were working for a high-tech startup when their conversations about their love for Tex-Mex food and tequila evolved into a discussion about starting a Mexican brewpub, which eventually turned into talk of starting their own brewery. After the tequila wore off, the friends decided to move forward with starting a brewery to brew Mexican-style beers in Texas.

Twisted X has hit the ground running since they opened their full-scale brewery in Dripping Springs, quickly getting beer out to the public and pushing it across the state and catching a lot of attention with their unique style of beers. Needless to say, the beers all pair perfectly with bold and spicy Tex-Mex dishes. The **Twisted X Premium Tex Mex Lager** is a great sessionable beer that is very easy to approach with a low 5.1% ABV. The beer has a light body, but it is not light on flavor. It is a great introductory beer for someone that is new to craft beer because its profile is light yet flavorful. It has a bouquet of straw and sweet malt and an earthy mouth with a light sweet malt balance. The hops are faint but still present, which makes this a great day-drinking kind of beer. For those looking to kick things up a notch, the **Fuego** Jalapeno Pilsner is a mouthwatering chile beer that is well balanced on the flavor of the chile without the gimmick of the heat. It is a well-balanced beer that is very easy to drink and pairs perfectly with a sizzling plate of fajitas. The beer is

Señor Viejo
Style: Schwarzbier
ABV: 8.2%
Availability: Year-Round

Señor Viejo is a beer that will both please and confuse your palate. The beer pours a heavy black with a thick creamy tan head. It has a heavy mouth feel that would make you think you were sipping on a bourbon barrel–aged stout or porter, but Señor Viejo is a dark German lager that has been aged in barrels used by Austin's own Dulce Vida Tequila for their Lone Star Edition Anejo tequila. The nose picks up a symphony of aromas from wood and chocolate to coffee and brown sugar. On the mouth you definitely get the taste of the barrel and the tequila-soaked wood comes through with flavors of roasted chocolate malt and vanilla. This is a great beer to enjoy a little warmer, because it opens up with a very creamy texture and releases more of the barrel essence. This might be one of my favorite beers in the state and pairs well as a dessert beer or even with a good cigar. It will even pair with a decadent dessert such as a *leche quemada* or even a rich chocolate cake drizzled with Cajeta, a Mexican caramel sauce. Dulce Vida translates to the sweet life, and the Twisted X Señor Viejo definitely makes life pretty sweet.

surprisingly crisp and refreshing but still leaves just the slightest warmth in your throat. I was pleasantly surprised by how much I enjoyed this beer, and I highly recommend it if you are venturing into chile-infused beers.

Twisted X is changing the game in Texas and doing things their own way. There are not many beers that are brewed to pair with Mexican food, but they have done a great job bringing some love to the south of the border flavors. I highly recommend stopping by their brewery if you're venturing into the Hill Country. Their brewery might be one of the nicest you will see in Texas, and their beers are definite crowd pleasers. Unlike most breweries that open their taproom on the weekend, Twisted X makes it convenient for guests as they are open every day. There is nothing better than a great beer on a clear day in the Texas Hill Country.

Brewpubs

AUSTIN BEER GARDEN BREWING COMPANY

1305 W. Oltorf, Austin, TX 78704; (512) 298-2242; theabgb.com; @TheABGB
Founded: 2013 **Founders:** Brian "Swifty" Peters & Amos Lowe **Brewers:** Brian "Swifty" Peters & Amos Lowe **Flagship Beer:** Hell Yes Helles **Year-Round Beers:** Hell Yes Helles, Industry Pils, Day Trip Pale Ale, Superliner IPA, Big Mama Red **Seasonals/Special Releases:** Gretchen's Brown, Rocket 100

Austin Beer Garden Brewing Company, or ABGB as the locals call it, is a brewpub born out of years of experience. Both owner/brewers Brian "Swifty" Peters and Amos Lowe were professional brewers in the Austin area before coming together to form ABGB. Swifty was one of the original co-founders of Live Oak Brewing Company

and later was the head brewer for Austin brewpub Uncle Billy's Brew & Que on Lake Travis, while Amos was the head brewer for Uncle Billy's original location on Barton Springs. After the Lake Travis Uncle Billy's location shut down, Amos and Swifty decided that they would go into business together and form a brewpub of their own.

Austin Beer Garden Brewing Company is in the Bouldin Creek neighborhood of south Austin. It is off the busy and popular South Lamar, nestled just off the street with a large outdoor beer garden. The brewpub is German in origin but the food is anything but. The mainstay is pizza, but not your traditional drunken late-night slice. Instead you will find amazing hand-tossed pizzas with locally grown toppings. The interior is lined with long tables for communal-style dining with a large stage for live music. Outside is a sprawl of picnic tables, lawn chairs, and wooden spools as makeshift tables.

ABGB makes some great pizza, so it is only right that the beer be just as good and pair perfectly. Luckily for us, ABGB has made beer and pizza that are phenomenal together.

THE BARBER SHOP
207 W. Mercer St., Dripping Springs, TX 78620; (512) 829-4636; barbershopbar.com; @BarberShopBar
Founded: 2011 **Founder:** John McIntosh **Brewer:** John McIntosh **Flagship Beer:** Mild Mullet **Year-Round Beers:** Bitter Anniversary, Station 7 Pale Ale, Mild Mullet, Bourbon Barrel Pandemic Porter

Dripping Springs is a small town just 30 minutes west of Austin. It is one of those towns you pass along a highway that can be easily missed with the blink of an eye. Just a block off the 290 highway sits a former gas station that at one time was used as a barbershop. Later, that barbershop closed its doors, and in 2011 John McIntosh purchased the building and turned it into a brewpub. Keeping the nostalgia of the building, John decided to call it The Barber Shop. Since opening many confused patrons have stopped in looking to have their ears lowered, but instead they're offered a beer. Stop in and you can even see the sign showing the ever-changing tally of how many times patrons have walked in looking to get a haircut. John likes to joke that keeping the name as The Barber Shop, "locals would never have to lie to their wives where they were going." They might have never come home with a haircut, but they did get a buzz.

The Barber Shop has that small-town feel where everyone seems to know each other, but newcomers are always welcomed and the bartenders will greet you with a friendly smile while you look over their taps. Using a 5-barrel brewing system, John

is making English-style ales that have turned local commercial beer drinkers into craft beer fans. While carrying some of the common light beers, the Barber Shop has 18 taps from other local and regional breweries, but when stopping don't miss a chance to try some of their homebrewed beers.

One of the most popular beers would have to be the **Mild Mullett.** It is a very light English mild session beer at only 3.4% ABV and has slight notes of toffee and roasted malts. John brewed a beer after his divorce, and it is ironically called the **Bitter Anniversary.** It is an English ESB hovering around 4.6% ABV and much like marriage it rides that line between sweet and bitter. One of John's favorites and one that takes more time to condition is his 6.5% ABV **Barber Shop Bourbon Barrel Pandemic Porter.** The Barber Shop will fill growlers of most beers, but when it comes to the Pandemic Porter there just isn't enough to go around.

Next time you are passing through Dripping Springs be sure to stop by The Barber Shop, and don't forget to ask for a haircut.

BLACK STAR CO-OP PUB & BREWERY

7020 Easy Wind Dr., Austin, TX 78752; (512) 452-2337; blackstar.coop; @BlackStarCoOp
Founded: 2010 **Founders:** Steven Yarak, Jeff Young & Johnny Livesay **Brewer:** Chris
Hamje **Flagship Beer:** High Esteem **Year-Round Beers:** Recalcitrant Dockhand, Elba,
High Esteem, Vulcan **Seasonals/Special Releases:** Waterloo, Epsilon, Hubris

Black Star Co-Op is the first cooperatively run brewpub of its kind; it gives its members and employees ownership of the brewpub and gives everyone an equal voice. One of the original goals of Black Star was to take care of its members and the community at large. Aside from the great beer and amazing food, Black Star is known for their rule that tipping isn't accepted. They take pride that they can pay their employees a livable wage without having to make them work for tips. Its original pioneers were Steven Yarak, Jeff Young, and Johnny Livesay, but the community is the true founder of Black Star.

The brewery puts out many different beers throughout the year, and they are broken down as Rational and Irrational. The Rational beers are more of the regulars that follow the original recipes, while the Irrational beers are more on the experimental side of things. This gives the brewer a chance to try new things and expand the roster of in-house beers. **High Esteem** is one of the great Rational beers brewed at Black Star. It is a 4.7% ABV American pale ale that is brewed with 40 pounds of local Goodflow Wildflower Honey. It is a sessionable pale beer that isn't too extreme, one I find to be a great starter beer for a novice beer drinker. It has a sweet malty nose that follows onto the palate with hints of grass and bread and leaves a clean finish. I find it pairs great with their Black Star Burger, made with locally sourced brisket that they ground to form a juicy and mouthwatering patty. The tang from the house-made beer mustard is mellowed out by the clean honey finish from the High Esteem, and since both the burger and beer use locally sourced ingredients, the pairing becomes a perfect example of the co-op's philosophy.

Want to Be a Part of a Brewpub?

The co-op has over 3,300 members and they are always accepting more. For a small price you can obtain one membership share of the brewpub. Other benefits include equal voting rights to elect board members, helping to plan the long-term goals, and a subscription to their newsletter that announces special events and beer releases. For more information about becoming a member, head over to blackstar.coop for all the details.

For a delicious meal and some great beer, stop in to Black Star Co-Op and see the difference that a community makes.

DOUBLE HORN BREWING COMPANY

208 Ave. H, Marble Falls, TX 78654; (830) 693-5165; www.doublehornbrewing.com; @DoubleHornBrew

Founded: 2011 **Founders:** Dusty & Tracy Knight **Brewer:** Eric Casey **Flagship Beer:** Guero Wheat **Year-Round Beers:** Guero Wheat, 1855 Pale Ale, Over/Under Amber **Seasonals/Special Releases:** Black Dan IPA, Mo Dat IPA, Stout Scout, Watermelon Wheat, Dunkel

Marble Falls–based Double Horn was founded by Dusty and Tracy Knight, inspired by Dusty's love for good beer. He worked full time for a computer software company and was an avid homebrewer who enjoyed trying new beers as he traveled for work. When Dusty and his wife moved from Austin to Marble Falls, they found that there was a lack of craft beer in the Hill Country. It inspired him to come up with a business plan to start a brewpub where patrons could get good beer with what Dusty calls upscale American pub grub. In 2011 the brewpub finally opened, making way for Marble Falls to give patrons their first taste of craft beer.

Since Double Horn's owner Dusty remains with his full-time career, he brought on head brewer Eric Casey to take over the brewing duties. Eric has created very approachable, likable beers that complement the great selection of food they serve perfectly. Eric's indoctrination into craft beer came back at the old Bitter End brewpub in Austin while Eric was attending the University of Texas and earning a degree in microbiology. Eric took a trip to Europe where he discovered a wide range of beer styles and decided to delve further into the craft.

Double Horn Brewing Company focuses on craft beer and their selection of wines, but their food is also second to none. With their great selection ranging from burgers and sandwiches to steaks and salads, they have made sure to cover the bases to ensure their customers leave happy. The chicken fried steak is always a safe bet and more than filling for any appetite. Their steaks will make you think you are dining at a fine steakhouse. Double Horn has fulfilled Dusty's original dream to make upscale American pub grub and is a great place to stop in for a few pints and a great meal.

FAUST BREWING COMPANY

240 S. Seguin Ave., New Braunfels, TX 78130; (830) 625-7791; faustbrewing.co; @FaustBrewingCo
Founded: 1998 **Founders:** Vance Hinton & Mike Crowe **Brewer:** Ray Mitteldorf
Flagship Beer: Altered States German Altbier **Year-Round Beers:** Faust Golden Ale, Walter's Ghostly Pale Ale, Mike Crowe IPA, Vinny's ESB **Seasonals/Special Releases:** Ray's Damnation Barley Wine, Oktoberfaust Marzen Lager, Hell Fire Irish Red, Dullahan Stout

New Braunfels is a quiet Texas town with strong German ties. In a normal week it can seem a little deserted, but it becomes a very popular destination during the summer months with tourists tubing the river and the first two weeks of November for their annual Wurstfest, which celebrates the rich German culture of the town. Even if you pass through New Braunfels in a normal week, you can find the historic Faust Hotel, which is open all year round. Established in 1929, the hotel still carries that old-time charm and is even reportedly haunted. Owners Vance Hinton and Mike Crowe decided to install a brewpub in the back of the hotel to offer guests the feel of a German pub. The dark solid wood bar greets patrons as they belly up to the bar and a window into the brewery offers a view of the beautiful shiny copper kettles.

In 2011 owners Vance and Mike brought on head brewer Ray Mitteldorf, who had experience brewing for the Dodging Duck Brewhaus in Boerne and Two Rows Restaurant & Brewery in Houston. Ray has worked hard to bring some very big

beers to such a small town. Brewing a mix that rides along the line of German- and American-style beers, Ray has been given freedom to experiment and explore new recipes. **Walter's Ghostly Pale Ale** is a sign of respect to the ghost that reportedly haunts the hotel. The smooth-drinking pale comes in around 5.2% ABV and with a mild citrus bit from the hops. One of the biggest sellers for Faust is their **Oktoberfaust,** which is brewed fresh every year just in time for the big German fall festival. At 7.5% ABV, Oktoberfaust is very easy drinking with a malt-forward beer that would easily compete with some of the well-known commercial German Märzen lagers.

Faust is currently in the process of opening a larger full-scale brewery just a few blocks down from the hotel. This would give them the opportunity to explore the possibility of distributing their beers. The hotel brewpub will still be operating while Ray focuses on the project down the road. If you make it out to the annual Wurstfest in downtown New Braunfels, don't forget to stop by and see what Faust has brewing.

FREDERICKSBURG BREWING COMPANY

245 E. Main St., Fredericksburg, TX 78624; (830) 997-1646; yourbrewery.com; @EstensonsRandR

Founded: 1994 **Founder:** Richard Estenson **Brewer:** Rick Green **Flagship Beer:** Enchanted Rock Red Ale **Year-Round Beers:** Peace Pipe Pale Ale, Pioneer Porter, Enchanted Rock Red Ale, No So Dumb Blonde, Harper Valley I.P.A. **Seasonals/Special Releases:** Haupstrasse Helles, Hoppy Holidaze, El Hefe, Oktoberfest

Fredericksburg is another popular German town in the Hill Country. Every year tourists across Texas flock to the small town to celebrate Oktoberfest at the downtown Marktplatz, which is German for market square. While the town is overwhelmed for the festival, you can visit on any normal weekend to find tourists strolling down Main Street to visit unique shops and authentic German restaurants. One of the most popular places for beer lovers is Fredericksburg Brewing Company. With a bold presence on the strip, Fredericksburg serves up authentic German and classic southern dishes while head brewer Rick Green brews delicious German-style lagers.

The **Enchanted Rock Red Ale** is the biggest seller. At 5.3% ABV, this award-winning beer is big on flavor and is dedicated to the Enchanted Rock granite rock formation just 15 miles north of Fredericksburg. The beer has an even blend of malts and a light hop bite. It is a great complement to their "Best Reuben in Town" sandwich that brings out the rich flavor of their pumpernickel bread and takes off

Oktoberfest!

Since 1981, the German town of Fredericksburg, Texas, has hosted the largest Oktoberfest event in the state every year, on the first weekend of October. Held at the MarktPlatz in downtown Fredericksburg, the event brings German food, great beer, traditional music, and local vendors together. The event has grown over the years and become a very popular tourist destination, and getting a hotel is nearly impossible. If snacking on bratwurst and pretzels aren't enough, then head just down the street to Fredericksburg Brewing Company for a complete meal along with delicious German-style beer brewed onsite. With the heightened amount of traffic during the event, you might need to wait for a table, but head back into their indoor beer garden and enjoy a pint or two while singing old drinking songs. For more information about Oktoberfest in Fredericksburg, be sure to visit oktoberfestinfbg.com. *Prost!*

the tanginess from the Russian dressing. The **Harper Valley I.P.A.** is a much larger beer in flavor and comes in at 6.2% ABV. The hoppy British-style ale has a blend of Munich and Crystal malts with a strong kick from the Amarillo, Chinook, and Palisade hops. While untraditional for German-style beers, this is a great beer for the Sausage Sampler that seems to cut through the grease of the sausages and brings together a complexity of flavors that makes you want to yell *prost!*

If you are in Fredericksburg, make sure you stop in for a great beer and a delicious meal. It is a great place to go after a day of hiking around Enchanted Rock or an afternoon of shopping along the strip. They sell flights of beer so you can try all of their offerings, and they sell growlers of beer to go. So why not take some beer back home to enjoy while telling your friends about your experience?

KAMALA BREWING / WHIP IN
1950 S. I-35, Austin, TX 78704; (512) 442-5337; kamalabrewing.com; @WhipIn
Founded: 2012 **Founders:** Amrit & Dipak Topiwala **Brewer:** Kevin Sykes **Flagship Beer:** Bitterama **Year-Round Beers:** Visha Viter Pale, Bitterama, Brahmale, Parvati Pale Ale, Sita's Saison **Seasonals/Special Releases:** Austonerweisse, Shiva Stout, Brown Sahib

The Whip In is just a couple exits south of downtown Austin. It is many things: a grocery store, bottle shop, bar, restaurant, concert venue, and home to Kamala Brewing Company. The story of the Whip In goes back to 1986 when Amrit and wife

Chandan purchased the store, where they sold gas and rented out B movies. Amrit decided to add beer to his inventory, and the community took notice. Sales started to increase, so Amrit and Chandan continued to seek out new and rare beers as well as boutique wines. Whip In became known for their bottle selections. Chandan was famous for her Gujarati cuisine from the Gandhi region in India. Employees and friends encouraged her to share her traditional recipes with the community, and she found that her dishes were well received by their customers, thus launching a new aspect to their business. As years passed, Whip In's popularity grew and eventually they became one of the most popular bottle shops and bars in Austin.

With the craft beer community exploding in Texas and the success of their business, Amrit and Chandan's son Dipak approached them with the idea to convert the Whip In into a brewpub. Amrit believed in Dipak's vision, and they began planning the expansion of the Whip In. With a relatively small building, adding a full brewing system was going to be difficult, so they settled on adding a small ½ barrel system. The Whip In officially unveiled Namaste Brewing in 2012, and within that first year they headed to the Great American Beer Festival (GABF) in Denver, where they won Gold for their **Bitterama** in the "Herb & Spice" category. Fresh off of their high from taking home Gold at the GABF, Namaste Brewing was hit with a cease and desist letter from Delaware-based Dogfish Head over the use of Namaste, which is the name that Dogfish uses for one of their beers. It was an unfortunate setback for the Whip In, but they refused to let it stop them. Once past their legal setback, Namaste changed their name to Kamala Brewing Company. You would think that a name change would confuse customers and hurt business, but they found that the new name brought more attention to the brewpub and their business continued to prosper.

Kamala has continued to work on new recipes with their head brewer Kevin Sykes. Their goal is to incorporate beer with food and refine how they intersect with each other. They strive to use local and seasonal ingredients to brew their beer whenever possible. Much like the Indian fusion food that is served in the kitchen, the beer too is a crossing of styles between English and Belgian

with a twist. Their mission is not necessarily to surpass other breweries by brewing the common beer styles in Texas, but rather to brew beers with unique and interesting flavors while experimenting with different ingredients. A great example of their unique style is their **Bitterama,** which is an 8.2% ABV classic ESB that they brew with Earl Grey tea, or their **Brahmale,** which is a 9.5% ABV post-colonial IPA that they brew with local GoodFlow honey, lemongrass, and grapefruit peels. A personal favorite of mine is their winter seasonal **Shiva Stout.** It is a big 12% ABV imperial stout that is nearly black in color with a light tan head. It is brewed using bourbon-reduced dates and oatmeal, which give this beer a beautiful aromatic nose of roasted malts, bourbon, and chocolate. As you go in for the sip, your palate dances with the flavors of bourbon, vanilla, and burnt toffee that is smooth and creamy. The alcohol is present with a minor warming finish that makes this a beautiful bold beer.

Whether you are just arriving in Austin or heading out, make the Whip In a stop on your agenda. Enjoy one of the beers brewed in house or one of their 72 guest taps and pair it with one of Chandan's delicious dishes. They have a large array of beers available for purchase in their coolers, or you can have a growler filled up when you are ready to go. Whip In makes for a memorable experience that blends unique dishes and great craft beer.

NORTH BY NORTHWEST RESTAURANT & BREWERY
10010 N. Capital of Texas Hwy., Austin, TX 78759; (512) 467-6969; nxnwbrew.com; @NXNWBrew
Founded: 1999 **Founder:** Davis Tucker **Brewer:** Don Thompson **Flagship Beer:** Northern Light **Year-Round Beers:** Northern Light, Duckabush Amber, Py Jingo Pale Ale, Okanogan Black Ale, Bavarian Hefeweizen **Seasonals/Special Releases:** Prost Pilsner, Beerliner Weisse, Dark Side IPA, Holiday Ale, Oktoberfest, Barton Kriek

North by Northwest Restaurant & Brewery (often shortened to NXNW) is in the Gateway area of north Austin and was founded by restaurateur Davis Tucker, who also owns Austin's laid back craft beer establishment, Red's Porch. Davis designed NXNW after establishments in the beer-centric Pacific Northwest, where many brewpubs and microbreweries got their start. He wanted to combine craft beer and good food in a fun and inviting atmosphere. Opening its doors in 1999, NXNW took the combination of food and beer to the next level with a large menu of delightful upscale dishes created by executive chef George Powell.

Davis Tucker has a long history in the Texas beer industry. Davis was one of the co-founders of Austin's original brewpub, The Copper Tank, until he parted ways with the company in 1996 to focus on his own projects. The Copper Tank was located

The Beerliner

Created by Red's Porch and North by Northwest founder Davis Tucker, the Beerliner is an old 1974 tour bus that has been decked out as a rolling beer peddler. With 4 beer taps, an industrial kitchen, and three flatscreen TVs, it's used as a rolling tailgating party during the University of Texas football season. Every year Davis and his friends ride their bicycles on a 1,400-mile journey from Austin to Denver to the Great American Beer Festival with the Beerliner following along. This trek is in honor of Davis's longtime friend and North by Northwest brewmaster Don Thompson, who battled prostate cancer. The ride raises money for cancer awareness while spreading their love for Texas craft beer. Leading up to the ride, the Beerliner team hosts fundraisers and events for men to learn about prostate health as well as get a free prostate exam. For more information about the Beerliner and their great cause visit 1400miles.com.

in a bustling area of popular bars and nightclubs in downtown Austin that appealed to the younger college crowd instead of craft beer aficionados, and the brewpub went bankrupt and went out of business in 2005. Davis saw these setbacks and used his knowledge to combine an equal commitment to both the beer and food with NXNW. Don Thompson came on as the head brewer for NXNW after moving from Plano, Texas, where he and his wife founded Reinheitsgebot Brewing Company in 1982, which was the first microbrewery in the Southwest. With Chef Powell running the kitchen and Don heading up the brewing, Davis has an all-star team that has put NXNW on the map for the last 15 years.

Don explores using local ingredients to create one-of-a-kind, memorable beers with head brewer Kevin Roark that complement the food served at NXNW. The **Duckabush Amber** is the most popular beer that they keep on tap and is a great entry-level beer that pairs well with most dishes. Duckabush is a sessionable 4.5% ABV amber ale with a deep golden color and a light white head. It has a bouquet of caramel, malt, and nuts, and a very light flavor of malts and toffee with a light-hop bitterness. The beer finishes dry and is overall a very light easy-drinking beer.

North by Northwest has long been a respected brewpub in Austin. They've recently expanded to open a new location on the south side of town with head brewer Hayden Winkler, formerly of Real Ale Brewing. There have been no talks, but

I hope to see Davis expand NXNW outside of Austin and into other cities around the state. There aren't many things better in life than their Pork Chop Porterhouse and a cold beer. Be sure to stop in for a great meal and wash it down with their great beer at either location.

PECAN STREET BREWING

106 E. Pecan Ave., Johnson City, TX 78636; (830) 868-2500; pecanstreetbrewing.com; @ PecanStreetBrew
Founded: 2011 **Founders:** Tim & Patty Elliot **Brewer:** Sean Elliot **Flagship Beer:** Screw Loose Blonde **Year-Round Beers:** Screw Loose Blonde, Ten Penny Nail, County Jail Pale Ale, Guilty as Charged IPA, Simcoe Hoppy Session Ale, Catcher in the Wheat **Seasonals/Special Releases:** Holiday Ale, Javelina Brown Ale, Chain Gang Oatmeal Stout

Johnson City is a small town most notable as the hometown of the thirty-sixth president, Lyndon Baines Johnson. One of the biggest tourist attractions for the area is the birthplace and ranch of the former president just the next town over in Stonewall, but many come for the old antiques shops and the exceptional local art scene of Johnson City. In the center of town you will find Pecan Street Brewing, owned by husband wife duo Tim and Patty Elliot. They purchased the old building

supply store where town folks would congregate to socialize and gossip and turned it into a brewpub. Though they specialize in pizzas, burgers, and sandwiches, it is the beer that their son Sean Elliot is brewing that keeps the locals coming back and keeps that community spirit alive.

As you enter the brewpub, you are greeted by friendly smiles ready to welcome you and find you a seat. Just behind the bar is a window looking into the brewhouse where Sean is hard at work experimenting with new ideas and recipes for his beers. As you walk to the back of the building, you might be shocked to see a large open concert hall where locals enjoy the sounds of live music every week. Just outside is the beer garden where you can soak up some sun and enjoy the beauty of the small Hill Country town.

Head brewer Sean is an avid beer lover who learned the brewing craft while studying in Europe and brought back his skills to Pecan Street Brewing. In many small towns the craft beer scene is overrun by the usual commercial beers, so Sean has crafted beers with full flavors but that are still easy enough on the palate for a novice beer drinker. The most popular beer is the **Screw Loose Blonde,** which is a very light 5.2% ABV blond ale with a crisp flavor of malt and grass. This is a perfect beer for warm Texas afternoons or could even go well with a salad. For someone looking for something with more of a bite, the 7% ABV **Guilty as Charged IPA** has a nice strong hoppy aroma and a very clean citrus bite on the mouth with a well-balanced blend of malt characteristics, while the **Simcoe Hoppy Session Ale** comes in at only 4.5% ABV and gives the big hoppy aroma, but takes it easy on the mouth for those that aren't into the big hop flavors. After you've enjoyed their great food and a night of live music, pick up a growler of your favorite Pecan Street brew so you can remind yourself of the good times to be had in Johnson City.

PINTHOUSE PIZZA
4729 Burnet Rd., Austin, TX 78756; (512) 436-9605; pinthousepizza.com; https://twitter.com/PinthousePizza
Founded: 2012 **Founders:** Ryan Van Biene, Nic Van Biene, Kyle Detrick, Ned Lavelle & Tyler Norwood **Brewer:** Joe Mohrfeld **Flagship Beer:** Calma Muerta **Year-Round Beers:** Man O' War, Calma Muerta, Iron Genny, Bearded Seal, Old Beluga, Nitro Seal, Fallen Cask IPA **Seasonals/Special Releases:** Calypso, The Dude, Blind Jake, Burro's Breakfast, The Admiral, Sw'Elsinore, Jaguar Shark

Pinthouse Pizza is in the Rosedale neighborhood of Austin and was founded by five longtime friends: Ryan Van Biene, Nic Van Biene, Kyle Detrick, Ned Lavelle, and Tyler Norwood. The friends all felt like their individual careers were just not the right fit for them, and when they took a step back they realized that they all shared

an interest in pizza and beer. The friends and partners designed a plan around a brewpub that would feature fine beers brewed in house along with artisanal pizza. They brought on head brewer Joe Mohrfeld, who was originally the brewer for Odell Brewing in Fort Collins, Colorado, and Pinthouse Pizza opened its doors in the fall of 2012.

Pinthouse Pizza was built to be a neighborhood family establishment where you could gather over a couple beers and great pizza. In the kitchen the pizzas are all made from scratch using locally grown and organic produce when possible. The dough is made fresh daily and bakes up wonderfully with a crisp yet chewy crust. The pizzas follow the usual American fare, but they like to keep things interesting by having weekly specialty pizzas with unique ingredients. For libations, they have 40+ guest taps of beer available for your liking including the mainstays brewed by Pinthouse and any seasonal or special releases. You can order by the pint, pitcher, or go for the spread and order a flight, but don't forget to take home a growler filled with their great beer. The head brewer Joe Mohrfeld designed American craft beer recipes with English inspirations. The beer is loaded with choice ingredients but balanced to give a full flavor but still remain sessionable with lower alcohol contents. The **Calma Muerta** is a session ale that Joe has brewed with a great hop-forward mouth that tastes of grapefruit and pine yet mildly bitter and has a great floral nose of citrus and malt. With an ABV of only 4.8%, the Calma Muerta is a beer that you can drink a few of without feeling weighed down, and it goes great with their Hill Country pizza that is topped with cheese, bacon, spinach, mushrooms, and ricotta cheese. A personal favorite is **Man O' War,** a 6.5% ABV IPA that pours a dark golden color with a light white head. It has a nose that is bursting with citrus and pine that surprisingly doesn't quite follow onto the mouth. The beer is shockingly smooth without that overwhelming hop bitterness. Joe wanted to get away from the palate-wrecking IPAs on the market and make a beer that is loaded with hops for a great bouquet but still remains rather light on the mouth. It is a perfectly balanced beer that I find to be quite enjoyable, and it pairs great with their Works pizza that is loaded with fresh veggies and succulent meats.

There are two minor things to note about Pinthouse: parking and seating. The parking lot is small and cramped. Pinthouse shares the lot with neighboring businesses, so you might have to circle a few times on the weekends. Also, the seating is rows of picnic tables that patrons communally share, so you will have to be okay with sharing the space especially during the busy hours.

WIMBERLEY BREWING COMPANY

9595 Ranch Rd. 12, Wimberley, TX 78677; (512) 512-3299; wimberleybrewingcompany.com
Founded 2008 **Founders:** Holly & Bruce Collie **Brewer:** Bruce Collie **Flagship Beer:** Peggy's Cream Ale **Year-Round Beers:** Hefeweizen, Peggy's Cream Ale, Blonde, Drop the Rabbit, Chimay Style, Amber, IPA, Red Bitter, Porter F4 Phantom

If the name Bruce Collie sounds familiar, it is probably because Bruce was an offensive lineman and two-time Super Bowl champion with the San Francisco 49ers. After he hung up his shoulder pads and left behind a life of bad decisions, Collie became a born-again Christian and landed in the small town of Wimberley looking for solace. With the help of his wife Holly and their thirteen children, they run Brewster's Pizza where you can find Bruce brewing the beers out back in a brewpub called Wimberley Brewing Company.

Bruce had a dream of shops and restaurants that would bring people to his little slice of heaven, and he designed and built a wooden strip of buildings. In what seems like a rural area, the land kind of just pops out at you. Step inside Brewster's Pizza and you will find delicious handmade pizzas and hand-crafted beer brewed by Bruce himself. As you step into the bar, you will be surrounded by a shrine to Bruce's

past football career. Pictures of the old days when Bruce took the field and jerseys with the Collie name hang proudly. Chat with Bruce long enough and he might even show you his 5½-carat Super Bowl ring. While Bruce will always remember the gridiron days, today he is a family man who lives a simple life of brewing beer while his wife and children run the restaurant.

Brewster's Pizza tosses up some very serious brick oven pizzas that are complemented perfectly by their beers. While most of the beers brewed are light bodied and very easy drinking, they all hover between 5.4 and 7.9% ABV. Their **Red Bitter** is a 7.9% ABV fruity and malty brew with a bitter hoppy finish that pairs well with their Supreme Pizza. Another great pairing I would recommend would be the **Blonde** with the veggie loaded Omnivore Pizza. The Blonde is an easy-drinking traditional blonde ale at 5.9% ABV and has crisp notes of fruit and citrus. If you can't manage to save room for dessert, you can always opt for the **Porter F4 Phantom** with its heavy flavor of roast coffee and dark chocolate. It is a perfect way to complement a great meal.

The small town of Wimberley is easy to miss. Many people come in for the small shops and antiques stores, but I suggest making a stop at Brewster's for some amazing pizza, good beer, and to meet a football legend. That sounds like a pretty good trip to me.

Beer Bars

BANGER'S SAUSAGE HOUSE & BEER GARDEN
79 Rainey St., Austin, TX 78701; (512) 386-1656; bangersaustin.com; @BangersAustin
Draft Beers: 104 **Bottled/Canned Beers:** 15

Banger's Sausage House & Beer Garden is located along the popular Rainey Street in Austin. It is a street of old houses that have been converted into bars and restaurants. Banger's has become a mecca for great beer and delicious house-made sausages and boasts one of the largest outdoor beer gardens in the area.

The inside dining room is rather small with a handful of tables, but the real experience is outside in their large open beer garden where you will find rows of communal picnic tables, a stage for live music, and a fenced-in dog park for your four-legged friend to socialize as well. Inside, the bar is a 27-foot-long butcher-block surface that separates the patrons from the 103 taps of beer that embellish the back wall of the bar. They keep many of the local breweries on tap such as Adelbert's, Hops & Grain, 512, and Austin Beerworks, along with other popular craft offerings from breweries across the country. Following the trend of minimalist design, the typical brewery-embellished tap handles have been replaced by plain wooden taps that are numbered to the corresponding row of offerings listed on chalkboards hanging above the taps.

While Banger's might be known for their grand selection of craft beers, they are also recognized for their magnitude of delicious house-made sausages: from the usual bratwurst, andouille, and old-fashioned hot dogs to their creative exotic sausages such as Duck, Bacon and Fig, Chicken, Spinach, and Sundried Tomato. Banger's is really setting the bar high when it comes to gluttonous culinary pairings with craft beer. Banger's is a must-see for anyone stopping in Austin. Enjoy the outdoors on the patio with a pint and you will understand why Austinites love this city so much.

BILLY'S ON BURNET
2105 Hancock Dr., Austin, TX 78756; (512) 407-9305; billysonburnet.com; @BillysOnBurnet
Draft Beers: 36

Billy's on Burnet is located in the Rosedale neighborhood of Austin. They take pride in serving good food and a great selection of craft beers. Inside is small with a greasy spoon dive feeling, but outside on the wooden deck is a great place to enjoy a few beers.

Billy's has been known for frequently bringing in popular craft beers, and they make lip-smacking, hand-shaped burgers for a flawless pairing. The menu reads like a doctor's warning of foods to stay away from, but life is short so indulge. There is a long list of appetizers, burgers, and sandwiches, but you might be pretty shocked to see their rather large assortment of veggie options.

Billy's boasts that they have the "Happiest Happy Hour" in the city, and with beer prices ranging from $1.50 to $2.75, they can make even the most frugal drinker a happy camper. This is a great neighborhood bar, so the majority of the customers are locals that live in the surrounding communities. There is no dress code as Billy's is just your classic burger bar that happens to support and sell local craft beers. It is a great place to get away and mingle with the locals.

BLACK SHEEP LODGE
2108 S. Lamar Blvd., Austin, TX 78704; (512) 707-2744; blacksheeplodge.com; @blacksheeplodge
Draft Beers: 26 **Bottled/Canned Beers:** 130

Black Sheep Lodge is a small neighborhood bar with an inviting sports vibe. They specialize in craft beer and burgers while screens are scattered across the bar for optimal viewing pleasure. Outside is a large covered patio with plenty of seating and in the side room they have a couple of pool tables, a shuffleboard table, and a few arcade games to help pass the time. This place is popular not only for their beer selection and great food, but also for their happy hour specials, especially on Wednesday when they feature cheap can beers for only $1—but don't expect anything more than the commercial fizzy water. If you want the good stuff they have it, but it's going to run you just a little more than a dollar. But don't worry: A few beers here won't break your bank.

Black Sheep Lodge is a great bar for gathering with friends over happy hour, watching sports, or just enjoying a good beer and a bite. Hamburgers are what they are known for, but they have other options as well such as a Carnitas Sandwich, Tex-Mex style pulled pork piled high on a bun and topped with slaw and green chiles. This delicious sandwich has a little kick, so it will pair perfectly with a nice citrus-forward IPA. Their Chili Cheese Dog is another great hit that is messy and delicious; I usually pair it with a pale ale and some extra napkins. The burgers are somewhat no frills without over the top extras, but one bite and you will see that the flavors are out of this world. Perfectly seasoned fresh beef grilled to precision keeps customers coming back. You can kick back with almost any beer style, but a light saison or Belgian goes perfectly with their seared burgers. One warning: Black Sheep is on a busy street surrounded by a residential neighborhood, so parking can be a pain at times. Be sure to look out for street signs and careful crossing the busy intersections.

THE BREW EXCHANGE
706 W. 6th St., Austin, TX 78701; (513) 366-5727; brewexchangeaustin.com; @72beers
Draft Beers: 72 **Bottled/Canned Beers:** 50+

The Brew Exchange is an interesting and unique concept mixing beer and the stock market. Not the actual stock market, but above the bar is an electronic streaming stock ticker. It is synced up with the cash registers and as beers are purchased the prices fluctuate. It is all about buying low and passing high. Every beer that is purchased changes the price for other beers of that style. It is a fun twist on a night at the bar that doesn't require a financial background, but be careful, there are no bailouts in real life. Prices can get quite high at times when the market is on an upswing, but what goes up must come down in the roller coaster world of the markets, so buy a beer at the right time to get the best buy for your buck.

The bar is mainly standing room only with a few tabletops and a few booths. On the weekends this place can get rather busy, as it is in the middle of the West 6th Street nightlife district. Expect to see the occasional frat guys and drunken bachelorette parties strolling in off the strip. Happy hour is a great time to take advantage of the beers because the prices are usually low. Flatscreen TVs adorn the walls for your sports needs and a DJ spins live on the weekends for the party crowds. This is a fun bar for a younger crowd looking to have a good time while seeking good beer.

CHICAGO HOUSE
607 Trinity St., Austin, TX 78701; (512) 358-6202; thechicagohouse.com; @TheChicagoHouse
Draft Beers: 22 **Bottled/Canned Beers:** Occasional Specialties

Chicago House is right in the middle of the action in downtown Austin. It doesn't quite fit with the area, which is full of nightclubs and shot bars, but Chicago House has committed to bringing craft beer to the popular tourist nightlife destination. It is owned by famed Doug Guller of ATX Brands, who owns many popular and successful bars in and around Austin.

Chicago House has just one focus: 22 taps of fine craft beer that are constantly rotating. They have a full bar, but it is secondary to the beer selections. They are the only bar in town that features a set price for all of the beers at only $5, except during happy hour when the price is dropped to $4. This is a bargain when they have rare and specialty beers on tap. While the bar might have a different vibe than the neighboring bars, it is a great chance for tourists to get a taste of good beer without having to wander off the main strip.

Chicago House has a small menu of food available that is made at Guller's other neighboring bar, Parish Underground. The Chicago House was originally a hotel dating back to 1885 and was later used as a boardinghouse. The building has lived many different lives, but I expect that Chicago House will be around for a while. When you need to get away from the madness that can sometimes be found along the row of bars on 6th Street, stop in for a pint or two at Chicago House.

CRAFT PRIDE
61 Rainey St., Austin, TX 78701; (512) 428-5571; craftprideaustin.com; @CraftPride
Draft Beers: 56 **Bottled/Canned Beers:** 125+

Craft Pride is located along the popular Rainey Street in Austin, a row of old houses that have been converted into a small nightlife destination of bars. Craft Pride might as well have been named Texas Pride, because they have 54 gorgeous

taps and two cask engines of beer brewed solely in the Lone Star State. Craft Pride also has a small bottle shop with a pretty remarkable selection, or if you just want to take home some good Texas beer, they offer growler fills of nearly any of the beers on tap. When new breweries break into the Austin market, it is likely that Craft Pride will be the first to tap a keg.

The bar is somewhat rustic with a multitude of different wooden boards paneling the walls. The back of the bar is an attention grabber with its row of tap handles along a flat black wall. Up above the bar is a board with the current offerings on tap. Out back there is a small stage where they occasionally feature live music, and tables that spread around the back patio and wrap along the side of the building to the front.

Craft Pride is well regarded in the Texas craft beer community for their dedication to Texas beer, and they host many events with local breweries including firkin tappings and special release parties. A word to the wise when visiting: Rainey Street is a popular nightlife area, so it gets busy on the weekends and parking is very limited. Don't let this deter your visit, because Craft Pride is the only establishment in Austin where you can sample beers from across Texas in one place.

THE DIG PUB
401 Cypress Creek Rd., Cedar Park, TX 78613; (512) 996-9900; thedigpub.com;
@TheDigPub
Draft Beers: 36 **Bottled/Canned Beers:** 15

The Dig Pub is located just 20 minutes northwest of Austin in Cedar Park. It is a unique bar that makes you feel as if you are drinking in an Egyptian pyramid. The bar was founded by husband and wife Todd and Christy Wink, who opened the bar to specialize in craft beer, boutique wine, and unique eats. The food for the most part is handheld, but they have a small selection of salads for the leaf eaters. While the menu consists mainly of burgers and sandwiches, this isn't just your average pub fare. The Dig Pub is going big on flavor with dishes such as their Totes Magoat Cheese Burger that starts with a 1/3-pound Angus beef patty and is layered with pancetta, shallots that have been caramelized in port wine, and finished with creamy honey-whipped goat cheese. One bite of that burger and you will see why Dig Pub is a cut above the rest. If you are looking for something to snack on as you peruse your way through their beer taps, the Beer Cheese is another great selection. They use Twisted X Lager to create a creamy delicious batch of queso topped off with tomatoes, bacon, and chives. If you want to make that Beer Cheese come to life, I suggest pairing it with Twisted X's Fuego when they have it on tap.

Todd and Christy have come up with a unique vibe for their establishment that perfectly combines great food with a great selection of wine and craft beers. This is helping local Cedar Creek residents who want a place to hang out without having to drive into Austin. This is a great place to visit and I always look forward to returning for another great meal.

DRAUGHT HOUSE PUB & BREWERY

4112 Medical Pkwy., Austin, TX 78756; (512) 452-6258; draughthouse.com; @DraughtHouse
Draft Beers: 76 **Bottled/Canned Beers:** 12

Draught House Pub & Brewery is well known in Austin for the beers they pour and their support for the craft beer community for over 45 years. In 1995, they decided to convert the bar into a brewpub, and they started to brew their own beers while continuing to sell some of the best beer available in the state. From the outside the place makes you think you flew over the pond and stepped into an authentic German pub. Inside the place is dark and has a slight musty smell from the years of spilt beers. While you can belly up to the bar and enjoy your pints, there is only one line to order your drinks, and on busy nights it can extend out the door. If the atmosphere inside is too dark, you can always head outside and catch a table on the patio, but don't be surprised to see patrons scattered in the parking lot with their own lawn chairs or tailgating setups with food included.

The brewing at Draught House has been put on a long hiatus, but they have plans to start brewing again soon. In the meantime they continue to support craft beer and host events nearly weekly with different breweries. They have 76 taps of beer and usually carry around a dozen specialties or rare beers in bottles, and on Sunday they have $3 pints of Texas beer. Draught House Pub has become an Austin icon for craft beer love, so make sure they are on your itinerary for your next trip to the state capital.

EASY TIGER BAKE SHOP & BEER GARDEN

709 E. 6th St., Austin, TX 78701; (512) 614-4972; easytigeraustin.com; @EasyTigerATX
Draft Beers: 35 **Bottled/Canned Beers:** 5

Easy Tiger is on the famous 6th Street in downtown Austin. From the street it looks like some out of place French bread shop that clashes with the surrounding shot bars and nightclubs, but as you enter the doors and make your way downstairs, it's as if you discovered a speakeasy of good beer and choice quality food. The downstairs dining and bar area is rather tight, but you can make your way out the back door, which spills out into a large outdoor beer garden that overlooks Waller Creek just below.

Everything is made fresh in house, from the bread that is baked upstairs to the house-made sausages. The filling bread and hearty sausages are the perfect combination for a day of beer indulgence while enjoying the outdoor beer garden. Easy Tiger is a far cry from the surrounding bars and one of the few places in downtown that don't price gouge during special events. Their taps might be limited, but they do focus more on popular national craft brands with a few locals scattered in. Be sure to order a giant pretzel to go with your beer, and don't forget their homemade beer cheese, which will change your life. Easy Tiger is a low-key place that is great for all occasions and inviting for all. If you are in downtown Austin and need a refuge from the insanity of 6th Street, then Easy Tiger is a great place to kick back. Don't forget to pick up some fresh bread on your way out.

HAYMAKER
2310 Manor Rd., Austin, TX 78722; (512) 243-6702; haymakeraustin.com; @HaymakerAustin
Draft Beers: 40 **Bottled/Canned Beers:** 120+

Haymaker is in east Austin in the old Cherrywood neighborhood along Manor Road. It is owned by the same group that established another Austin hop spot, Black Sheep Lodge. Haymaker is a nod to the old neighborhood bars of the Midwest and northeastern US. It is a place that focuses on "Darn good poutine, ice cold beer and big burly sandwiches." This might not be the place for a vegan or anyone on a diet. The house specialty is a large plate of poutine, which is a popular Canadian dish consisting of fries, brown gravy, and Wisconsin cheese curds, but they put a southern take on the dish by using cream gravy instead and adding bacon. Either dish goes great with crisp lager or a citrus-forward IPA. Flatscreen TVs adorn the walls, making this a great place for watching sports and rooting on your favorite team. They have 40 taps of frequently revolving beers that range from local favorites to mainstream craft selections from across the country. Be warned, on big sporting event days this place gets very crowded and it has become the official watch party headquarters for the US Men's National Soccer Team, so plan accordingly.

HI HAT PUBLIC HOUSE
2121 E. 6th St., Austin, TX 78702; (512) 478-8700; hihatpublichouse.com; @hihatph
Draft Beers: 24 **Bottled/Canned Beers:** 10

The Hi Hat Public House is just outside of downtown in east Austin, in a retail space below an apartment complex. It is an oasis down at the end of East 6th Street past all of the bars and nightlife in an up and coming industrial area that is being converted into upscale living spaces. The bartenders at Hi Hat are always friendly and inviting so you will never feel pressured or judged. They are more than happy to talk beer with you and help you find something you might like from their wall of 24 taps. The kitchen is whipping up great food from light bites to a small selection of upscale pub grub that should satisfy a foodie's soul without breaking the bank. Dishes include steamed mussels, a confit duck sandwich, and shrimp mac & cheese. Hi Hat occasionally features beer dinners with different breweries and a specialty menu to complement the beers. They even have a great brunch on the weekends that is served until 6 p.m., so no need to feel guilty about drinking with your plate of eggs at 11 a.m. Though they only have 24 taps, they focus on keeping a strong, constantly rotating selection of beers, and they always make room for the local breweries. Hi Hat is a great hidden gem that is definitely worth venturing off the beaten path for. If you are only planning to stop in for a few beers, do yourself a favor and order a giant pretzel, which comes along with their creamy house fondue and beer mustard—because there is always room for a pretzel when you're drinking.

HOPFIELDS

3110 Guadalupe St., Austin, TX 78705; (512) 537-0467; hopfieldsaustin.com; @hopfieldsaustin
Draft Beers: 43 **Bottled/Canned Beers:** 15+

Hopfields is on the drag just north of the University of Texas campus in Austin. It is a small French bistro with an emphasis on craft beer and traditional French comfort food. Unlike craft beer bars that put all of their focus on the beer, owners Bay and Lindsay Anthon wanted the food to be just as important. To keep things interesting, the menu changes weekly and features a specialty dish to pair with the latest tapping from their wall of 42 beers. Hopfields has perfectly combined their food and beer and has made their establishment a haven for both craft beer fans and foodies alike. Hopfields is also one of the only places in town that serves brunch daily from 11 to 3 p.m. They have great dishes like Moules Frites and Catalana Fish Stew, and many have praised the Pascal Burger as a complement to a good beer. The burger is piled high with Camembert cheese, cornichons, and caramelized onions, a combination that I find pairs great with a Belgian tripel. The dining room is rather small, so I recommend arriving early on the weekends to beat the dinner rush. Guests typically hang around for a while conversing and sipping on beer and wine. The interior has a cozy feeling reminiscent of a French home mixed with a gastropub. It makes for a great date night or just an intimate place to gather with a small group of friends. While it is located near the college, the crowd is a little older and mature so don't expect to be greeted by

large frat gatherings. Hopfields is a must when looking for a great beer selection and a memorable meal. As a last-minute tip, Hopfields also sells and fills growlers: So if you find a beer you like, take some to go to continue the evening at home.

RED'S PORCH

3508 S. Lamar Blvd., Austin, TX 78704; (512) 440-7337; redsporch.com; @RedsPorch
Draft Beers: 25 **Bottled/Canned Beers:** 50

Located on South Lamar in Austin, Red's Porch is an outdoor drinker's paradise with a gorgeous view of the Green Belt hiking trails. Red's focuses on the laid back vibe of Austin with a large outdoor space and an open yet covered second-story dining room. They focus on great food with a phenomenal selection of beers.

Red's Porch was founded by restaurateur Davis Tucker, who is also behind the Austin brewpub North by Northwest, and he has brought his same focus on beer and food to Red's. The menu has a vast selection of dishes from giant burgers that are perfectly grilled to Tex-Mex inspired dishes and even a selection of down home southern comfort favorites. As if Red's food wasn't impressive enough, they put just as much effort into the bar. The beers are carefully selected with a great selection of locals and great happy hour prices. They do a great job with their craft cocktails and margarita selections as well. Red's always feels inviting.

There are plenty of activities to pass the time with your friends like the bean-bags outside and the small seating area in the back of the dining room with board games and shuffleboard, a great way to play for drinks. Lastly, every Thursday night is Pint Night at Red's. They tap a beer from the featured brewery and give away glassware with the purchase of a beer. This is a great way to stock your cupboard with swag from your favorite breweries. Red's has everything you could want, and I highly recommend a stop when in Austin.

THE SILO ON 7TH
1300 E. 7th St., Austin, TX 78702; (512) 524-0866; siloonseventh.com
Draft Beers: 16 **Bottled/Canned Beers:** 50

The Silo on 7th is a relatively new bar in Austin that took almost 4 years to come to life. Owner Dave Rightmer broke ground on land that was formerly Tony's Tortilla Factory, which was built in the early '20s. The name Silo on 7th came from the use of the repurposed corn silo that stands proudly facing out along 7th Street in east Austin. The neighborhood has seen a renaissance as of late due to the heavy growth of residents. Bars and restaurants have started to pop up all across the east side of town, but none are like Silo on 7th.

The Silo is known for their burgers, which are made with fresh never frozen beef and only the freshest ingredients. In fact, everything on the menu except for the buns is made in house. Aside from food they feature a full bar with an impressive selection of whiskeys, but the display fridge stocked with beer grabs your attention along with the neatly arranged taps of beer. Much of the beer is Texas brewed, but they also carry popular beers from across the country. Head upstairs onto the rooftop patio for a stunning view of Austin's downtown skyline just as the sun starts to set and continue drinking into the evening as the stars shine bright above Texas. They are currently expanding their tap selections including adding more taps in their rooftop patio bar.

Keep in mind the Silo is only open till midnight on weeknights and 1 a.m. on Saturday, so plan accordingly if you are looking to drop in for burgers and beer. On a very positive note, the Silo is one of the only bars in the east side nightlife district that has their own free parking lot. How can you beat free parking, craft beer, and an open air patio with a view of the Austin skyline?

WRIGHT BROS. BREW & BREW

500 San Marcos St. #105, Austin, TX 78702; (512) 493-0963; thebrewandbrew.com;
@thebrewandbrew
Draft Beers: 38 **Bottled/Canned Beers:** 12+

Wright Bros. Brew & Brew is just a couple blocks east of downtown Austin. It was founded by brothers Matthew and Grady Wright, along with their friend and business partner Matthew Bollick. They focus on two things: good beans and good beer. They feature a full espresso bar along with 38 taps of the best craft beer available in the area.

The bar has a sleek design that is modern yet minimalistic. A row of shelves holds small chalkboards listing their current beer offerings. Large roll-up doors allow the space to open up and come to life with a great industrial feel. You won't find much in the way of marketing on the walls or even tap handles; instead you will find a row of plain black handles that make the guests pick their beer by choice with-

out the influence of visual marketing. No need to feel pressured though, the bartenders are very knowledgeable and are great about helping their consumers find a beer of their liking. Wright Bros. also features growler fills and even sells bottles and cans to go. It's a great place for a quiet evening of conversation over beers or to focus and get work done with a hot cup of choice bean coffee.

Bringing together coffee and beer appeals to nearly everyone and makes Brew & Brew a great place to visit without the rowdy noisy crowd. They also feature hot pressed sandwiches utilizing bread and pastries from Easy Tiger, which is located just a few blocks away. When in Austin stop in to Wright Bros. Brew & Brew for a relaxed experience and see how much more you focus on your beer when not distracted with marketing influences.

Austin—Pub Crawls

Austin is home to some of the best craft beer bars in the state. When most people think about bars in Austin, 6th Street is the first thing that comes to mind. For the craft beer fan, however, you will have to look elsewhere for your fix. You will need to venture out into the neighborhoods of Austin to find a great treasure trove of craft beer. You could come up with countless pub crawls in this city due to the number of bars in each area of town. Here are a couple great crawls to check out next time you are in Austin.

Austin—South Lamar

Red's Porch, 3508 S. Lamar Blvd., Austin, TX 78704; (512) 440-7337; www.redsporch .com; @RedsPorch. Red's Porch off South Lamar is a great place to start any pub crawl. The scenic view of the Greenbelt trails from the second floor balcony shows the

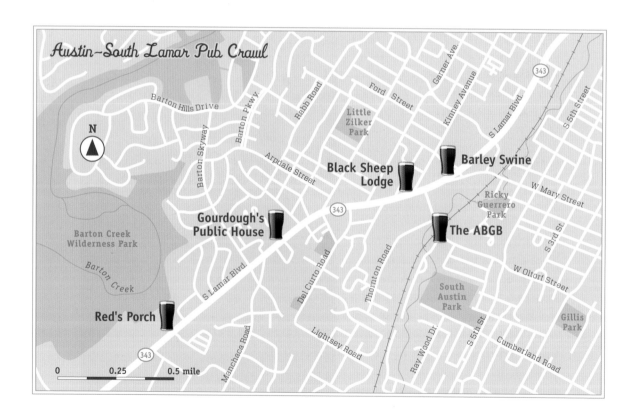

natural beauty of Austin. Aside from nature, Red's has a great selection of craft beers and a delicious menu of food offerings to pair with your beer. Red's is made for people to lounge around and spend hours hanging out playing washers or board games. This is another great chance to challenge your friends for rounds of beers.

Gourdough's Public House, 2700 S. Lamar Blvd., Austin, TX 78704; (512) 912-9070; gourdoughspub.com; @gourdough. If you have never heard of Gourdough's food truck, then you are missing out. They now have a brick and mortar establishment that also serves some great beers. They are famous for their doughnuts, but not just any doughnuts—these are massive doughnuts topped with some serious toppings like bacon and fried chicken. I hope you saved room for dessert, because you're going to need a lot of extra room to take down one of their decadent creations. Go with a big bold stout or a mellow Belgian to pair with your sweets.

Black Sheep Lodge, 2108 S. Lamar Blvd., Austin, TX 78704; (512) 707-2744; black sheeplodge.com; @blacksheeplodge. Black Sheep Lodge is one of the best sports bars in the city. They have screens throughout the building including a large projected screen in the back room. They have over 100 beers to choose from while you're hanging out. If watching sports is not your thing, you can also keep yourself entertained with billiards or shuffleboard. Wednesdays are popular nights at Black Sheep when they feature $1 can beers, but unfortunately, this does not include any craft beer selections. Be warned, during major sporting events, the bar gets really busy and finding a seat can be hard. If you are planning a large gathering, you will need to be aggressive to take over a table.

Austin Beer Garden Brewing, 1305 W. Oltorf, Austin, TX 78704; (512) 298-2242; the abgb.com; @theabgb. There isn't much in life better than pizza and beer. Austin Beer Garden Brewing brings the two greatest things together in a great way. Inside community tables pack the room where guests relax with friends. Outside, industrial wooden spools are used as makeshift tables for those that enjoy the outdoors. They occasionally feature live music to keep guests entertained, as if their beer wasn't enough.

Barley Swine, 2024 S. Lamar Blvd., Austin, TX 78704; (512) 394-8150; barleyswine .com; @BarleySwine. After a long day of beer tripping, there is no better way to end the crawl than with a great meal. Barley Swine is an upscale gastropub where prices are a little on the high side, but you get a meal that you will remember and they have a nice selection of draft and bottled beers to pair with your food. If you're with friends and I hope you are, share a large bottle and cheers to Austin and their great bars dedicated to craft beer.

Hill Country

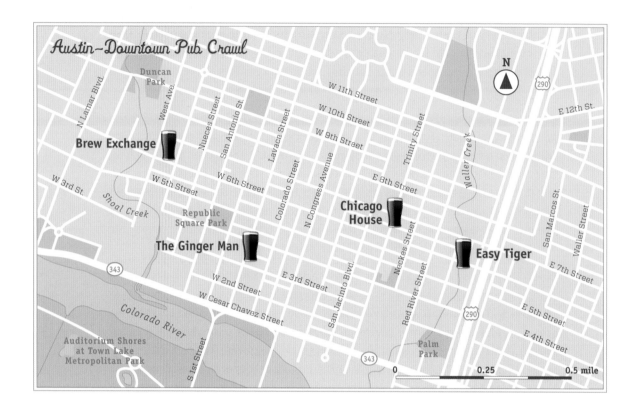

Austin—Downtown Pub Crawl

Austin—Downtown

Easy Tiger Bake Shop & Beer Garden, 709 E. 6th St., Austin, TX 78701; (512) 614-4972; easytigeraustin.com; @EasyTigerATX. Easy Tiger sits nonchalantly on 6th Street just a couple blocks from the main tourist area and its shot bars and night-clubs. It is a relaxed bar that greets patrons through the bakery on the street level entrance, but the bar is located downstairs and spreads out to a large outdoor beer garden. Start the pub crawl off right by layering your stomach with some of their fresh pretzels, beer cheese, and a nice saison or Belgian wheat.

Chicago House, 607 Trinity St., Austin, TX 78701; (512) 358-6202; thechicago house.com; @TheChicagoHouse. Chicago House is located just off of 6th Street and is like an oasis in the middle of the madness. Craft beer can get expensive, but at Chicago House all beers are $5 except during happy hour when they drop the prices down a dollar. They keep the taps constantly rotating and they do a great job bring-ing in rare or specialty seasonals to keep patrons coming back. The bartenders are very knowledgeable about the beers on tap, so should you have any questions they would be glad to help and are more than willing to offer a sample to help you find a beer you like.

The Ginger Man, 301 Lavaca St., Austin, TX 78701; (512) 473-8801; aus.gingerman pub.com; @AustinGingerMan. The Ginger Man got its start in Houston, but the Austin location has been bringing in patrons for years. They have 50 taps of unique beers and they constantly feature different breweries with glassware giveaways. The Ginger Man is an English-style pub that is rather dark inside, but they have a nice small patio out back. This is one place where you will need to be surrounded by good company, otherwise the place can seem a little dull. Due to their great selection of beers, it makes for a great stop for beer lovers visiting downtown.

The Brew Exchange, 706 W. 6th St., Austin, TX 78701; (512) 366-5727; brewex-changeaustin.com; @72beers. The Brew Exchange is right in the middle of the bars and nightlife on W. 6th Street, so it gets rather loud and busy on the weekends. If you have ever wanted to play the stock market, then this is the place for you. Tap into your inner Gordon Gekko and decide when to buy and when to pass. A scrolling ticker above the bar shows the prices of beers and each beer that is sold changes the prices of beers in that style. At times beer prices can get high, so you will have to wait for the market to plummet to get a great deal. The ticker is not tied to the real stock market; it is just a fun way to buy beer and end a pub crawl.

Hill Country

Prairies & Lakes

BREWERIES

Cedar Creek Brewery	26
Cobra Brewing Company	5
Community Beer Company	21
Deep Ellum Brewing Company	25
FireWheel Brewing Company	14
Four Corners Brewing Company	23
Franconia Brewing Company	2
Lakewood Brewing Company	13
Martin House Brewing Company	9
903 Brewers	1
Peticolas Brewing Company	19
Rahr & Sons Brewing Company	12
Revolver Brewing	6

BREWPUBS

Zio Carlo Magnolia Brew Pub	11

BEER BARS

The Bearded Lady	10
The Common Table	22
Dallas Beer Kitchen	18
Dancing Bear Pub	27
Flying Saucer Draught Emporium	8
The Holy Grail Pub	4
LUCK	24
Meddlesome Moth	20
Oak St. Drafthouse & Cocktail Parlor	3
The Old Monk	15
Rodeo Goat	7

BEER BARS cont.

Strangeways	16
World Beer Co.–The Bottle Shop	17

Prairies & Lakes

The Prairies & Lakes region of Texas is a long area that stretches from the Oklahoma border above Dallas down to almost as far south as Goliad. This region is where craft beer cities such as Dallas and Fort Worth are changing the game and breweries are rapidly growing. From the wide open spaces to the booming urban cities, the region is thriving, with growth both in population and in its appreciation for craft beer.

While writing this book I found it almost impossible to keep up with all of the new breweries popping up throughout the region. The Texas craft beer scene has helped bring new jobs to Texas as well as adding millions of dollars to the state's economy. Austin, which is located in the Texas Hill Country, is often noted as the craft beer capital of Texas, but the areas in and around the Dallas–Fort Worth metroplex are quickly catching up and could soon surpass every other city in the state when it comes to breweries. Not only has there been a large growth of breweries and brewpubs, but there is even a large group of craft beer bars that are dedicated to supporting local beer and helping their patrons learn about new beers. For those looking to road-trip through this region to visit the breweries and hunt for beer, I suggest you plan accordingly. The area is very spread out and just circling Dallas could take all day. Be sure to check brewery websites to ensure they are open and assign a designated driver because it's going to be a long ride.

Breweries

CEDAR CREEK BREWERY

244 E. Cedar Creek Pkwy., Seven Points, TX 75143; (214) 502-9795; cedarcreekbrewery
.com/; @cedarcreekbeer
Founded: 2012 **Founder:** Jim Elliott **Brewer:** Damon Lewis **Flagship Beer:** The Lawn
Ranger Cream Ale **Year-Round Beers:** Scruffy's Smoked Alt, Elliott's Phoned Home
Pale Ale, The Lawn Ranger Cream Ale, Dankosaurus IPA **Seasonals/Special Releases:**
Spinning Mule Robust Porter, Clover Kicker Saison, Fisticuffs English Barley Wine, Belgian
Style Dubbe **Tours:** Fri 4 to 9 p.m., Sat 12 to 9 p.m., Sun 12 to 6 p.m. **Taproom:** Yes

Cedar Creek is a brewery born out of determination. Owner Jim Elliott is a man
with patience, because getting the brewery started was a lengthy process that
involved moving locations a few times due to issues with real estate permits. The
brewery was finally built in Seven Points and was named after the nearby Cedar
Creek Lake.

Elliott knew for a long time that he wanted to own his own brewery. He left his former job as a high school teacher to fulfill his dreams and thankfully today, Cedar Creek is a fully operating brewery. The brewhouse is largely repurposed from dairy equipment, and brewer Damon Lewis has taken over and helped create award-winning beers.

Cedar Creek's center of attention is session beers with low alcohol content that you could spend the day drinking without feeling full and bloated. They have accomplished brewing session beers with full flavors and impressive stylings. Owner Jim Elliott always wanted to see his name on a beer, so he took the opportunity with **Elliott's Phoned Home Pale Ale.** The 5.1% ABV pale ale is a blend of American hops and malts with German yeasts. It makes for a smooth-drinking pale that is rich in malt with a clean light hop bitterness. **The Lawn Ranger Cream Ale** is the perfect beer for the Texas heat. It's a light and crisp cream ale that has a bready keenness with slight hop characteristics. It is both refreshing and fulfilling on a hot summer day. Maybe this is all you need to get motivated to mow the lawn in the summer. Cedar Creek beers can be found across Texas, but you can stop in to the brewery

Beer Lover's Pick

Dankosaurus IPA
Style: IPA
ABV: 6.8%
Availability: Year-Round

The Dankosaurus is a remarkable IPA that is a nod to the trendy West Coast–style IPAs. With strong citrus characteristics from the hops, the beer is very multifaceted with a blend of US two-row and German Munich malts that gives it its velvet charming complexity. Fifteen pounds of blended hop varieties go into every batch and give this citrus bomb an explosion of flavor with each sip.

The Dankosaurus is the fourth year-round beer to be released from the north Texas brewers, and thankfully it can be found across the state. I prefer to let this beer warm up a little to let the hop oils release a little and really come forward in the beer. Owner Jim Elliott suggests pairing with spicy food and pungent cheese, but I have found Dankosaurus also pairs well with burgers and steak. This beer is very close to being a palate wrecker, so it clears your taste buds with every mouthful. Dankosaurus easily goes into my top five for IPAs in Texas.

Thursday through Sunday to get a taste of their beer in the freshest form available. While they still have some hurdles to jump over, Jim assures that they will soon be selling growler fills, which would be a great souvenir to bring home from Cedar Creek.

COBRA BREWING COMPANY

146 Whatley Ave., Lewisville, TX 75057; (972) 221-2337; cobrabrewingco.com; @CobraBrewing
Founded: 2013 **Founders:** Bill & Sharon Shaw, Neil & Danielle MacCuish **Brewer:** Neil MacCuish **Flagship Beer:** Hoppy Dazed **Year-Round Beers:** Hoppy Dazed, Best Mistake Stout, Dawn of the Dank, Golden Girl **Seasonals/Special Releases:** Angry Leprechaun, Drunkin Pumkin, Nitemare Before Xmas, Jack Froth, Sumthin Strawberry, Banana Hammock **Tours:** Fri & Sat 6 to 10 p.m. **Taproom:** Yes

Cobra Brewing Company is just 30 minutes north of Dallas in Lewisville. It is owned by a family of New York transplants, Bill and Sharon Shaw along with their son-in-law and daughter Neil and Danielle MacCuish. The family has strived to work together and bring their affection for craft beer to north Texas. Bill started his brewing experience with a Mr. Beer homebrewing kit while Neil learned the crafts of brewing and winemaking from his father. Bill ran a taekwondo studio that he eventually closed, but brought along his cobra logo when the family formed Cobra Brewing Company.

Best Mistake Stout

Style: Triple Chocolate Stout

ABV: 7.3%

Availability: Year-Round

The Best Mistake Stout is definitely a great mistake. When the head brewer Neil Mac-Cuish was working on the recipe, he tried several different experiments that didn't quite come out as he wanted. Neil finally decided to try something wild and added brownie mix to the batch. The beer has a medium body that has a rich nose of cocoa and even a hint of molasses with a clean mellow flavor of chocolate and malt. The beer isn't overly sweet but still gives you a noticeable chocolate awakening to your palate. I am a fan of this beer because it is bold yet still approachable year-round no matter the weather. I like to let this beer warm up so that all of the flavors in the beer can open up. This is only sold in the DFW, so you will need to visit a local bar or hit the brewery to enjoy a pint.

Cobra Brewing follows a unique trend in brewing by using dairy vessels for brewing, with the exception of a few components. This not only saves money, but it also gives the yeast more room to thrive without being cramped in the usual conical fermenter. Neil has created the recipes by experimenting. While the beers stay true to style, he wants to brew a variety of different beers to keep consumers interested. Along with the range of beers, Cobra wanted fans visiting the brewery to have a fun experience unlike the standard tours most breweries have available, so they have pool tables, pinball machines, cornhole, and even live entertainment.

Neil brews such a wide range of beers that it is impossible to categorize them. The goal was to make good beer that they liked and they figured the public would like as well. Due to their location, they have to make beers that are approachable for those who are new to craft beer. The **Golden Girl** is a light easy-drinking beer that can still be respected for its overall presence. The beer is a 6.4% ABV golden ale that is light golden in color and has a semisweet profile of malt with a very light bite from the German Hallertauer hops. The **Banana Hammock** is similar to the **Golden Girl** because of its easy-drinking style. It is a light 4.8% ABV hefeweizen that is very light on banana esters but still gives you that crisp citrus and malt profile typical of hefeweizen-style beers.

Cobra Brewing Company is still in its beginning stages as a brewery, but the owners have come a long way. They are dedicating their time to make sure the beer is consistent and that their followers remain interested in their beers. This is a great brewery to check out after a day on Lake Lewisville, since they are open on the weekends from 6 to 10 p.m. along with local food trucks to keep you fed. This is a really nice family that just wants to connect with the community and spread their love for beer.

COMMUNITY BEER COMPANY

1530 Inspiration Dr., Dallas, TX 75207; (214) 751-7921; communitybeer.com; @CommunityBeerCo

Founded: 2013 **Founder:** Kevin Carr **Brewer:** Jamie Fulton **Flagship Beer:** Mosaic IPA **Year-Round Beers:** Public Ale ESB, Vienna Lager, Community Witbier, Mosaic IPA, Community Pale Ale **Seasonals/Special Releases:** Regalement Spiced Winter Ale, Ascension Coffee Porter, Minivan Wheat Wine, Glenstemmons Scotch Ale, Inspiration Belgian Dark Strong Ale, Trinity Tripel, Texas Pils **Tours:** Sat 2 to 5 p.m. **Taproom:** Thurs 5 to 9 p.m., Fri & Sat 5 to 10 p.m.

Community Beer Company had a dream not only to brew beer for the people of the Dallas–Fort Worth metroplex, but also to give back to the community that they love. Community works with local nonprofits and even offers local artists the opportunity to display and sell their art during brewery tours. While many breweries only open their taprooms during the day, Community offers late evening hours and they even have beers that are only available onsite. The large taproom features a large projected screen, pool table, and other forms of entertainment, as if enjoying their beers wasn't enough.

While Community Beer Company is relatively new, they have really made the state take notice with their award-winning beers. In just their first year, they brought home a gold medal at the Great American Beer Festival for their **Public Ale ESB** and a gold medal for their **Community Witbier** at the 2014 World Beer Cup. The **Vienna Lager** is a great beer to start off with at Community. It is a light-drinking 5.2% ABV beer that is brewed to style as a German lager, and they even design the water profile to mimic that of Bavaria. The beer ferments for weeks slowly at cold temperatures to make a fine crisp beer that is light on the palate with flavors of malts and faint hop bitterness. This is a great introductory beer for people who usually prefer mass commercial lagers.

Community Beer Company is a fun brewery where the employees believe in the mission to brew great beers and support the local community. Their dedication to

Mosaic IPA
Style: IPA
ABV: 7.5%
Availability: Year-Round

While Community Beer Company makes a great lineup of beers, I am really impressed with their Mosaic IPA. With floral notes of citrus and fruits, the Mosaic IPA has a very bold malty citrus bomb of flavor. The blend of Mosaic and other undisclosed American hop varieties makes for a surprisingly smooth-drinking IPA that should impress both beer aficionados and the novice newcomer to craft beer. This IPA is one that I find grows even more delicious as it warms up; the malt complex becomes a little sweeter and gives the drinker the full forward flavor of the blended hops. While this IPA is 7.5% ABV, it has a whopping 85 hoppy and delicious IBUs that will catch up to you if you're not careful. Mosaic hops have become a very popular hop variety as of late but can be hard to come by. Thankfully Community has a connection to make Mosaic IPA a year-round treat.

Prairies & Lakes

local nonprofits and artists speaks volumes for their character, and the beers that they are brewing are remarkable. Their taproom is open Thursday through Saturday with weekly tours Saturday afternoons. I highly recommend you check them out and see why they are turning heads in Texas.

DEEP ELLUM BREWING COMPANY
2823 St. Louis St., Dallas, TX 75226; (214) 888-3322; deepellumbrewing.com; @deepellumbrewco
Founded: 2011 **Founder:** John Reardon **Brewer:** Jeremy Hunt **Flagship Beer:** Deep Ellum IPA **Year-Round Beers:** Dallas Blonde, Deep Ellum Blonde, Pale Ale, Rye Pils, Double Brown Stout, Dreamcrusher 2X Rye IPA **Seasonals/Special Releases:** Cherry Chocolate Double Brown Stout, Numb Comfort, Oak Cliff Coffee Ale, Four Swords Belgian Quad, Neato Bandito, Wealth & Taste, Labor of Love **Tours:** Thurs 6 to 8:30 p.m., Sat 12 to 3 p.m. **Taproom:** Yes

Deep Ellum Brewing Company is both named after and located in the historic Deep Ellum neighborhood of Dallas. The industrial neighborhood has a long history of a thriving nightlife scene, music, and arts. Owner John Reardon found his affection for beer while attending college in Colorado and learned homebrew-ing. After college John returned to Dallas where he owned a couple of bars, but he decided as the Texas craft beer scene started to explode that it was time to jump on the market. Along with friends, John sold his bars and put all of his dedication into opening a brewery of his own.

Deep Ellum Brewing follows the attitude of the neighborhood and they like to do things their way. They went against the norm and worked to brew beers that they liked instead of brewing beers to win medals. The beers are mainly hop forward and in your face with bold flavors. They felt like making big bold beers was the best way to represent the area. The **Dreamcrusher 2X Rye IPA** is a great example of their bold style. The once seasonal beer has gained a lot of popularity, which has pushed it to become a year-round release. The 8.5% ABV double IPA is a big beer with a strong bitter citrus bite. The nose is overwhelming in a good way of hops, and once you take a sip your taste buds will be in for a treat with this malty citrus bomb of a beer. The rye gives a notable complexity to the malt for a well-rounded beer. No beer represents the money in Dallas more than Deep Ellum's **Wealth & Taste.** The 9.5% barrel-aged Belgian golden strong ale is brewed with muscat grape juice, grapefruit

Double Brown Stout
Style: Baltic Porter
ABV: 7%
Availability: Year-Round

I am not a big fan of browns, but Deep Ellum's Double Brown Stout is a smooth Baltic porter that has a medium body with rich notes of chocolate and molasses. The beer is very malty and even has a creamy mouth feel that leaves no off-putting after-tastes. It doesn't really follow the style of Baltic porters but is more of a stout, but I believe that is what they were going for. The beer is very easy to drink year-round and is paired great with red meats and barbecue. I enjoy opening it up as it warms to room temperature to release the notes of chocolate, earth, and pecans on the nose. This beer is a little on the sweeter side but not overbearing and can be appreciated by everyone from novice craft beer drinkers to craft beer fanatics. If you are on the adventurous side, I would suggest pouring a little over some vanilla ice cream or going all out and making a beer float.

peel, rose hips, and chamomile flowers before they age it in chardonnay oak barrels. The muscat is very noticeable but not overpowering on the mouth along with a fruity and citrus finish. You can undeniably taste the barrel in the beer, which gives the Belgian strong ale a gentle yet multifaceted finish.

When visiting Dallas, Deep Ellum Brewing Company and the surrounding Deep Ellum neighborhood is a must. Saturday afternoons at the brewery are a great time to try the beers and have a good time on their patio. Musicians are often performing and local food trucks are on hand selling food. Deep Ellum beers can be found across most of the state and they are currently in the process of expanding within the brewery, which hopefully means the beers will spill beyond the boundaries of Texas.

FIREWHEEL BREWING COMPANY

2806 Lawing Ln., Rowlett, TX 75088; (214) 725-9080; firewheelbrewing.com;
@FireWheelBrew
Founded: 2012 **Founder:** Brad Perkinson **Brewer:** Nate Breitzman **Flagship Beer:**
Midnight Ninja **Year-Round Beers:** Texas Pale Ale, Midnight Ninja, Liquid Assets, Special
#1, StrIPA, Inamorata **Seasonals/Special Releases:** Redneck Ninja, Das Achtzehn
Tours: Sat 11 to 3 p.m. **Taproom:** Yes

FireWheel Brewing Company is in the small town of Rowlett, less than 30 minutes northwest of Dallas. The brewery was founded by Dallas native Brad Perkinson, who graduated from UT-Dallas with a master's in finance. His obsession for beer came from a trip to Oktoberfest in Munich in 2009. It left him yearning to find better beer than the big three commercial brands in the States. It set him off to learn brewing and when he was laid off from his job in finance, he decided to take the leap of starting his own brewery. FireWheel Brewing was all self-funded by Brad, and he even built much of the brewhouse by hand.

FireWheel Brewing is the first brewery in Rowlett and is named after an area in neighboring Garland, Texas. Owner Brad and brewer Nate are big fans of malt and hoppy balanced beers, and beers that appeal to fans of bigger and bolder beers. With

no investors or loans, they brew what they want and have some pretty interesting beers in their lineup. The **Midnight Ninja** is an 8% imperial black ale that goes down smooth but with its higher alcohol content can sneak up on you and kick you in the face. The beer is dark in color with a soft brown head. It has a bouquet of toasted malts and toffee, but on the mouth it has hints of chocolate and even a little earth. The beer has a dry finish that keeps your taste buds interested. The **Texas Pale Ale** is a beer that represents Texas well. The 6% ABV pale pours in a rich amber color with a full white head. The nose is an opus of balanced malt and hoppy aroma. The mouth is citrus and earthy with a bitter clean finish. It is a very enjoyable beer that is very close to being an IPA. It is a well-received beer for an afternoon backyard barbecue.

FireWheel Brewing is in the process of expansion, and they are planning to make the move out of their current business park to a nearby freestanding full production brewery. Currently they are trying to keep up with the demand in the DFW area, but once they move to the new brewery and take on more brewing capacity they plan to expand into more markets in Texas. This is a brewery that I will keep an eye on as they continue to grow.

Beer Lover's Pick

StrIPA
Style: Strawberry IPA
ABV: 6%
Availability: Year-Round

I am usually not a fan of fruit in my beer, but that was until I tasted the StrIPA from FireWheel Brewing Company. The 6% ABV strawberry IPA is very refreshing beer that has a subtle sweetness and adds just the right amount of tartness to bring out the hops in the beer. Unfortunately, they were unable to find the right balance for the beer using fresh strawberries, so they have decided to go with a strawberry extract in the beer that can fool the taste buds into thinking that they are enjoying a fresh strawberry beer. This is a great way for people to tiptoe into the world of IPAs if they are put off by the bitter bite that is usually associated with the style. The strawberry extract gives the beer a citrusy mellow flavor with a clean malt finish. This may be a year-round beer, but it is definitely a summertime favorite. It is not overly sweet and does not leave any off-putting aftertastes. It can be paired with most dishes, but I find it to be a great addition to barbecue pork ribs.

FOUR CORNERS BREWING COMPANY

423 Singleton Blvd., Dallas, TX 75212; (214) 748-2739; fcbrewing.com; @fcbrewing
Founded: 2012 **Founders:** Steve Porcari, George Esquivel & Greg Leftwich **Brewer:** Zach
Petty **Flagship Beer:** Local Buzz **Year-Round Beers:** Local Buzz, El Chingon IPA, Block
Party, Rustic Red **Tours:** Sat **Taproom:** Yes

Four Corners Brewing Company is in West Dallas in the newly renamed neighborhood of Trinity Groves. This once industrial neighborhood has been converted into an up and coming arts and entertainment district by investors. The brewery was founded by friends Steve Porcari, George Esquivel, and Greg Leftwich. Steve and George were longtime friends who played in local bands together. They met Greg after competing in a homebrewing contest and quickly became friends over their shared love for craft beer.

The partners converted an old diesel mechanic shop into a large open space for their brewery along with a taproom that is open 7 days a week. Along with their head brewer Zach Petty, they have created beers that they consider "All Day Ales" that are balanced, true to style brews that are approachable and easy to drink in the Texas heat. They are the only brewery in Texas that is canning their beers in pop-top cans that remove the complete inner lid of the can. This was to allow the consumers to experience the beer with all of their senses and really explore the bouquet of the beers.

The flagship beer for Four Corners Brewing Company is their **Local Buzz,** which is a 5.2% ABV honey rye golden ale that uses locally produced honey. It is a nod to the local farmers of the neighborhood, from the farm to table restaurants to the backyard self-sustaining horticulturists. Local Buzz is smooth and delicately sweet with a touch of honey without being overpowering. The **Block Party** is a beer that was created by their original brewer, who made the beer for his neighborhood block party. It is a very light porter that has hints of chocolate roast malts. It is full bodied yet is still an easy-drinking beer for the warm weather. It is not overbearing or heavy so it can be paired with most dishes.

Four Corners Brewing started canning their beers in the spring of 2014, and ever since they have been swamped with demand. They have many other recipes in the works, but due to the lack of space they have had to focus on their four year-round beers. They are in the process of expanding their brewing capacity, which will allow them to expand into new markets and brew more recipes. Unfortunately, the beer is only available in the Dallas–Fort Worth area, so you will have to make the trek there to pick up a sixer, but once you pop the top on one of their cans you will see that it is well worth the trip.

Beer Lover's Pick

El Chingon
Style: IPA
ABV: 7.6%
Availability: Year-Round
El Chingon is Spanish slang for bad ass, and that is exactly what this beer is. The 7.6% ABV IPA is a bold slap in the face with a great citrus malty essence. It pours a deep hazy amber with a frothy white head and a nose of hoppy

goodness. This is a well-rounded balanced go-to IPA that you can drink all afternoon, but the slightly higher ABV will catch up with you. Following the brewery's Mexican theme, this beer pairs great with fajitas and spicy Tex-Mex dishes. The beer is quite refreshing and is a great example of the style. I always like to have this one on hand.

FRANCONIA BREWING COMPANY

495 McKinney Pkwy., McKinney, TX 75071; (972) 542-0705; franconiabrewing.com; @FranconiaBrew
Founded: 2008 **Founder:** Dennis Wehrmann
Brewer: Cam Horn **Flagship Beer:** Franconia Dunkel **Year-Round Beers:** Franconia Blonde, Franconia Lager, Franconia Kolsh, Franconia Wheat, Franconia Amber Ale, Franconia Dunkel **Seasonals/Special Releases:** Franconia Pilsner, Franconia Maibach, Franconia Kristal-weizen, Franconia Oktoberfest, Franconia Winter Wheat **Tours:** Sat 11 to 2 p.m. **Taproom:** No

Franconia Brewing Company is located in a business park in McKinney, Texas, which is about a 30-minute drive north of Dallas. The brewery was founded by German native and fifth-generation brewmaster Dennis Wehrmann. Dennis has a long family history of rich German brewing influences that he has brought with him, and it reflects in the beers brewed at Franconia. The brewery is named after the Franconia region in Germany, which is home to the most breweries in the world. Dennis moved from Germany to take a position as the brewmaster at local brewpub Two Rows. After 4 years working for the brewpub, Dennis decided it was time to make plans for a brewery of his own and that is exactly what he did.

Dennis has stayed true to his roots and brews beers that follow the strict Reinheitsgebot, also known as the German purity laws of brewing. The beers at Franconia are all true to style and one of the purest forms of German beer that you will find in Texas. While Dennis focuses on German-style beers, being in Texas he has even designed beers for Texas palates such as the **Franconia Amber Ale,** which is a classic Texas-style beer with a balance of malt and caramel that is unpretentious and inviting for all. Or the **Franconia Blonde** that pours a light hazy yellow that has a nose of grass and citrus. The beer is a clean blonde with a floral citrus mouth. If you really want to get a taste of a traditional hefeweizen from southern Germany, then you can go for the refreshing **Franconia Wheat,** a light sessionable 4.8% ABV hefe that has a delicate nose of bananas and clove. The mouth brings notes of light tart lemons and earth.

Franconia Dunkel

Style: Dunkel

ABV: 4.4%

Availability: Year-Round

One of the biggest misconceptions about beers is that dunkels are all dark wheat beers. Really the term dunkel means dark. Franconia Dunkel is a mix somewhere between a Munich dark lager and a schwarzbier that is brewed with two-row malts and Hallertauer hops. The beer is smooth and lightly carbonated with a faint chocolate and roasted malty mouth. The nose is light but you can detect the roast malts. The beer isn't very complex and is very approachable. It has a dry finish, which lets it pair with virtually any dish. It is a great beer to start your way into craft beers. I commend Franconia for going against the stigma of dunkels being dark wheat beers.

Franconia beers can now be found across the state, and they are continuing to break into new markets. They are all very approachable with low alcohol contents, which make all of the brews great session beers. This is a brewery worth checking out, and I am excited to see what Dennis has in store for special releases.

LAKEWOOD BREWING COMPANY

2302 Executive Dr., Garland, TX 75041; (972) 864-2337; lakewoodbrewing.com; @LakewoodBrewing

Founded: 2012 **Founder:** Win Bens **Brewers:** Jason Van Gilder & Shawn Vail **Flagship Beer:** Lakewood Vienna Lager **Year-Round Beers:** Lakewood Vienna Lager, Hop Trap Belgian IPA, Temptress Imperial Milk Stout, Rock Ryder Rye Wheat **Seasonals/Special Releases:** Punkle, Till & Toil, Zomer Pils, Legendary Series **Tours:** Sat 12 to 3 p.m. **Taproom:** No

Lakewood Brewing in Garland was established in 2012 by Belgian-born Win Bens. Most known for their **Temptress Imperial Milk Stout,** the brewery puts out a full line of impressive beers. While they don't limit themselves to strictly Belgian-style beers, the brews do have a Belgian flare that make them light and flavorful while at times still packing a high ABV. Lakewood is currently expanding their brewery because their current 30-barrel brewhouse is keeping them brewing two times a day, 7 days a week.

Punkle

Style: Dunkel

ABV: 5.5%

Availability: Autumn

There is no better time in Texas than just after the summer season starts to cool off. The temps drop from the upper 90s to the mid 70s and the trees start to change in color. For many breweries, they start to roll out their fall seasonals, many of which tend to be pumpkin-style beers, but Lakewood Brewing is going above and beyond. Their Punkle is a 5.5% ABV pumpkin pie dunkel that is a complement to the pie instead of a beer brewed with pumpkin in it. They brew a dark German lager and flavor it with allspice, cinnamon, ginger, and nutmeg. The beer has a roasted aroma with subtle hints of caramel and has a deliciously smooth flavor of sweet roasted malt and the pumpkin spices on the back end. I like to age this beer and wait for the dead of winter, but if you can't wait I would suggest tossing the beer in the fridge for about 20 minutes before opening just to give it a slight chill. This will allow you to get the full experience of the beer as it comes to room temperature. The spices come through more as it warms up, and it becomes a beer that will make you think of fall and crave a huge slice of pumpkin pie with a large dollop of whipped cream.

Along with the year-round and seasonal releases, Lakewood has a very special "Legendary Series" and "Seduction Series" of beers. Unfortunately, these beers are only brewed in very limited batches, so once they run out, there is no more. The Legendary Series are beers named after Belgian and local mythologies like **La Dame Du Lac,** which translates into the Lady of the Lake. Locals say there is a lady who haunts the region of White Rock Lake. She walks along the road looking for a lift. Legend has it when she is picked up she quietly sits in the back seat and eventually disappears leaving a wet spot. The legends vary as do the styles of the beers. For the Seduction Series, the brewers get to have fun tweaking their Temptress Imperial Milk Stout in different variations. One of the most memorable so far is their **Mole Temptress,** which was infused with chocolate, chiles, and spices. Sadly, this was a one-time batch, but hopefully the brewers will decide to bring this back once the brewery expands.

Lakewood has come a long way in such a short time, and with the upcoming expansion the sky is the limit. Their solid year-round releases, full-flavored seasonals, and sensational special releases are the perfect combination needed for a successful brewery. This is definitely a brewery to watch as they continue to grow.

MARTIN HOUSE BREWING COMPANY

220 S. Sylvania Ave. #209, Fort Worth, TX 76111; (817) 222-0177; martinhousebrewing .com; @MartinHouseBrew
Founded: 2013 **Founder:** Cody Martin **Brewer:** Cody Martin **Flagship Beer:** The Imperial Texan **Year-Round Beers:** Gateway XPA, Day Break, The Imperial Texan, River House, Pretzel Stout **Seasonals/Special Releases:** Salsa Verde, Turtle Power, SeptemberFest **Tours:** Thurs 6 to 8 p.m., Sat 2 to 5 p.m. **Taproom:** Yes

Martin House Brewing Company is just west of downtown Fort Worth in a warehouse with a spectacular view of the skyline. It was founded by Cody Martin, who originally worked as an engineer. It was a trip to The Ginger Man in Fort Worth that sparked his curiosity and left him wanting to explore new flavors and styles of craft beer. Cody started to learn homebrewing and quickly jumped from a 5-gallon extract brew to 10-gallon all grain batches in the matter of a month. Cody started to realize that beermaking had many similarities to his career in engineering and became obsessive about expanding his brewing. Cody and his wife Anna were living in Florida when he approached her about his interest in starting up a brewery, and she quickly laughed it off as a daydream. But after a while she realized that her sales and marketing background could be beneficial to the brewery. After a few years they decided to move back to Texas and Cody left his engineering career behind. He then brought on a couple of trusted friends, David Wedemeier and Adam Myers, to help him move forward on his brewery, and in 2013 Martin House rolled out their first keg.

From the beginning Martin House was very straightforward that they wanted to brew beers that they liked. They didn't worry about following strict guidelines, but instead they wanted to think outside of the box and brew big bold beers that would capture consumers' attention. While many breweries make suggestions for food pairings, Martin House suggests outdoor adventures customers can take part in to understand and appreciate their beers. From camping and rock climbing to kayaking and mountain biking, they want their fans to get out and really taste life both physically and in their beers.

Martin House Brewing has come a very long way in a short time brewing some very big beers with unique flavors. Many breweries make seasonal beers, but Martin House has opted to release a beer every month. As if summer wasn't hot enough in

Pretzel Stout
Style: Stout
ABV: 6.5%
Availability: Year-Round
Martin House is big about doing things differently, and their Pretzel Stout is a great example. The beer is a 6.5% ABV stout that is actually brewed with over 6 pounds of sourdough pretzels. This gives the beer a semi-salty light chocolate taste that is surprisingly flavorful. The pretzels give the beer a salty dry zest that keeps your palate wanting more. The beer is quite light on the mouth and warms up to release more of the chocolate flavors. It can be enjoyed in both warm and cool seasons since it is a year-round release. Martin House suggests pairing this beer with rock climbing, but I have plans for celebrating Oktoberfest and enjoying some bratwurst on a stick.

Texas, they have made a beer for the month of August called the **Salsa Verde,** an ale brewed with roasted hatch green chiles, tomatillos, cilantro, and lime that hit your mouth with a robust explosion of flavors. While it has a nose of fresh salsa, it is actually pretty delicious without being spicy. Martin House recommends pairing this beer with rope-swinging and chili-eating contests, but if you ask me I would pair it with fresh chips and queso. As far as their year-round beers go, you really can't go wrong.

Martin House currently keeps their beers floating around north Texas, but you will occasionally find them in bars in Houston and Austin. I am anxious to see their upcoming monthly beer releases and how the rest of the state welcomes their beers.

903 BREWERS
1718 S. Elm St., Sherman, TX 75090; (214) 243-8029; http://903brewers.com/; @903brewers
Founded: 2013 **Founders:** Jeremy & Natalie Roberts **Brewer:** Jeremy Roberts **Flagship Beer:** The Chosen One Coconut Ale **Year-Round Beers:** The Chosen One Coconut Ale, Roo's Red Ale, Breezy Blonde Ale, Crackin' Up Pecan Porter, Sasquatch Chocolate Milk Stout **Seasonals/Special Releases:** General Sherman's Brown Ale **Tours:** Sat 12 to 3 p.m. **Taproom:** Yes

903 Brewers is about an hour north of Dallas in the small town of Sherman. The brewery is named after the regional area code and is owned by husband and wife Jeremy and Natalie Roberts. An avid homebrewer, Jeremy decided to turn his love of brewing into a full business. Before jumping into the brewing business, Jeremy and Natalie were public speakers helping businesses with management and financial advice. Natalie supported her husband's dream and inspired him to pursue his passion to become a brewer. In 2013 they purchased space in an old building that was the first industrial warehouse in Sherman and was built in the mid 1800s. This history resonates and brings a sense of historic charm to the brewery.

Brewing on a small 7-barrel system has limited the amount of beer 903 can put out, but brewing daily has helped them keep the Dallas–Fort Worth region drinking well. While their most popular and flagship beer is the very easy drinking **The Chosen One Coconut Ale,** the beer that drinkers can't get enough of is the **Sasquatch Chocolate Milk Stout.** It packs a serious punch for big beer fans with its 10.7% ABV; this behemoth is rich and smooth with strong chocolate notes from the cocoa nibs and a velvety texture on the mouth. It goes down smooth without noticing the high ABV.

Jeremy has designed his recipes by trial and error and has done a great job of making some very serious beers that will impress both seasoned craft beer veterans

Beer Lover's Pick

Crackin' Up Pecan Porter
Style: Porter
ABV: 8.5%
Availability: Year-Round
903 Brewers are really bringing out that Texas pecan flavor in their Crackin' Up Pecan Porter. Using fresh locally grown pecans, this porter is sweeter than other similar porters without the bitterness from the pecans. It has a smooth texture on the mouth that doesn't leave a long-lasting flavor yet demands another sip. The roast malts make this a pecan pie in a glass, but just not as sweet. Thankfully Jeremy brewed this beer just right without being overbearing in sweetness and with just the slightest bite of hops. This is a well-rounded beer that Jeremy suggests can be paired with barbecue and steak, which might complement the smokiness from the meat. I think this is a great beer to age and I can only hope they plan to barrel it.

and novice newcomers. Sadly, due to their limited capacity the beer is only available in the Dallas region, but once they have room for expansion Texas will be in for a delicious treat.

PETICOLAS BREWING COMPANY

2026 Farrington St., Dallas, TX 75207; (214) 234-7600; peticolasbrewing.com; @Peticolas
Founded: 2011 **Founders:** Michael & Melissa Peticolas **Brewer:** Michael Peticolas
Flagship Beer: Velvet Hammer **Year-Round Beers:** Velvet Hammer, Royal Scandal, Golden Opportunity **Seasonals/Special Releases:** Wintervention, Great Scot!, Alfred Brown, The DUKE, Rye't On, Sit Down Or I'll Sit You Down, Irish Goodbye, Black Curtains, Belgian Tripel **Tours:** First and third Sat of the month, 1 to 3 p.m. **Taproom:** No

Peticolas Brewing Company was built on a love for homebrewing passed on from owner/brewer Michael Peticolas's mother. It was Michael's mother that first introduced him to the fun and excitement of drinking and sharing homemade beer, not the usual story of how someone first encounters homebrewing. As Michael grew a friend taught him how to brew on his own and eventually Michael and his wife Melissa came across an opportunity to invest in a startup brewery. After careful

Sit Down Or I'll Sit You Down
Style: Imperial IPA
ABV: 10%
Availability: Special Release

Sit Down Or I'll Sit You Down is a beast of a beer. The 10% ABV monstrosity dares you to be cocky and try to challenge it to a fight. The English malts blend wonderfully with the citrus from the hops for a superb experience in your mouth.

The beer is named after owner Michael Peticolas's brother Charlie, who was a police officer and was filmed on an episode of the show *Cops*. He arrested an uncooperative suspect. When Charlie lost his temper, he told the detainee "Sit down or I'll sit you down!" The episode became a long-running joke in the Peticolas family, so Michael decided a beer this big needed a name that would let its consumers know that it is a force to be reckoned with. It is not for beginners; the beer is a bold expression of an imperial IPA that boasts a noticeable bitterness that is calmed with the malty base for a velvety mouth feel that almost dares you to challenge it.

Unfortunately, Sit You Down is only a special release so you will have to stay tuned to their website for updates on future releases. It is a great beer to pair with spicy dishes. Michael suggests it be paired with Indian food, but I have yet to find anything that this doesn't pair well with. All I can do is hope that this eventually becomes a year-round release so I don't have to travel to Dallas and hoard bottles every time it is released.

consideration Michael thought why not just do it himself? With Melissa giving her husband her full support, the couple decided to go forth and break ground on what is Peticolas Brewing Company today.

Peticolas Brewing Company is widely known throughout Texas for their admired **Velvet Hammer.** The big 9% ABV red is a monstrous beer that is malt forward with notes of caramel and brown sugar without being sweet thanks to the floral hop bite. The beer is a foreboding rusty brown color with a cream white head. The **Golden Opportunity** is a sessionable easy-drinking golden ale with a low 4.6% ABV. It is a sweet malty beer with delicate hop bitterness, carbonated flawlessly for a crisp enjoyable beer.

Peticolas Brewing is a force to be reckoned with in Dallas. They are racking up awards at events, and they continue to grow and brew new recipes. The beer can only be found in the Dallas–Fort Worth area, so you will have to make a trip to sample their goods. Peticolas beers have occasionally popped up in the Austin market, but it is a rare occurrence.

RAHR & SONS BREWING COMPANY
701 Galveston Ave., Fort Worth, TX 76104; (817) 810-9266; rahrbrewing.com; @RahrBrewing
Founded: 2004 **Founders:** Fritz & Erin Rahr **Brewer:** Craig Mycoskie **Flagship Beer:** Texas Red **Year-Round Beers:** Rahr's Blonde, Ugly Pug, Texas Red, Stormcloud, Buffalo Butt **Seasonals/Special Releases:** Iron Thistle, Bucking Bock, Summertime Wheat, Gravel Road, Oktoberfest, Snowmageddon, The Regulator, Pecker Wrecker, La Grange, Angry Goat, Bourbon Barrel Aged Winter Warmer **Tours:** Wed 5 to 7:30 p.m., Sat 12:30 to 3 p.m. **Taproom:** Yes

Rahr & Sons Brewing Company is arguably the largest commercial craft brewery in north Texas. It is a partnership built with love between husband and wife, Fritz and Erin Rahr. Established in 2004, they have the structure of a company that has been around for much longer. Their beers have over fifty nationally recognized awards and their weekend tours are packing in well over 400 attendees every Saturday, and that's pretty impressive for a brewery that is only distributing within Texas.

Ugly Pug
Style: Schwarzbier
ABV: 5%
Availability: Year-Round

Ugly Pug was the original flagship beer for Rahr & Sons. The name came about from a poor ugly little pug by the name of Oscar who belonged to the mother-in-law of Fritz Rahr. The dog must have had a face only a mother could love, but he is forever immortalized on the bottles of Rahr & Sons' Ugly Pug. It is a very light drinking 5% ABV black lager with an aroma of roasted malts and coffee. On the mouth the beer is very light bodied with a deep dark brown color and has notes of bitterness from dark chocolate and light caramel flavors. It is a very enjoyable black lager that can be enjoyed all year thanks to its light body. It is great both for someone who usually prefers a commercial light beer and the craft beer enthusiast.

Some of the most recognized beers from the Rahr are the **Ugly Pug** black lager, which was originally the flagship beer from the brewery, but lately the **Texas Red** amber lager has become one of their biggest sellers. Texas Red is a well-balanced malty amber lager that has a light malt and sweet caramel profile with just an edge of hoppy goodness. The original **Rahr's Blonde** was the first beer commercially brewed at the brewery, and it is still a very popular beer for their fans. The traditional style Munich Helles-style lager is a bright blonde ale that is light on the mouth and has a semisweet malty flavor with very little bitterness. In 2010 a heavy snowstorm hit Fort Worth and accumulation of snow brought down part of the roof of the brewery. While it was a big hit to the brewery, they rebounded quickly, and in a tribute to the community that stood by them they brew the **Snowmageddon** oatmeal stout. The 8.5% ABV stout is surely going to warm you up with rich roasted malts and hints of coffee and chocolate. I prefer this beer at slightly below room temperature.

If you're planning to visit the brewery for a tour, you better arrive early, because they get filled up pretty quickly. Every week around 300 guests show up to taste fresh beer right from the brewery and learn about what makes Rahr & Sons so great. Rahr beers can practically be found all across the state so be sure to pick up a couple sixers to enjoy with your friends.

REVOLVER BREWING COMPANY

5600 Matlock Rd., Granbury, TX 76049; (817) 736-8034; revolverbrewing.com; @RevolverBrewing
Founded: 2011 **Founders:** Ron & Rhett Keisler **Brewer:** Grant Wood **Flagship Beer:** Blood & Honey **Year-Round Beers:** Blood & Honey, High Brass, Revolver Bock **Seasonals/Special Releases:** Sidewinder, Mother's Little Fracker **Tours:** Sat 12 to 3 p.m. **Taproom:** Yes

Revolver Brewing Company is just 35 miles southwest of Fort Worth in the town of Granbury, and it was founded by father and son team Ron and Rhett Keisler. Ron put in 30 years as a geologist with Marathon Oil while Rhett worked in corporate finance in Toronto. In 2009 after Ron retired, Rhett was feeling burnt out in his career and was looking for new ventures. Rhett decided to move back to Texas to escape the brutal winters and look for new opportunities. Rhett was inspired by the quick-growing craft beer movement in Texas and started to look into the industry. He put together a business plan and approached Ron with the idea of starting a brewery, but neither one of them had any brewing experience. They put out an ad out seeking a brewer who could help form the brewery and take the plans off the ground. Grant Wood, a brewer who had spent the past 16 years working with Boston Beer Company at the time, answered the ad and met with Rhett. The two instantly hit it off over beers and their plans for the brewery, and the Keislers eventually offered Grant the position as master brewer. It took Grant some time to mull over the offer and move his family to Texas to join Ron and Rhett to form a new brewery. In 2011 Revolver Brewing went live, but their kegs didn't roll out until 2012.

Once their beer hit the market, the public took notice and **Blood & Honey** was an instant sellout at many bars. Even today, Blood & Honey is still the biggest seller for Revolver. It is a very approachable beer that has a great flavor and is easy to drink. The 7% ABV American wheat pours a light golden color with a medium head. It has a fruity citrus nose with notes of coriander and spice. On the palate the beer has a sweet malty base with flavors of honey and orange with a soft bitter finish. It is a great beer that pairs with many dishes, and it finishes dry. The **Sidewinder** is what Revolver calls a Southwest pale ale, which comes in at an enjoyable 6.75% ABV. The beer is a seasonal release from the brewery that goes down perfectly in the warmer months thanks to its light body and flavor profile. It is brewed with agave nectar, citrus, and corn that is finished off with Citra hops, which gives the Sidewinder a clean balanced flavor. It has notes of the agave, biscuits, and citrus

Beer Lover's Pick

Mother's Little Fracker
Style: Stout
ABV: 7.75%
Availability: Fall

Mother's Little Fracker is a winter seasonal that is there to warm you up on those cold winter nights. It is a 7.75% ABV stout that pours a rich and deep brown with a tan head. The bouquet quickly gives off beautiful notes of roasted malts and coffee with just a hint of oats. On the palate the stout is on the sweeter side with a rich chocolate and coffee flavor with a minor hint of burnt caramel that is both creamy and delicious. It is hopped with Summit and Challenger hops that are present but seem to be overwhelmed by the roasted malt. The beer is a little light on the body, but it is still a filling and enjoyable experience. I find Mother's Little Fracker to be a great beer for the cooler temps, so grab a bottle to warm up.

that follow onto the palate with a floral hop finish. This is a very approachable and almost sessional beer, different from most other pale ales but still enjoyable. While it is brewed with unusual ingredients such as maize and agave nectar, it makes for a complex and interesting beer that almost anyone can enjoy.

Revolver Brewing has had a hard time getting their other beers in the hands of the public thanks to the success of Blood & Honey. Sometimes once you are known for something, it is hard to try something new, but Revolver has worked hard to show the state that they have some other great beers as well. Luckily, the beer is pretty easy to find across the state. Be on the lookout for any upcoming special releases and try to stop by the brewery to see what is new on tap.

Brewpub

ZIO CARLO MAGNOLIA BREWPUB

1001 W. Magnolia Ave., Fort Worth, TX 76104; (817) 923-8000; ziocarlobrew.com; @ZioCarloBrew

Founded: 2011 **Founders:** Carlo Galotto, Adam Gonzales & Austin Jones **Brewers:** Carlo Galotto, Austin Jones **Flagship Beer:** Roman Empire Strikes Back! ESB **Year-Round Beers:** 1011 Amber Ale, Roman Empire Strikes Back! ESB, Single Phase Pale Ale, Roman Empire Bitter ESB **Seasonals/Special Releases:** Vivaldi Series, Rowdy Stout, Salt in the Biertieg Asch Gose, Batch Limit Berlinerweisse, Smoke Wheat Eryday

Fort Worth is a booming yet quiet city that has exploded recently in the craft beer community. Zio Carlo Magnolia Brewpub has been a long time in the making, but since the doors opened in 2011 they have worked hard to be the go-to spot in the community for fine craft beers and homemade food.

Zio Carlo is a partnership between Carlo Galotto, Adam Gonzales, and Austin Jones. Together, the partners' backgrounds have been part of what has made Zio Carlo's such a success. Carlo is an Italian-born immigrant who has brought family recipes to make the house-made pizzas that you can smell throughout the building. The intoxicating scent of a fresh pie pairs perfectly with the beers they are brewing. **Smoke Wheat Eryday** is a sessionable German-style Grodziskie wheat beer that's only 2.8% ABV. With the low alcohol content, you would think this would be a bland lifeless beer, but surprisingly this light beer comes with a very clean and refreshing flavor that works as a great palate cleanser when pairing with food. The beer has bright citrus notes and subtle hops characters that make it a very easy beer to enjoy over and over again. The most popular beer for Zio Carlo's is the **Roman Empire Bitter ESB.** This 6% ABV ESB-style beer has a very light body with a great blend of sweet malt and delicate hop bitterness, while the more intense **Roman Empire Strikes Back! ESB** is more aggressive and comes in at 8.5% ABV.

Zio Carlo believes smaller is better and is very selective about the beers they keep on tap. Out of the 16 taps they tend to have 6 house-brewed beers on the roster. Go ahead and enjoy some of their guest taps, but I can guarantee it's the house brews that are going to really keep your attention.

Pub Church

If you feel like it has been way too long since your last confession, stop by Zio Carlo's on Sunday at 5 p.m. for pub church. Two Lutheran congregations teamed up to host services at the brewpub over craft beer and pizza. They are not worshipping beer; this is a laid back group that praises the gospel and takes the word of the Lord seriously. I guess when you really think about it, a church is just a building; it is the prayers that are spoken and the faith of the congregation that really matters in the end. Why not worship over a pint? The idea was that for many, a typical church feels stuffy and very uptight. The services held at Zio Carlo by Calvary Lutheran Church and Trinity Lutheran Church let their parishioners attend in an environment that is fun and inviting. The pastors noticed that young people were starting to leave their church, and they decided it was time to break tradition and reach out to people, whether it is in a house of God or a house of ales.

Beer Bars

THE BEARDED LADY
1229 7th Ave., Fort Worth, TX 76104; (817) 349-9832; beardedladyfw.com;
@BeardedLadyFW
Draft Beers: 30 **Bottled/Canned Beers:** 175+

The Bearded Lady is in an old house built in 1926 in the Southside neighborhood of Fort Worth along Magnolia Avenue. This bar isn't a freak show or a circus-themed establishment, but you will probably run into a lot of guys there rocking a burly beard and tattoos. The Bearded Lady focuses on craft beer and killer food. With almost 200 beers to choose from, they offer some of the best beers from across Texas and beyond. The food is unlike anything you will see at your usual craft beer pub. Here they make some pretty intricate dishes such as the Bearded L.U.S.T Burger, which they stuff with roasted poblanos and feta cheese, then top with grilled onions, avocados, and lettuce on a brioche bun, or their delicious tangy and spicy pork wings. The Bearded Lady is a great place to hang out with friends and get a great meal and good beer. The space is rather small, but it still has a great environment that is warm and inviting for all. The Bearded Lady is definitely a special gem that I consider a must when visiting Fort Worth. The staff is friendly and very knowledgeable about beer, so you never feel pressured or judged when you're not sure what to order.

THE COMMON TABLE

2917 Fairmount St., Dallas, TX 75201; (214) 880-7414; thecommontable.com;
@Common_Table

Draft Beers: 28 **Bottled/Canned Beers:** 60+

Common Table is in the trendy Uptown Dallas area, surrounded by a spread of great bars and restaurants. But none can even begin to compete with the beer selection here. When you arrive at Common Table, it's hard to decide whether you want to claim a spot on their beautiful outdoor patio or head inside to escape the naturally occurring Texas heat. Inside the horseshoe-shaped bar takes center stage and almost draws you in for a drink, but the host staff are more than willing to find you a table if you're not a fan of bellying up to the bar. The staff is friendly and they are great about remembering your name. If they find out that it is your first visit, they will be excited to go over the beer menu, which is an album sleeve that is filled with listings on both front and back. With such an extensive beer list it can be almost overwhelming, but the bartenders are very attentive and are great about helping you find a beer that fits your tastes. While the bar usually has a steady crowd, they are most busy on Saturday and Sunday afternoons for the brunch crowd that hijacks the patio with music blasting overhead. This isn't the usual quiet craft beer bar. They are all about having fun at Common Table, but they get serious when it comes to the beer and the food. Don't think that just because they have put so much attention in the beer menu that the food is a second thought. You can go for the beefed-up normal pub fare like massive burgers or stacked sandwiches, or you can order a few plates to share like the Avocado on the Half Shell with lobster and chive oil or the Mussels and Frites, which is steamed in saison beer. The Common Table is definitely a great place to check out while in Dallas, so take a break from shopping and enjoy a beer or two.

DALLAS BEER KITCHEN

1802 Greenville Ave., Dallas, TX 75206; (214) 484-2481; dallasbeerkitchengreenville.com;
@FollowDBK

Draft Beers: 30 **Bottled/Canned Beers:** 50

Dallas Beer Kitchen is inconspicuously nestled within the row of bars and restaurants in the popular Lower Greenville area of Dallas. The front of the building is bold and white with a roll-up glass garage door and a very simple painting of their name in block letters. The outside of the building doesn't give you a lot to think about, but when you step inside you get a different, more inviting perspective. The

building is long and narrow with ominous red and cream walls and a few nostalgic photos of years past. A few tables are neatly lined in rows and there are a couple high-top tables along the wall opposite the bar. While minimalistic, the bar is nice and feels like a modern take on an old school speakeasy. The bar area itself is rather small and seems tight to work behind, but it has not stopped them from slinging great beer.

The kitchen cooks up an appetizing variety of foods, from snacks to small plates and entrees such as burgers, sandwiches, and build your own mac 'n cheese. This isn't your standard pub fare; the flavors are bold and the presentations are striking. The bartenders here are friendly and willing to help you decide what to eat and drink along with pairing suggestions. This is a quiet place that differs from the noisier bars along the street. People are here for the beer, not for the nightlife. Due to the city ordinance they are only open till midnight, so plan accordingly and don't miss a chance to grab a bite. This can be a great place to start your evening on Lower Greenville if you are planning to continue socializing past 12.

DANCING BEAR PUB

1117 Speight Ave., Waco, TX 76706; (254) 753-0025; facebook.com/WacoCraftBeer; @Dancingbearpub
Draft Beers: 16 **Bottled/Canned Beers:** 30

The Dancing Bear Pub is just a few blocks from Baylor University in Waco. The small bar packs a big punch when it comes to craft beer. In a town like Waco, many people are springing for the usual commercial beers, but for those who have a love for something different the Dancing Bear Pub is there for them. The bar is small and parking is almost nonexistent, but once you're inside you will be pretty amazed with the selection of beers. The bartenders are friendly and a great help when you need help selecting a beer. The ambiance of the building is rather simple with beer paraphernalia decorating the walls. Out back there is a patio where most people like to hang out on nice days. Most of the patrons are locals and college students, but you will find the occasional tourist searching for good beer. Owner Paxton Dove is a board member for the Texas Tavern League, which is an organization run by local craft beer bars throughout the state that are spreading the love of craft beer through education and special events. Paxton is well respected in Texas and well connected to the local craft beer scene. You will find many of the beers at the Dancing Bear are brewed in state. They have a love for supporting local beer and if you stop in they will share that love with you.

FLYING SAUCER DRAUGHT EMPORIUM

111 E. 3rd St., Fort Worth, TX 76102; (817) 336-7470; beerknurd.com; @FlyingSaucerFW
Draft Beers: 70 **Bottled/Canned Beers:** 200+

The Flying Saucer Draught Emporium is probably one of the most known craft beer bars in the state. With seven locations, including Houston, Dallas, Austin, and San Antonio, the Flying Saucer is bringing one of the largest selections for fine craft beer and delicious food. It was founded in 1995, with its original location in Fort Worth, by restaurateur Shannon Wynne, who also owns the Meddlesome Moth in Dallas and Rodeo Goat in Fort Worth. In 1993, Shannon saw the craft beer movement start to grow in Texas and instead of deciding to open a brewery or brewpub of his own, he decided to open a bar that would celebrate all craft beer. It was not an easy task at the time to find such a wide variety of beers but Shannon pushed to get the Flying Saucer opened and it has been a big hit since day one. With locations in six states, each location focuses on the local beer scene while still offering a large selection of beers from across the globe. The name Flying Saucer comes from Shannon's collection of commemorative and antique plates, which hang on the walls of each location. The collection includes brass plates earned by patrons known as Beerknurds. You might be asking yourself, what is a Beerknurd? They are patrons who have joined the club at Flying Saucer and who are encouraged to experiment with different breweries and beer styles. They must drink 200 different beers in order to earn a brass plate on the wall in the Ring of Honor. Every location has its walls adorned with the plates of its local Beerknurds who have completed the challenge, and many have earned multiple plates. Today there are over 200,000 Beerknurds who are exploring the world of beer. Thanks to Flying Saucer, it has become a great unpretentious place to both learn about and try new beers. If you love craft beer and want to have your name forever immortalized on the walls of your local Flying Saucer, sign up and start your journey. Shannon and his Flying Saucer team are always looking into new locations so keep your fingers crossed that you will get a location near you soon.

THE HOLY GRAIL PUB

8240 Preston Rd., Plano, TX 75024; (972) 377-6633; holygrailpub.com; @HolyGrailPub
Draft Beers: 48 **Bottled/Canned Beers:** 100+

Out in the suburbs of Dallas in the city of Plano sits an oasis of great craft beer. The Holy Grail Pub offers a modern take on the classic English pub. There is a long outdoor seating area that is covered from the elements, while inside is a large dining room that offers a delicious array of food to go with their beer selection. This is a great bar to bring newcomers to craft beer because the bartenders and waitstaff are well versed on the beers they carry and the menu breaks down the selections by style. As for the food menu, there is a wide variety that can satisfy practically anyone, but be warned—the portions are hearty. The clientele is a mix ranging from mid-20s to mid-50s, and most are locals that live out in the area. Holy Grail is great for locals and visitors alike. While beer is the focus here, their food is something worth checking out as well. The menu is a more upscale take on pub food without being pretentious. There is a great selection of burgers and sandwiches that pair perfectly with the beers they keep on tap, and should you need a suggestion, you can always count on your waiter or bartender.

LUCK

3011 Gulden Ln. #112, Dallas, TX 75212; (469) 250-0679; http://luckdallas.com/;
@LUCKdallas
Draft Beers: 40

LUCK, which stands for Local Urban Craft Kitchen, is a unique concept. It is in the up and coming Trinity Groves neighborhood of Dallas just over the Margaret Hunt Hill Bridge. Trinity Groves is a large art, dining, and entertainment warehouse strip that has been converted into restaurants with different owners and different themes. LUCK put their focus into the beer first and built a menu to follow. They wanted food that would flatter the beer, and they definitely take their beer seriously. If you are new to the north Texas beer scene you're in luck, pun intended, because they only carry locally brewed beers, many of which you cannot find in other parts of the state. You can order a flight of four beers and make your way through the variety of local beers, or you can order by the pint. Once you have found the beer that you enjoy, you can even take home a 64-ounce growler to go. The menu at LUCK is small and the options are limited, but what they do have is pretty stellar. From sharable plates to entrees, you will find the portions are large and the flavors are just as big; after all, everything is bigger in Texas.

MEDDLESOME MOTH

1621 Oak Lawn Ave., Dallas, TX 75207; (214) 628-7900; mothinthe.net; @MothDallas
Draft Beers: 40 **Bottled/Canned Beers:** Over 85

The Meddlesome Moth is just a few miles outside of downtown Dallas in the Design District. Block by block you will find high-end home decor and furniture stores along with some very popular Dallas restaurants. The Meddlesome Moth is owned by the famed Dallas restaurateur Shannon Wynne, who also owns the wildly popular Flying Saucer Draught Emporium. From the beers they carry to the upscale food coming out of the kitchen, Meddlesome Moth has set the bar high when it comes to the gastropub experience. Even though this is a restaurant, they have given careful attention to the beer they carry, including shipping their own firkins to breweries to be filled with a special batch that they tap every week. They stand by their opinion that if you have seen a beer in a commercial, then you won't find it here. The bartenders are very knowledgeable about the beers that they carry and will give you samples to help you find a beer you like. Beer director Matt Quenette is also level-two Cicerone-certified, one out of only a handful in the state, so you can expect to get a very in-depth lesson in beer if you are in need of help.

Aside from the bar, the dining room is large and open. Three large stained glass panels of Elvis Presley, Chuck Berry, and Jerry Lee Lewis salvaged from the original Hard Rock Café in Dallas steal your attention as you head to your seat. The food is not your usual greasy pub grub; instead you will find upscale sharable plates and the menu even suggests beer style pairings. The beer menu reads like a long wine list with great tasting notes, and their full bar mixes up peculiar cocktails. The Meddlesome Moth is definitely changing the game in Dallas for other gastropubs.

OAK ST. DRAFTHOUSE & COCKTAIL PARLOR
308 E Oak St., Denton, TX 76201; (940) 435-0404; oakstreetdrafthouse.com; @oakstdrafthouse
Draft Beers: 72 **Bottled/Canned Beers:** 100

Oak St. Draught House is on a very quiet street in the third oldest house in town, just a block away from the Denton City Hall. From the outside it appears to be nothing more than an old country house with the accompanying furniture on the porch and children's toys decorating the front yard. Step inside and you will get the same nostalgic sense that you stepped back into the past, except for the fact that where the kitchen probably stood now stands a bar and 72 taps of fine craft beer, half of which are beers brewed in Texas. Chalkboards list the current beers on tap, and they ask that you order by the number, because instead of the usual array of

logoed beer tap handles you will see hand-blown glass pipes adorning the taps. Head out to the backyard and you will find a large beer garden with plenty of picnic tables and seating. Tall old trees offer just the right amount of shade to enjoy an afternoon of beer drinking. The crowd is a younger mix of college students and locals gathering for a few beers while chewing the fat. This is a great bar that feels warm and inviting. You will not feel pressured as you look over the beers, and the bartenders are happy to pour a sample so you can find a beer that you will enjoy. This is the kind of place where everyone knows each other, so order a beer and socialize with the locals.

THE OLD MONK
2847 N. Henderson Ave., Dallas, TX 75206; (214) 821-1880; oldmonkdallas.com; @OldMonkDallas
Draft Beers: 23 **Bottled/Canned Beers:** 75

The Old Monk is on historic Henderson Avenue in east Dallas. The bar is surrounded by a bustling nightlife, boutiques, and old antiques shops. The Old Monk is an Irish pub with a very authentic setting. Some of the light fixtures came from a monastery in Pennsylvania, and the back bar came from an old chemist's shop in England. The interior has dark wood throughout and it seems a little dark, but outside they have a large wraparound patio that is covered on one side. The bar has a focus on German and English-style beers, but they do keep a shorter list of American favorites and local beers on tap as well. The food menu is quite large and offers many different

options. The most popular dishes are their Belgian Style Steamed Mussels that are steamed in Hoegaarden Belgian White Ale, or their take on the traditional fish and chips. They even have an extensive list of traditional burgers, sandwiches, cheese boards, and snacks. With so many different varieties of beer, they have worked to make a menu that can please everyone. The weekend afternoons are very popular, and like many bars with patios, outdoor space is prime real estate for an afternoon of brunch and beer. The Old Monk also features a full bar, and in true Irish fashion they have a large selection of whiskeys. Unlike the bar's namesake, you will not find much silence or solitude. This is a great bar to get together with friends for pints and good times. The mood is friendly and it carries that vibe of fun spirited drinking that goes along with an Irish pub.

RODEO GOAT

2836 Bledsoe St., Fort Worth, TX 76107; (817) 877-4628; rodeogoat.com; @rodeogoatfw
Draft Beers: 20 **Bottled/Canned Beers:** 100+

Only in Texas will you find a place like Rodeo Goat, and no city is more fitting than Fort Worth. The city is known for its historic stockyards and cowboys living up to the Texas stereotype with 10-gallon hats and boots. As for Rodeo Goat, the bar is far from a country bar. While it is rodeo themed, they put their focus on burgers and beer. From the outside you don't get much of an impression, but once you walk in you see the large dining room with plenty of tables. Just above the bar is the stuffed mascot Billy Goat Shaver, forever immortalized in a bucking stance with his saddle on. Outside you will find a large patio with picnic tables in true beer garden fashion. If you are an indecisive person, you are going to have a hard time picking a beer because they have a great selection with 20 taps to choose from and over 100 bottles and cans they keep constantly in rotation. Choosing a burger to go with that beer is another battle. They have eighteen mouthwatering burgers on the menu and every 2 weeks the chefs add two more that go head to head to see which is the most interesting burger. In Texas they take their meat seriously, so don't expect some no frills burger. The meat is ground in house and the accoutrements are out of this world. For Billy Goat Shaver's sake they don't actually feature any goat burgers, just pure Texas beef. Rodeo Goat is the kind of place you can spend all day enjoying burgers and beers while taking in a few rounds of cornhole on the patio.

STRANGEWAYS

2429 N. Fitzhugh Ave., Dallas, TX 75204; (214) 823-7800; facebook.com/
Strangewaysdallas; @StrangewaysBar
Draft Beers: 40 **Bottled/Canned Beers:** 120

Strangeways in east Dallas sure has seen some strange times in its day. The building was a former Mexican cantina that experienced some really sketchy periods, but after it closed its doors it was purchased by current owner Eric Sanchez, who named the bar after the '80s band The Smiths' album *Strangeways, Here We Come*. With the help of friends and family, Eric completely gutted the building and completely changed its vibe, decorating the building with eclectic vinyl art figurines and even a wall dedicated to The Smiths. The neighborhood itself is quickly becoming a trendy haven for late 20-somethings thanks to the booming gentrification. Some call Strangeways a dive bar and many working in the service industry would like to keep this place as their own secret, but it's hard to consider a place a dive when it is named as one of the best bars in *Draft* magazine's "America's 100 Best Beer Bars 2013." They have over a hundred bottles and 40 taps of some of the best beer available in Texas on constant rotation, so you can expect to try something new on every visit. The kitchen is just as impressive with a Latin fusion take on classic burgers and even some delicious tortas to keep your stomach full as you work your way through their beer list. Even if beer isn't what you are looking for, they have a full bar with a great selection of whiskeys and tequilas. Eric is currently in the process of opening a Belgian bar next door to feature wines, Belgian beers, and a menu designed to complement the drinks. While Strangeways will keep appealing to the craft beer crowd, the new bar will have a quieter and more intimate setting.

WORLD BEER CO.—THE BOTTLE SHOP

2116 Greenville Ave., Dallas, TX 75206; (214) 828-2873; wbcbottleshop.com;
@WorldBeerCo
Draft Beers: 24 **Bottled/Canned Beers:** Over 500

Nowhere in Dallas will you find a better bottle shop than at World Beer Co. They have over 500 beers to choose from, and they are all proudly displayed along the wall in singles so you can make your own sixer. If you ask real nicely and prove your devotion to craft beer, they might be able to let go of some hidden treasures they have locked away in their climate-controlled storage room. Unfortunately, this room is off limits to the public, but they do have some very hard to find special releases and rarities that would make even the biggest beer hoarder look like an amateur. If you're looking to hang out and just have a few beers, World Beer Co. offers 24 taps of great beer, many of which were brewed in Texas. They have a very friendly, knowledgeable staff that is unpretentious and very helpful when you need some advice and can spend all evening talking about the beers they carry. For anyone who is on the hunt for a beer that is available in the state, World Beer Co. will have it, so stop in for a couple pints and make a few sixers to take back home.

Dallas—Pub Crawl

allas is a big city and things tend to be really spread out. It makes it rather difficult to put together a pub crawl that doesn't have you crossing all over town. Luckily, east Dallas has a great neighborhood that is booming with bars and restaurants specializing in craft beer. You will need a cab to make the pub crawl a success, but the total trip is less than 3 miles. A major plus about bar hopping in Dallas is that many of the north Texas breweries don't distribute outside of Dallas, so this is a great chance to try local beers.

The Old Monk, 2847 N. Henderson Ave., Dallas, TX 75206; (214) 821-1880; old monkdallas.com; @OldMonkDallas. The Old Monk is an old Dallas bar focused on European beers more than local craft, but they still have a great selection of beers. The food is your normal pub fare, but it is still delicious. I find their brunch to be an exceptional way to kick off a Sunday Funday if you have that luxury. This is a

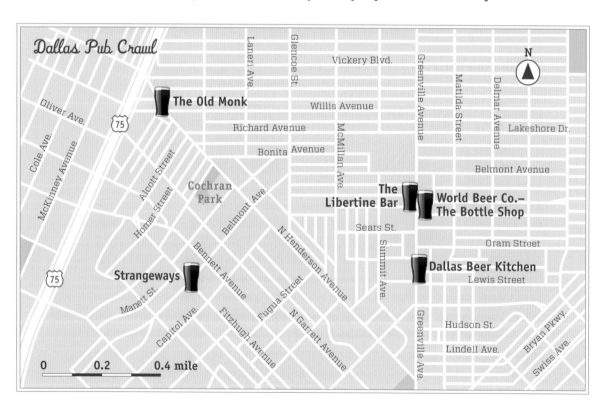

great starting point to kick off an east Dallas pub crawl, so order your beer and be prepared for a day of good beer.

Strangeways, 2429 N. Fitzhugh Ave., Dallas, TX 75204; (214) 823-7800; facebook. com/Strangewaysdallas; @StrangewaysBar. Strangways is one of my favorite bars in Dallas. Located in an old neighborhood that is going through gentrification, the bar is a solid brick building decorated with unique art and a small shrine to '80s singer Morrissey. They have a great selection of beers available and their food is just as impressive. The staff is really friendly and they are more than willing to help you find a beer that you will like. Industry workers like to escape to Strangeways when it's their turn to drink, so don't be shocked to see a waiter or bartender from a spot along the crawl here.

Dallas Beer Kitchen, 1802 Greenville Ave., Dallas, TX 75206; (214) 484-2481; dallas beerkitchengreenville.com; @FollowDBK. The Dallas Beer Kitchen is located along the popular Greenville Avenue in Lower Greenville, which has a row of bars and restaurants that have gone through numerous changes over the years. Be warned there is an ordinance that keeps many of the bars from staying open late, and Dallas Beer Kitchen is one of them. They close at midnight, so if you are doing a night crawl make sure you leave yourself enough time.

The Libertine Bar, 2101 Greenville Ave., Dallas, TX 75206; (214) 824-7900; libertine bar.com; @libertinebar. The Libertine is an old bar along Lower Greenville that is grandfathered in and does not have to obey the ordinance about closing early. The Libertine is approved to go the full night and close at 2 a.m. The bar is long and narrow with a very diverse mixed crowd. The bartenders can seem rushed at times, but since the bar stays full it is easy to understand their pain. Make sure you know what you want when you get to the front of the bar; this will catch the bartenders' attention and hopefully they will remember you next time you're in line.

World Beer Co.—The Bottle Shop, 2116 Greenville Ave., Dallas, TX 75206; (214) 828-2873; wbcbottleshop.com; @WorldBeerCo. There is no better way to end a pub crawl than to end at a bar that is also a bottle shop. This is a great chance to possibly take home some of the new beers you discovered on the crawl. The bottle shop is a big "make your own sixer" place and lets you decide what you want to take home. Don't forget to have a couple pints on the spot and try to talk your way to their special collection of rare and specialty bottles.

Prairies & Lakes

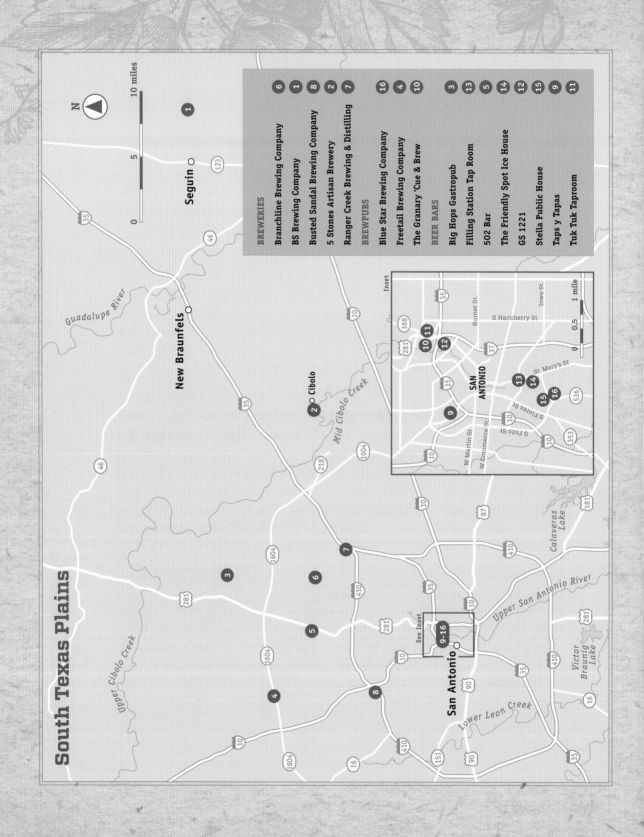

South Texas Plains

BREWERIES

⑥	Branchline Brewing Company
①	BS Brewing Company
⑧	Busted Sandal Brewing Company
②	5 Stones Artisan Brewery
⑦	Ranger Creek Brewing & Distilling

BREWPUBS

⑯	Blue Star Brewing Company
④	Freetail Brewing Company
⑩	The Granary 'Cue & Brew

BEER BARS

③	Big Hops Gastropub
⑬	Filling Station Tap Room
⑤	502 Bar
⑭	The Friendly Spot Ice House
⑫	GS 1221
⑮	Stella Public House
⑨	Taps y Tapas
⑪	Tuk Tuk Taproom

N

10 miles

Guadalupe River

Seguin

New Braunfels

Cibolo ②

Mid Cibolo Creek

Upper Cibolo Creek

Inset

SAN ANTONIO

Burnet St.
S Hackberry St.
Iowa St.
St. Mary's St.
S Flores St.
W Martin St.
W Commerce St.
S Frio St.

1 mile

⑩ ⑪
⑫
⑬ ⑭
⑮ ⑯
⑨

③

⑥

⑦

⑤

④

⑧

⑨-16
See Inset

San Antonio

Upper San Antonio River

Lower Leon Creek

Calaveras Lake

Victor Braunig Lake

South Texas Plains

The South Texas Plains stretch from San Antonio down to Laredo along the Mexico border. The region is rather small when it comes to craft beer, but San Antonio has exploded onto the scene with a rapidly growing craft beer following. With plans for new breweries opening soon, San Antonio has been a great birthplace for new bars and restaurants centered on craft beer. There has been some growth in small towns around San Antonio, where breweries such as 5 Stones Artisan Brewery in Cibolo and BS Brewing in Seguin are popping up. But for now the epicenter for the region is San Antonio. When visiting San Antonio you will find that there is more to the city besides the Alamo, the Riverwalk, and amazing Mexican food. Craft beer is the new reason to visit San Antonio, so get to exploring.

Breweries

BRANCHLINE BREWING COMPANY

3633 Metro Pkwy., San Antonio, TX 78247; (210) 403-2097; branchlinebrewing.com;
@BranchlineBrew
Founded: 2013 **Founders:** Jason & Laura Ard **Brewer:** Paul Ford **Flagship Beer:**
Evil Owl Amber **Year-Round Beers:** Evil Owl Amber, Shady Oak Blonde Ale, White Cap
Coconut Cream Ale, Woodcutter Rye IPA **Seasonals/Special Releases:** River Bend Citrus
Pale Ale, Oso Knotty Oyster Stout, Menger 32 Pumpkin Ale **Tours:** Second Sat of the
month **Taproom:** Yes

Founded by Jason and Laura Ard, Branchline Brewing Company is in the northern
Uptown area of San Antonio. The Ards' story goes back to when Laura bought
Jason a homebrewing kit as a gift. Jason quickly became fascinated with brewing
and learned new techniques to advance his knowledge. Once he got the brewing
down, he knew that he wanted to one day open a brewery of his own. Jason and

Evil Owl Amber
Style: Amber
ABV: 5.24% ABV
Availability: Year-Round

The Evil Owl Amber is the signature beer for Branchline and rightfully so. It is a great go-to amber ale that has a balanced medium body with an equally balanced malty and hoppy profile. The beer pours a rich amber in color with a medium off white head. The nose is that of grains and caramel, and it features an easy malt base with hoppy dry finish. I find it to be a great beer with Tex-Mex, barbecue, or practically anything. It is not a very powerful beer and does not have an over the top profile of hop bitterness, so it makes for a great introductory full-flavored beer.

Laura decided the time was right to go forward with his dream and they brought on head brewer Les Locke. Jason had originally named his company Old Boxcar Brewing, but he was issued a cease and desist letter from Pennsylvania-based Boxcar Brewing Co. before the brewery was in full production. Jason tried to reason with the other brewery over the name, but to avoid legal issues he decided changing the name would be the best route. He finally settled on Branchline Brewing Company, which was in honor of his late grandfather. Jason often reminisced about his childhood, when he would hear the trains running through his grandfather's ranch. In 2013, Branchline Brewing Company opened their doors and quickly worked to get their beers out to the San Antonio market.

From the very beginning, Jason's vision for Branchline was to brew high-quality handcrafted beers with local and regional ingredients when possible. He wanted beers that were light enough to appeal to the new craft beer drinkers yet still full flavored with unique styles that would appeal to the craft beer aficionados. They launched with their three core beers, **Evil Owl Amber, Shady Oak Blonde Ale,** and **Woodcutter Rye IPA.** Branchline instantly caught the attention and affection of local San Antonians, who praised the new brewery's beers. In the summer of 2014, brewer Les Locke announced that he would be leaving the brewery. Paul Ford had parted ways with 5 Stones Artisan Brewery in neighboring Cibolo when he started to volunteer with Branchline. Jason hired Paul as their new head brewer. When Paul came on board they added the **White Cap Coconut Cream Ale** to their year-round rotations. The beer is a 5.2% ABV cream ale that pours a bright hazy yellow with a light white head. The flavor profile is creamy and semisweet with a malty base and flavors that are reminiscent of white chocolate. For the hot Texas weather, Branchline features their **Shady Oak Blonde Ale,** which is brewed with locally sourced Texas wildflower honey. It is a light 4.45% ABV American-style blonde ale that is perfect all year round. It gets an added sweetness from their honey but is dry with a pleasant lightly bitter hop finish. Like many of their beers, it is simple, well balanced, and can be appreciated by most any palate.

Branchline is quickly expanding and doing a great job of educating locals about craft beer. Their monthly open house tours gain big turnouts with local food trucks selling gourmet food. Plan your trip to San Antonio for their tours on the second Saturday of the month. With Paul Ford taking over the brewing, they are working on new recipes as well as planning for sours and barrel-aged beers. Their beers can be found in bombers, cans, and on draft around San Antonio, Houston, and Austin. They have plans to expand distribution, but they want to focus on keeping up with demand from their current accounts. Branchline has become a hometown favorite and participates in many local events to gain exposure. Be sure to keep them on your radar as they continue to grow.

BS BREWING COMPANY
1408 Old Lehmann Rd., Seguin, TX 78155; (830) 660-8124; bsbrewingtx.com; @BS_Brewing
Founded: 2012 **Founder:** Brian Schmoekel **Brewer:** Brian Schmoekel **Flagship Beer:** Seguin Ale **Year-Round Beers:** Seguin Ale, College Chronic Red Ale, Pecan Ale with Honey, Imperial IPA **Seasonals/Special Releases:** Seguin Ale Pecan Reserve, Caedmon's Ale **Tours:** Upon Request **Taproom:** No

BS Brewing Company might sound like the initials of an innuendo, but they are actually the initials of owner Brian Schmoekel. BS Brewing is located practically in the middle of nowhere in Seguin, Texas. In a small metal building on his family's ranch, owner Brian Schmoekel brews almost daily on his 5-barrel brewhouse. The brewery is no frills and gritty, but Brian's passion to make great beer has brought him success.

Brian was a finance major who graduated from nearby Texas State University. Numbers were fun to Brian, but he had a higher calling to serve his country. He enlisted in the US Marine Corps, and his service included tours to the Middle East. Upon his return, Brian had an idea to start a brewery and talked it over with his father, who gave him permission to break ground on the family land.

Brian has worked hard to create beers that can be enjoyed by all. When you hear **College Chronic Red Ale,** you might think it refers to marijuana, but Brian said it is in reference to the chronic pain and agony that college can sometimes be. This 6.2% ABV red ale is sweet and malty with a mellow bite from the three different hop varieties. The **Pecan Ale with Honey** is a semisweet ale that gives you a hint of honey without the overpowering flavor. The pecans shine through on the mouth and give you notes of vanilla and slight caramel. Brian is working on a barreling program, and I can only hope that he makes a barrel-aged pecan ale with honey. Brian is keeping his beer true to Texas with locally grown pecans and honey from nearby Gretchen Bee Ranch. As BS Brewing continues to grow, I expect there to be an explosion of new flavors to experience. Still in its beginning stages, BS Brewing is a brewery to watch.

BUSTED SANDAL BREWING COMPANY

7114 Oaklawn Dr., San Antonio, TX 78229; (210) 872-1486; bustedsandalbrewing.com; @bustedsandal

Founded: 2013 **Founder:** Michael DiCicco **Brewer:** Jeff Kuhle **Flagship Beer:** Slippery Rock IPA **Year-Round Beers:** 210 Ale, Fire Pit Wit, Slippery Rock IPA, El Robusto Porter **Seasonals/Special Releases:** El Gourdo Pumpkin Porter, Negra Noche, Sandal Buster Double IPA, Bourbon Barrel El Robusto, El Diablo **Tours:** Wed through Fri 5 to 9 p.m., Sat 2 to 9 p.m. **Taproom:** Yes

Busted Sandal Brewing Company is in the Balcones Heights neighborhood in northwest San Antonio and was founded by Mike DiCicco in 2013. After serving for the US Air Force in the early '90s, Mike worked in the IT industry and got into homebrewing with his friend Rob Garza. Mike and Rob spent their time brewing and exploring new beers. They found that San Antonio lacked a craft beer scene and would often spend time drinking at the Blue Star Brewing Company, as it was the only establishment in San Antonio at the time to get fresh craft beer. The friends often took the short road trip to Austin to enjoy the beers at the local brewpubs. On one particular trip after a long night of drinking, they came upon a busted sandal. To many it would just be another piece of trash left discarded in a parking lot, but for Mike and Rob, it was an epiphany. Over beers the friends made up a whole back-story about the lone busted sandal and wondered about the life that sandal lived and where it had been. In Texas where the weather allows people to wear sandals 10 months out of the year, a busted sandal is a celebration because it has reached the end of its journey. It has been all over the place and has lived many fun experiences. The friends often reminisced about the sandal and it became an inside joke that stuck with them for years. Eventually that joke turned into a dream when Mike decided to mortgage his house and take out as many personal loans as possible to form Busted Sandal Brewing.

Today the Busted Sandal Brewing Company is brewing away in a small office park, pushing their beer to local establishments as well as national chain restaurants. Many of the beers they brew were designed by Rob Garza, who has been with Mike since the beginning to help make Busted Sandal the brewery it has become today. Their **210 Ale** is a nod to the city of San Antonio, named after the city's area code. Mike calls the 210 Ale a blonde ale, but in reality, it is a kölsch-style recipe that they pitched with English ale yeast. It is a smooth, very easy drinking 6.1% ABV ale that has a medium golden body and has a delicate nose of malt. On the palate the 201 Ale has a light body that is malty and semisweet. The carbonation is on the light side but still finishes crisp and refreshing. I would highly suggest 210

El Robusto Porter
Style: Porter
ABV: 7.4%
Availability: Year-Round

The El Robusto Porter is one of the three porters brewed by Busted Sandal and the only one available year-round. It is a dark medium-bodied porter that comes in around 7.4% ABV but drinks smooth and light on the mouth. The bouquet of the porter is wonderfully roasted with the usual notes of chocolate and coffee. On the mouth the beer is creamy and delicious with notes of sweet malts, dark chocolate, dates, burnt caramel, and coffee that are reminiscent of an espresso or cappuccino. It is a complex and enjoyable robust porter that I find to be full flavored, yet it is light enough to be enjoyed year-round. It opens up to become sweeter and smoother like that of a lighter-bodied stout. I think Busted Sandal has done a great job on this porter, which is even more impressive when they put the beer into a bourbon barrel to age and it becomes an even more complex porter with deeper notes of flavor. I am hoping to see the El Robusto Porter expand outside San Antonio so the rest of Texas can taste what I find to be one of the best porters in the state.

Ale for someone looking for an approachable go-to beer. For someone looking for a beer with a little more of a bite, the **Slippery Rock IPA** is the solution for you. Coming in with a slightly high ABV of 7.1%, the beer has a great nose of hops and caramel that resonate off of the light white head. On the palate the beer comes to life with a balanced blend of malt and citrus flavoring hops for an enjoyably smooth IPA without overbearing bitterness. I find it to be a great representation of the BJCP (Beer Judge Certification Program) style guidelines for what an American IPA should be and a very enjoyable IPA even for those who are not typically fans of the style.

Busted Sandal has come a long way in a short time. At their 1-year anniversary they named Jeff Kuhle head brewer, and he plans to take the brewery to the next level. They are expanding within their small location with expectations to almost double their capacity, and they are adding a canning line to help get their beer into more establishments including retail stores. As they build out, their brewery tours will be temporarily put on hold, but the taproom will continue to be open 3 days a week to get your Busted Sandal fix. Currently their beer is only available in and around San Antonio, but their beers are definitely worth the trip. They expect to have cans on retail shelves by the summer of 2015, and their brewery expansion should be completed by then as well. Next time you are exploring the world of Texas craft beer, rock your sandals and have an adventure. Who knows where you will end up.

5 STONES ARTISAN BREWERY

850 Schneider, Cibolo, TX 78108; (210) 380-8215; 5StonesBrewing.com; @5StonesBrewing

Founded: 2012 **Founder:** Seth Weatherly **Brewer:** Seth Weatherly **Flagship Beer:** Aloha Pina **Seasonal Beers:** Aloha Pina, Rhubarb-Cherrylicious, Camo, Manmosa, Merry Christmas, Norma Jean, Flower Child, Sleepy Hollow **Tours:** Check Website **Taproom:** No

5 Stones Artisan Brewery is just outside of San Antonio in Cibolo. It is a nano-brewery with a 3-barrel brewhouse founded by homebrewing hobbyist Seth Weatherly. While many of the Texas breweries release a standard core of beers consisting of the usual blonde, pale ale, IPA, and stout, 5 Stones is taking a different path by making beers that are technically seasonal. They rely on seasonal fruits and produce to make their interesting concept beers.

Since 5 Stones is working on such a small setup, their beer distribution is limited to the San Antonio and Austin areas, but it hasn't stopped Weatherly from

Beer Lover's Pick

Camo
Style: Pale Stout
ABV: 7.8%
Availability: Fall/Winter

Camo is a beer that is rightly named. If you were blindfolded and handed the beer, you would think you were sipping on a heavy dark stout, but you would be fooled because the beer is actually medium golden in color. It has notes of cocoa and roasted malts on the nose and the mouth is created with stout malt from Ireland along with flaked barley, wheat, and oats that give this beer a malt-forward base with hints of chocolate and coffee. It is a smooth delicious treat that you wouldn't expect from a pale-colored stout. It is a surprise to the palate when your eyes are expecting something else.

grabbing some attention. Their first release and most popular beer is **Aloha Pina,** a 6.4% ABV American golden ale brewed with fresh pineapples and jalapenos. The beer pours a light golden color with a sweet citrus nose. On the mouth the pineapple is actually lighter than I had expected, but it still felt clean and invigorating. On the back end the jalapeno beckons its little head with light warmth on the back of your throat. The beer is an interesting concept that came to Seth over a Hawaiian Fire Pizza when someone stated, "Dude, you need to brew a beer with pineapple and jalapeno!" and that was when the idea was born. The **Manmosa** is another interesting and surprisingly great concept. It is a 5.8% ABV wheat ale that is loaded with fresh oranges and orange zest. It pours a hazy orange color with a medium-bodied head. It has an aroma of orange peels with an addition of straw. The beer has a bitter orange flavor that closely rides the line of perfume but is still enjoyable. The wheat helps mellow the beer out for a soft finish. No longer must men be forced to drink champagne mimosas for brunch, thanks to 5 Stones.

I am very interested in seeing how 5 Stones evolves. They are currently in between brewers, so I am curious how the recipes will change and what additions will be made. They plan on hosting regular tours, but in the meantime you will have to follow their website or social media outlets for upcoming announcements.

RANGER CREEK BREWING & DISTILLING
4834 Whirlwind St., San Antonio, TX 78217; (210) 775-2099; drinkrangercreek.com; @rangercreek
Founded: 2010 **Founders:** Dennis Rylander, Mark McDavid & TJ Miller **Brewer:** Holland Lawrence **Flagship Beer:** Mesquite Smoked Porter **Year-Round Beers:** Lucky Ol' Sun, OPA, Mesquite Smoked Porter, La Bestia Aimable **Seasonals/Special Releases:** Ranger Creek Small Batch Series, Strawberry Milk Stout, Love Struck Hefe, Red Headed Stranger
Tours: Sat 2 to 4 p.m. **Taproom:** Yes

Ranger Creek Brewing & Distilling is in the Uptown neighborhood of San Antonio and was founded by friends Dennis Rylander, Mark McDavid, and TJ Miller. The group met each other working for a company in San Antonio and often met up for drinks after work. They all shared an affection for beer and whiskey, and would often get together to homebrew beers. It wasn't long before the business school grads started looking at their hobby of homebrewing in an entrepreneurial light. They started to work on a business plan for the brewery, but the idea of starting a whiskey distillery was just as exciting. Since they were torn on choosing between beer and whiskey, the partners decided to go with both and in 2010 they launched Ranger Creek Brewing & Distilling. They were one of the first craft microbreweries

in San Antonio as well as the only brewery to distill whiskey in the state, and they dubbed themselves the first "brewstillery" in Texas.

Ranger Creek is widely respected for their beers thanks to their original head brewer Rob Landerman, who created many of the core beers. Rob left Ranger Creek in 2012 to form his own brewery with his wife in Boise, Idaho. With their new head brewer Holland Lawrence, Ranger Creek brews a beer that can appeal to nearly anyone. From light easy-drinking beers to beers that are bolder and more robust, it is this concept that has helped them gain popularity in San Antonio and beyond. The **Lucky Ol' Sun** is a drinkable 5.5% ABV Belgian-style golden ale and is named after the Johnny Cash song "That Lucky Old Sun." While it is a year-round release, Lucky Ol' Sun is a perfect patio-weather beer. It pours as a hazy light yellow with a yeasty nose from the Belgian yeast with notes of honey and bread. On the palate the beer tastes of malts and slight honey with a delicate back end of hop bitterness. This is a great sessionable beer for a day of drinking outdoors and barbecueing in true Texas fashion. The **Mesquite Smoked Porter** is probably the most popular beer from Ranger Creek, and it is used to distill their bourbon. The beer is a 6.4% ABV porter inspired from German styled *rauchbiers* (smoked beer). They go the extra mile by smoking the malts used in the beer in house over Texas mesquite wood. The beer has a silky medium body with a dense black color. It has a beautiful nose of roasted malts and oak that follow onto the mouth with notes of dark chocolate and dark roasted coffee. It tends to have a faint bitter finish, but I find the Mesquite Smoked Porter to be a great beer to enjoy slowly.

Ranger Creek is a must for both craft beer fans and whiskey aficionados. Their beers can be found mainly in San Antonio as well as Austin and Houston with other markets scattered in between. They offer tours every Saturday from 2 to 4 p.m., and you can even sample their whiskey. They occasionally host bottling and labeling events on their distillery side, allowing volunteers to help with the bottling and labeling process and walk away with a bottle for their time. You will need to check their website for postings about upcoming volunteer opportunities. For you beer hunters, keep your eyes peeled for their specialty **Small Batch Series** of beers. They release the one-off beers sporadically with different recipes that are usually perfect for aging. I highly recommend picking up a bottle if you happen to see them sitting on a shelf, and while you are at it grab a couple bombers of their year-round offerings.

Strawberry Milk Stout
Style: Milk Stout
ABV: 5.6%
Availability: Spring

The Strawberry Milk Stout is a spring seasonal from Ranger Creek that is brewed with 500 pounds of Texas-grown strawberries from nearby Oak Hill Farms in Poteet. The beer is a dark yet light-bodied beer that I could closely relate to a dark chocolate–dipped strawberry. I was expecting the strawberries to be more present in the flavor profile, but it is enjoyable nonetheless. The roasted malts seem to overpower the strawberries and give more of a chocolate flavor on the palate, but the fruit seems to reappear on the end. While this is a milk stout–style beer, it works great as a spring seasonal because it still has a drinkable light body no matter the time of year. Let this beer open up by taking it out of the fridge 20 minutes before drinking. You will find that the beer grows a little sweeter and you can taste more of its complexity.

Brewpubs

BLUE STAR BREWING COMPANY

1414 S. Alamo St., San Antonio, TX 78210; (210) 212-5506; bluestarbrewing.com; @BlueStarBrewCo

Founded: 1996 **Founders:** Joey & Magdalena Villarreal **Brewer:** Joey Villarreal
Flagship Beer: Flying Pig Extra Pale Ale **Year-Round Beers:** Flying Pig Extra Pale Ale, Texican Lager, Spire Stout, Scottish Ale, Pilsner, Cinco Peso Pale Ale, Wheat Head, Raspberry Geyser, Close Encounter **Seasonals/Special Releases:** King William Ale, Dunkelhead, Maennerchor Marzen, Pilsner, English Mild

Located along the banks of the San Antonio River near the King William neighborhood of San Antonio, Blue Star Brewing Company was founded by Joey Villarreal and his wife Magdalena. Joey originally picked up homebrewing while in college at University of Texas San Antonio, where he studied biology. In the beginning, Joey opened the neighborhood bar Joey's in 1988. It was a trip in 1992 to Cleveland, Ohio, that exposed Joey to his first brewpub and sparked his interest in the concept. He later went on to visit Great Lakes Brewing Company, and he was inspired to design a brewpub of his own. Joey went on to spend the next four years working on his business plan, and in 1996 Blue Star Brewing Company opened its doors. His vision was to feature casual dining along with handcrafted beers.

Blue Star is now the oldest brewpub in San Antonio, and the complex surrounding the brewpub has grown into a popular arts and entertainment district that also features the beautifully updated San Antonio Mission Trail that runs along the San Antonio River. The food at Blue Star is your average pub grub array of burgers and sandwiches with the exception of dishes such as their Turkey Plate, which is like a healthier Thanksgiving platter, or the Shrimp & Grits, which is jumbo blackened shrimp served over organic cheese grits. Overall, the food is decent but a little on the pricey side. They have the traditional styles of beers that you will find at other brewpubs except for the **King William Ale**, which is a larger barley wine–style beer that hovers close to 9% ABV. It has a strong boozy profile that is softened with a sweet body of sweet caramel malts and fruity notes. With the popularity of sour beers on the market, Blue Star has brewed their **Raspberry Geyser.** It is a 3.8% ABV wild ale that has been aged 2 years; they brew it with fresh organic raspberries. A geyser is a lambic style of beer also known as a fruit beer. It is made blending young lambics aged 1 year and old lambics aged 2 to 3 years. This is a great introductory beer for those looking to get into sour beers. It is light and refreshing with a very light mouth feel but isn't too sour or bitter. The lower ABV makes this a beer that you can drink all day.

When traveling through San Antonio, stop by Blue Star Brewing Company to grab a meal and a few beers. They offer beer flights, which I recommend so you can get a sample of all the beers they make. Blue Star also offers beers to go once you have found the beer that is to your liking. As long as you haven't indulged too much, you can head next door to the Blue Star Bike Company to rent a bike and check out the history sites along the 20-mile stretch of the San Antonio Mission Trail. A last piece of advice: The brewpub closes at 3 p.m. on Sunday and 7 p.m. on Monday, so plan accordingly when creating your itinerary.

FREETAIL BREWING COMPANY
4035 North Loop 1604 W #105, San Antonio, TX 78257; (210) 395-4974; freetailbrewing .com; @freetailbrewing
Founded: 2008 **Founder:** Scott Metzger **Brewer:** Jason Davis **Flagship Beer:** Freetail Ale **Year-Round Beers:** La Rubia, Rye Wit, Freetail Ale **Seasonals/Special Releases:** Ananke, La Muerta, Old Bat Rastard

Freetail Brewing Company is in northern San Antonio and was founded by San Antonio native Scott Metzger. It was on a New Year's Eve ski trip in Colorado that he made a promise to himself that he would one day open a brewpub in his hometown of San Antonio. That dream would come to reality in 2008 when he brought on chef Gary Butler and head brewer Jason Davis to open Freetail Brewing Company. Scott's mission was to "[bring] the pursuit of better stuff to fruition for our customers, employees and community in everything we do." Since day one they have worked to make food that pairs wonderfully with the beers they brew and have ensured it is something that their patrons can stand behind. Aside from the brewpub, Scott has been a very vocal opponent of the outdated Texas Alcoholic Beverage Commission laws, which have long restricted the growth of small breweries and brewpubs in the state.

Head brewer Jason Davis came on board with years of brewing experience that Scott needed to make Freetail a success. Jason got his start as a dishwasher at Waterloo Brewing Company, which was the first brewpub in Texas. He worked hard and moved his way up as an assistant brewer for the brewpub, eventually landing a job brewing for the former legendary Celis Brewing. It is his years of experience and his creation of over one hundred recipes at Freetail that has helped them gain their success in the Texas craft beer community. Chef Gary Butler has helped boost Freetail's popularity by creating a delicious array of pizzas, baked pastas, and sandwiches from the kitchen that all pair perfectly with Jason's beers. Together Scott and his team have helped grow the craft beer scene in San Antonio, and they have now expanded to a second location not far from the King William neighborhood in south San Antonio. The second location should give Freetail the capacity to brew more beer and package the beer for retail sales.

Many of Freetail's beers are light and easily approachable. The go-to for many is the **Freetail Ale,** a 4.8% ABV American amber ale with a rich copper body. It has a nutty malty aroma with a hint of hops that follows onto the palate with a sweet caramel flavor and a hop bitter finish. It can go with any dish. Freetail is also known for their **Spirulina Wit,** an ominous mint green–colored hazy beer that gets its color from blue-green algae. The nose of this brew brings hints of spinach and grass that follow onto the palate and is unique to say the least. The Spirulina Wit was noted by *Bon Appetit* magazine as one of the Top 10 Strangest Beers in America.

When you are in San Antonio, Freetail is a great place to check out. Since they also have a location on the south side, it makes stopping in convenient. Order a pie and take a flight but don't forget to take a few bottles to go.

THE GRANARY 'CUE & BREW

602 Avenue A, San Antonio, TX 78215; (210) 228-0124; thegranarysa.com; @TheGranarySA

Founded: 2012 **Founders:** Timothy & Alex Rattray **Brewer:** Alex Rattray **Flagship Beer:** Rye Saison **Year-Round Beers:** Rye Saison, IPA, Brown Ale **Seasonals/Special Releases:** Blackberry Berliner Weisse, Black IPA, Coffee IPA

The Granary is located on the historic grounds of the former Pearl Brewery just outside of downtown San Antonio and was founded by brothers Alex and Timothy Rattray. The Granary is a farm-to-table-style barbecue joint that combines succulent smoked meats and craft beer. Everything is made in house and only top-quality and humanely raised meat is used here. They make everything from the bread and pickles to the pies and beer. The beers are all made to pair with the food they serve, and they are treated with the same respect as the food, using only the finest ingredients.

Today the grounds of the Pearl Brewery have been restored and converted to a massive entertainment district with shops, cafes, bars, and restaurants. In 2012,

the Rattray brothers formed their brewpub in the former home of Ernst Mueller, who was the chief cooper (barrel maker) for the historic Pearl Brewery. Chef Timothy has a vast background in the kitchen working under James Beard–nominated chefs in a nationally acclaimed French restaurant. Alex found his taste for beer while studying abroad in London. Upon his return to the States, Timothy bought Alex a homebrewing kit, and it sparked Alex's brewing obsession.

The Granary is most known for their barbecue, which is technically sold only during lunch. For dinner the place becomes an almost fine dining experience with dishes like Beef Clod, Veta La Palma Grey Mullet, and Brisket Ramen. The dining experience is as top notch as is the beer. I find the **Rye Saison** to be a great beer to pair with most of their dishes as it has a smooth flavor profile that finishes dry and welcomes a fresh palate for each new bite.

The grounds of the old Pearl Brewery are something to see. The area has become a revamped tourist stop with restaurants and shops along with a hotel and apartments. While many of the old buildings are getting a modern twist, stepping into The Granary is like traveling back in time. No trip to San Antonio should be complete without a visit here.

Pearl Brewery

The Pearl Brewing Company was founded in 1952 on the grounds of the old San Antonio Brewing Association, which was established in 1881. Pearl Beer was a major competitor for Lone Star Brewing Company just down the road. Both brands were eventually picked up by Pabst, which ended up closing the Pearl Brewery in 2001. Pearl Brewery land was purchased by developers, who have converted the 23-acre site into a tourist destination with restaurants, shops, and bars operating out of the old buildings. The Granary 'Cue & Brew is located in the house of the old chief cooper for the Pearl Brewery. The main brewhouse is being converted into the Hotel Emma, which is expected to open in 2015, and Culinary Institute of America has opened a campus on the grounds of the brewery that is helping to create future chefs. Pearl Beer is still sold throughout the state, but it is no longer brewed in San Antonio.

Beer Bars

BIG HOPS GASTROPUB

22250 Bulverde Rd. Suite 106, San Antonio, TX 78259; (210) 267-8762; bighops.com;
@BigHopsGastro
Draft Beers: 51

Big Hops Gastropub is just one of the Big Hops establishments from Rob and Kylie Martindale that are keeping San Antonio flowing with good beer. Big Hops is a craft beer bar where you can enjoy your beer and take it home too, but the gastropub adds the food element that is hard to beat when enjoying a good beer. Many of the taps here are dedicated to the local Texas-brewed beers from Saint Arnold and Ranger Creek to Busted Sandal and Deep Ellum.

The Martindales know that San Antonians like good beer, and along with that the gastropub offers a great variety of decadent dishes that will leave your mouth watering. The appetizers range from a cheese plate with great offerings for beer pairing to the gut-busting Big Hops WTF!? (What the Fries) which is their own take on the Canadian dish poutine. If you're in the mood for something a little fancier, they have mussels that pair perfectly with a Belgian tripel or their sweet and spicy Asian Wings & Rice with a side of bacon fried rice that goes delightfully with a bitter citrus IPA. This place isn't for someone that is watching their figure. Craft beer certainly isn't helping anyone lose weight, so you are going to need a hearty meal to keep drinking. Don't forget to pick up a growler of your favorite beer on the way out. Beer is usually better than a doggy bag.

There are three Big Hops locations around San Antonio, all along the north side of town. The Big Hops Gastropub is a must when you are looking for amazing food and beer, while the other two locations focus on pints and growlers. Since many of the smaller or up and coming breweries dedicate their beer to draft, this is the place to get growler fills to go. They offer fills of 16-ounce, 32-ounce, and 60-ounce pours. I can only hope they get a Crowler (can filling machine) soon so they can sell canned draft beers that travel easier and stay fresh longer. I often look forward to my trips to San Antonio to stop in at one of the Big Hops locations to see what is on tap. No trip to the Alamo City would be complete without them.

FILLING STATION TAP ROOM
701 S. St. Mary's St., San Antonio, TX 78204; (210) 444-2200; thestationsa.com
Draft Beers: 25 **Bottled/Canned Beers:** 2

Blink and you could miss it. The Filling Station Tap Room is a small former gas station turned into a growler filling location in the King William neighborhood of San Antonio. The gas is gone, but now they are filling growlers of premium beer alongside a small yet delicious selection of sandwiches and pizzas. The space is small so it can quickly get crowded, and street parking isn't very abundant so you might want to avoid the lunchtime rush at the cafe portion of the establishment. While it might seem like they have a focus on food, the beer is the focal point for the craft beer fans who stop in for a fill.

There may be other bars in town with more beer, but you will not receive the one-on-one attention and the knowledge that they have at the Filling Station. This is a great place to go if you are new to craft beer or are interested in trying new things. The bartenders are well versed in craft beer and very knowledgeable

about the beers they have on tap. Next time you are in San Antonio, grab your growler and take it in for a fill, or pick one up here and enjoy your beer on your own time.

502 BAR
502 Embassy Oaks, San Antonio, TX 78216; (210) 257-8125; 502bar.com; @502Bar
Draft Beers: 26 **Bottled/Canned Beers:** 40

Mixing live music and craft beer, the 502 Bar in San Antonio is an unusual yet awesome venue. Usually when you're at a concert you expect to pay $8 for some flavorless fizzy commercial brew, but at 502 you can rock out with your favorite stout. The music is the reason many come here, but craft beer fans have taken note of their dedication to the good stuff and this has become a craft beer destination in San Antonio. Every week their website is updated with the latest offerings on tap along with great little write-ups and tasting notes. The beers are reasonably priced and the offerings are hard to beat. No longer will concertgoers feel like they are getting ripped off paying too much for cheap beer. The venue books all genres of music from local bands to national touring artists, which is great for the bands, who get a sample of the beers brewed in Texas. While it might not be for the good beer, you can always get a beer and a shot for $5. If you are in San Antonio and looking for a place to catch live music, then look no further than the 502 Bar. Plus, you'll get to enjoy some great craft beer while you're there.

THE FRIENDLY SPOT ICE HOUSE
943 S. Alamo St., San Antonio, TX 78205; (210) 224-2337; thefriendlyspot.com; @thefriendlyspot
Draft Beers: 76 **Bottled/Canned Beers:** 250+

Don't ever let anyone tell you San Antonio isn't a friendly city. If they do it is probably because they have never spent an afternoon or evening drinking good beers at the Friendly Spot. There isn't much to the place; it is an outdoor establishment shaded by large trees. Two buildings designate the bars and kitchen along with a covered indoor area for those that want to escape nature's elements. The rest of the grounds is littered with tables and chairs for a plethora of seating for all. They carry some of the best beer selections you will find in the Alamo City with many from local brewers like Ranger Creek and Branchline, along with many selections from popular

breweries across the country. They do have food available, but it mainly consists of finger foods and appetizers to keep your belly full while indulging on their taps of great beer.

The Friendly Spot is located in a residential neighborhood, so they close at midnight and parking can sometimes be a pain. But I highly recommend checking this place out while in San Antonio. They have a screen displaying the beers available along with an updated website that shows all of the beers they currently have on tap. This place is laid back and relaxed with a friendly, casual vibe. It is a family- and pet-friendly establishment, so don't expect a rowdy brooding crowd, though children are scarce once the sun starts to set.

GS 1221
1221 Broadway St., San Antonio, TX 78215; (210) 251-3184; gs1221.com; @GS1221TX
Draft Beers: 30 **Bottled/Canned Beers:** 20

GS 1221, which is short for Growler Station and the address of the building, is located along Broadway at the bottom of the luxurious 12Welve 2Wenty1 Lofts in downtown San Antonio. GS 1221 is a dream come true for any craft beer fan that has ever wanted to live above a bar, but even if you don't live in the lofts you are still welcome to take advantage of the bar.

Inside the bar is very minimal when it comes to atmosphere, but it still feels modern and inviting. Along the wall is a timeline of the disciplines of craft beer. Aside from the mural, a few TVs, and a board listing the beers on tap, you won't find much in the form of advertisements. The focus at GS 1221 is the beer and the Pegasus CrafTap growler filler, which is the only one in the city. The system removes the air as the growler is filled, which will keep your beer fresh for almost a month. There are 30 beers on tap to choose from with a focus on Texas breweries, but you will also find popular beers from across the country. Outside is a large open patio that is dog friendly, and food trucks are constantly parked across the street to line your stomach as you're indulging on great beer. Parking is limited to the street, so on busy nights it might be better to grab a cab, plus after an evening of beer you shouldn't be driving anyway.

If you are planning to stop in for a few pints, do yourself a favor and have a growler filled up to take home. If you don't have one, GS 1221 sells them for only $6.50 and many of the beers can be filled for under $20. Fair warning for you planners, GS 1221 closes around 10 p.m. through the week and 11 p.m. on weekends, so if you are looking for a place to spend the evening you might want to choose a secondary bar for after GS 1221 closes.

STELLA PUBLIC HOUSE
1414 S. Alamo St., San Antonio, TX 78210; (210) 277-7047; stellapublichouse.com;
@STELLASouthtown
Draft Beers: 20 **Bottled/Canned Beers:** 40

Stella Public House is located in the Blue Star Arts Complex in San Antonio. The complex is just south of downtown but still runs along the San Antonio River. Stella is a "Farm to Pizza" concept making hand-tossed pizzas with only the freshest local ingredients. Everything that goes onto these pizzas is local and both the cheese and sauce are made in house. Aside from the pizza, Stella is helping to push the craft beer movement in the Alamo City. They have 20 rotating taps of American craft beers along with 40 bottles and cans to choose from.

Inside of Stella you are greeted by the roaring wood-burning pizza oven and the cooks prepping each pizza with careful detail. The atmosphere is warm and alluring with the feel of an Italian villa without being cheesy. Stella would make for a great date spot as they have done a great job of making pizza and beer seem romantic. Outside the patio offers a great place for happy hour gatherings when the weather is nice. The food is delicious and the rotating taps keep their beer offerings interesting. This is a great place to check out when visiting San Antonio.

TAPS Y TAPAS
1012 N. Flores St., San Antonio, TX 78212; (210) 277-7174; tapsytapas.com;
@tapsytapas
Draft Beers: 24 **Bottled/Canned Beers:** 15

Taps y Tapas is located in this historic 1883 Charles Ochse house in the Five Points neighborhood of San Antonio. It is one of the last remaining limestone homes in the area and Taps y Tapas is preserving the building and offering patrons a reflective dining experience. Inside is small and quiet with tables encompassing each room. Out back is a large space where live music is featured and tables are covered by umbrellas and the natural shade of trees. At night the outdoor area is a great setting for a romantic dinner or just a place for casual conversations with friends over drinks. The food is an upscale take on Mexican street food with a modern gourmet twist.

Taps y Tapas is owned by Denise Aguirre and Noel Cisneros, who originally started their business with The Point Park & Eats. The Point is a foodie destination with a gathering of San Antonio gourmet food trucks and a bar featuring craft beer. They teamed up with Chef Luciano Valadez, who gained recognition with his food

truck Texasada Mexican Street Food, and together the partners are bringing a culinary and craft beer medley that is a perfect pairing.

I find Taps y Tapas to be a great place to visit when in San Antonio. I tend to stay away from the tourist traps downtown to seek out genuine Mexican food, which I have found at Taps y Tapas. The atmosphere is breathtaking and has such a homey air. I have been in Texas all my life, so you would think I would be used to the heat, but during the summer you will find me indoors. But come fall and spring, the Taps y Tapas backyard is such an amazing place to be. They perpetually rotate their beers, so I suggest stopping in often for a pleasurable dining experience and superior beer.

TUK TUK TAPROOM
1702 Broadway St., San Antonio, TX 78215; (210) 222-8277; tuktuktaproom.com; @TukTukTapRoom
Draft Beers: 72 **Bottled/Canned Beers:** 50+

Tuk Tuk Taproom is a collaboration between friends David Gilbert and Steve Newman, who have different backgrounds but similar tastes. They blend together Asian street fare with craft beer, culminating in a perfect balance for a great business plan. Chef David cooks with an upscale gourmet spin on Asian street food dishes, while Steve brings his experience from another craft beer venture he owns with his wife, the Friendly Spot, and the food truck park the Alamo Street Eat Bar. Steve is also highly recognized for his knowledge and engineering of state of the art tap systems for bars and restaurants. Having Steve involved in a bar lets you know that you will only find great beer and some of the cleanest and best-designed taps in Texas.

The prices can vary depending on if you want appetizers or a real meal. It can get expensive, so don't expect the usual cheap pub burger here. Chef Gilbert is no greasy spoon cook; he has a long background of culinary experience that you wouldn't find in just any old gastropub. He learned cooking from his grandfather, who owned a butcher shop. He has worked for a Michelin-starred restaurant in Amsterdam, he was the chef for luxury hotels like the Ritz-Carlton and Beverly Hilton, and he is even a best-selling author of the book *Kitchen Vagabond*. You might be wondering what all of this has to do with craft beer, but it is the attention to detail and the dedication that both partners put into their work that make Tuk Tuk Taproom a must visit in San Antonio. The beers that Steve keeps on tap are perfect complements to the food Chef David has coming out of the kitchen, and the flavors mix perfectly for a well-rounded experience.

San Antonio—Pub Crawl

San Antonio is another city that is very spread out when it comes to putting together a pub crawl. There are great locations up north near Alamo Heights and lots of bars rounding out the south side of town such as the King William neighborhood. San Antonio roads can be confusing, so it is best that you use a cab to get around on this pub crawl—drinking and driving is never a good idea. Also be sure to eat as you explore the great bars of San Antonio.

Alamo Street Eat Bar, 609 S. Alamo St., San Antonio, TX 78205; (210) 227-2469; alamostreeteatbar.com; @AlamoEatBar. It is only fitting to start any pub crawl with a full stomach, so why not start at a food truck park that serves craft beer? The Alamo Street Eat Bar is an urban food truck park bringing together different eclectic food trucks and a bar that sells beer. While the selection of beers is rather small,

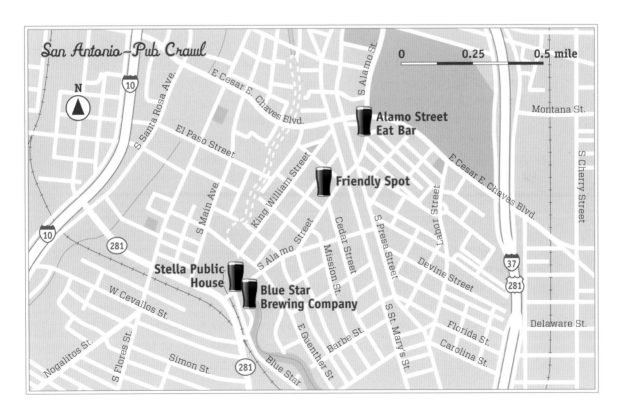

they tend to have some great beers from time to time. After all, we have only just begun and there is a lot of great beer ahead. Make sure to support the local food truck scene and grab a bite while you're sipping on your beer.

The Friendly Spot Ice House, 943 S. Alamo St., San Antonio, TX 78205; (210) 224-2337; thefriendlyspot.com; @thefriendlyspot. When the Friendly Spot first opened, it did not get a friendly welcome from the surrounding residential neighborhood, but those days have come and gone. Today the Friendly Spot has become a laid back outdoor bar that has an impressive selection of over 300 beers to choose from. There is an area to spread out with tables to lounge at while going through their taps. The bars are located in old shipping containers. This is a great afternoon bar to hang out with friends over beers.

Stella Public House, 1414 S. Alamo St., San Antonio, TX 78210; (210) 277-7047; stellapublichouse.com; @STELLASouthtown. Stella Public House is located in the Blue Star Arts Complex. They make some of the best wood-fire pizzas you will find in the city and have a great craft beer selection. Whether you are hungry or not, there is always room for pizza to go with your beer. The place has somewhat of an upscale feel, but don't worry; the staff is really friendly and they love talking about beer. I find this to be a great spot, so check it out when in Southtown, plus it is located in the same complex as the next stop.

Blue Star Brewing Company, 1414 S. Alamo St., San Antonio, TX 78210; (210) 212-5506; bluestarbrewing.com; @BlueStarBrewCo. The Blue Star Brewing Company was about all there was in the way of craft beer for a long time in San Antonio. It has even been the inspiration for some of the people that went on to start their own breweries. They make a wide variety of beers for pretty much any palate, and I can almost guarantee you will find a beer that you like. If you decided not to eat at the other spots along the crawl, the food here is decent, but it can get rather expensive. So if money is tight, save it for the most important thing, beer. A great thing about Blue Star is that if you can't decide on one of their many offerings, you can get a flight of every beer they have on tap. Be warned this is the best route to take, but it will definitely put you in your place because they can have 10 beers or more at any given time.

Beer Festivals

For the longest time beer festivals were almost nonexistent in the state, but over the last 5 years, Texas has seen an explosion of events looking to spread the gospel of craft beer. Gone are the days of walking from booth to booth sampling beers; today's festivals go all out with educational experiences, live music from national touring artists, and food pairings from some of the most respected local chefs. No matter what region of Texas you live in, there is a festival for you. From as far west as El Paso to a beach resort in Galveston, festival promoters are helping attendees learn about the wide array of beers available in Texas. There is no better way to experience new beers in one place than attending a beer festival, so start planning. Here are just some of the biggest annual beer festivals in the state. Be sure to do your research as things tend to change, and with the way the craft beer movement has expanded, you might just find a new beer festival popping up near you.

February

BORDER BEER FEST
Laredo Civic Center, 2400 San Bernardo Ave., Laredo, TX 78040; borderbeerfest.com

The Border Beer Fest is the grand finale to a week of craft beer events around the city of Laredo. The festival, while sponsored by Anheuser Busch, keeps a solid focus on craft beer along with live music, Beerlympics, and food pairings from local restaurants. In a city where the craft beer scene is relatively small, the Border Beer Fest is working to spread their love of craft beer to the people of Laredo and the surrounding area. They have homebrewing and cooking seminars to educate attendees and inspire them to try their hand at making beer for themselves or learn how to cook using beer. The festival is growing every year and has done a great job of expanding the craft beer scene on the Texas-Mexico border.

March

UNTAPPED INDIE MUSIC & BEER FESTIVAL
Panther Island Pavilion, 395 Purcey St., Fort Worth, TX 76102; untapped-festival.com

The Untapped Indie Music & Beer Festival has become one of the fastest-growing beer festivals in the state. It is one part music festival, one part beer festival all rolled into one stellar event that is pulling in attendees from across Texas. For those who don't live in Fort Worth, fear not, they host the festival with different bands in Houston and Dallas in the fall. While it is worth mentioning that the festival is not associated with the Untappd beer app, many of the attendees use the app to check into their favorite new brews while booth hopping and sampling the best beers distributed in the state. Untapped draws one of the largest crowds in the state when it comes to beer festivals, and every year they are trying to go even bigger.

April

BIG TEXAS BEER FESTIVAL
Fair Park Automobile Building, 1010 1st Ave., Dallas, TX 75210; bigtexasbeerfest.com

The Big Texas Beer Festival got its start with inspiration from the Great American Beer Festival in Denver, Colorado. Festival organizers Chad and Nellie Montgomery wanted to bring a beer festival to Dallas that would get the whole city involved with events leading up to the festival itself. The event brings out a great collection of over one hundred breweries with a focus on the local north Texas spots. Many participating breweries will bring a couple of specialties or rare treats that they have kept hidden away. You never quite know what you will find at the Big Texas Beer Festival, but one thing is for sure, you will find great craft beer.

May

NORTH TEXAS BEER & WINE FESTIVAL
Irving Convention Center at Las Colinas, 500 W. Las Colinas Blvd., Irving, TX 75039; northtexasbeerfestival.com

The North Texas Beer & Wine Festival attracts guests from across the Dallas–Fort Worth metroplex to learn about and sample great craft beer and wines. Their mission statement is to "Educate people about craft beers in a responsible and ethical manner, promote craft beer culture and craft brewers, and recognize excellence in the industry," and they have done an amazing job. They are bringing in nearly eighty breweries every year along with over a dozen wineries. To help educate the public, the festival features homebrewing classes and chef-instructed cooking demos. There is live music for entertainment and a large gathering of vendors to satisfy your hunger while you spend the afternoon sampling beers.

WILD WEST BREW FEST

Villagio Town Center, 22764 Westheimer Pkwy., Katy, TX 77450; katybrewfest.com

The Wild West Brew Fest is held in the city of Katy, which is just west of Houston. The festival raises funds for local charities and organizations while bringing together a delicious collection of breweries.

June

THE BEST LITTLE BREWFEST IN TEXAS

126 W. Church St., Lewisville, TX 75057; bestlittlebrewfestintexas.com

Yet another Dallas-area beer festival, the Best Little Brewfest in Texas is working hard to separate themselves from the pack. This nonprofit event supports the Cloud 9 Charities, which in turn support many different organizations such as the Alzheimer Association and Teen Suicide Prevention. The event not only supports great local craft beer, but they also bring in big-name local bands along with local chefs and food trucks to make the festival complete. There is nothing better than sampling a collection of craft beer while supporting a great cause.

HOUSTON BEER FESTIVAL

Hermann Square Park, 513 Walker St., Houston, TX 77002; houstonbeerfestival.com

Quite arguably the largest beer festival in the state, the Houston Beer Festival is more like a giant party. The festival mixes national touring bands, tons of beer, and food vendors all on the steps of Houston city hall. It can seem like a frat party at times because it brings in a younger crowd, but if you can look past the loud music and beer pong tables you will find that they bring in all of the big names in the craft beer industry. The festival kicks off every year in June, which is usually one of the hottest months in Texas. There is nothing better than cooling down with a cold beer, but don't forget to hydrate.

September

TEXAS CRAFT BREWERS FESTIVAL

Fiesta Gardens, 2101 Jesse E. Segovia St., Austin, TX 78702; texascraftbrewersfestival.org

The Texas Craft Brewers Festival is a festival dedicated solely to Texas craft beer. If it is brewed outside of the Lone Star State, then you won't find it here. It is put together by the Young Men's Business League and the Texas Craft Brewers Guild. The guild is made up of people who work in the Texas brewing industry. Its mission is to promote Texas craft beer while educating the public about the qualities and attributes of craft beer and advancing the common interest of Texas craft brewers. The event brings in a large number of attendees looking to check out the latest offerings from breweries and to hear about the new breweries just getting established. Throw in live music and delicious food from local restaurants, and you have one of the best festivals in the state putting a spotlight on the great beer made in Texas.

BREWMASTERS CRAFT BEER FESTIVAL
Moody Gardens, 1 Hope Blvd., Galveston, TX 77554; (713) 557-5732; brewmastersbeerfest .com

The Brewmasters Craft Beer Festival is one of the older festivals in the state and lasts an entire weekend. The event kicks off every year on Labor Day weekend and takes over the grounds of Moody Gardens in Galveston. The festival is broken down into different events, starting on Friday with the BrewLicious Brews & Foods Pairing, which combines a delicious upscale culinary experience with great craft beers. Saturday plays host to the main event, the BrewHaHa Grand Tasting, which gives attendees the opportunity to sample over 400 craft beers from around the globe. I'd say if there is one great way to spend Labor Day weekend it would be attending this great beer festival.

October

FLYING SAUCER BEERFEAST
Flying Saucer, Ft. Worth; (817) 336-7470, Austin; (512) 454-8200, Garland; (972) 226-0725, Sugarland; 281-242-7468; beerknurd.com

The Flying Saucer Draught Emporium has long been a craft beer destination for beer lovers, and now they have a festival at a few of their locations across the state. The BeerFeast features forty brewers with over 60 beers for attendees to sample and the event always brings in large numbers. Many of the people that attend are new to craft beer, and the event offers a great chance to try something new. Hopefully it will create new Beerknurds who will one day earn a place for their own brass plate on the wall of their local Flying Saucer.

SUN CITY CRAFT BEER FESTIVAL

Downtown El Paso, El Paso, TX; suncitycraftbeerfest.com

El Paso is a rather new territory when it comes to craft beer, but the team behind the Sun City Craft Beer Festival is working hard to bring exposure to the demand for craft beer in west Texas. They bring out a very strong lineup of both regional and national breweries so residents can learn and sample new beers. It is a great event that features food trucks that alter their menu to pair with beers, live music to entertain the crowd, and art from local artists to bring together the whole community in one great event.

SAN ANTONIO BEER FESTIVAL

Maverick Park, 1000 Broadway St., San Antonio, TX 78205; sanantoniobeerfestival.com

The San Antonio Beer Festival brings out large numbers every year for their festival. Leading up to the festival, organizers put together a ton of great events to bring awareness to craft beer and promote the festival. The festival is the kind of event you can spend all day at, and the organizers even encourage attendees to bring blankets or lawn chairs. Attendees have the opportunity to sample from over 250 beers from breweries across the country. Plenty of San Antonio's popular food trucks are on hand to keep the attendees fed, and live music plays all day long to round out the fun and festive event. The San Antonio Beer Festival does a great job of supporting craft beer and bringing local awareness to the art behind the beer.

BYOB: Brew Your Own Beer

Clone Beer Recipes

Homebrewing is one of the greatest ways to expand your understanding of beer and can be as easy as brewing with cans of extract or as advanced as brewing all-grain batches. Homebrewing goes back thousands of years, and in Texas you can brew at your own home for personal use. I highly suggest visiting your local homebrew store as well as reading up online about homebrewing, and you will be creating great beers in no time. Here are a few great recipes to get you started on your new homebrewing hobby.

RANGER CREEK MESQUITE SMOKED PORTER HOMEBREW RECIPE

Ranger Creek's Mesquite Smoked Porter is a robust porter smoked with Texas mesquite.

OG 1.060–1.064

FG 1.010–1.012

IBU 20

SRM 40+

Maris Otter: 54%
Smoked Maris Otter: 29%
Crystal 60 L: 11%
Chocolate: 3.5%
Black: 2.5%
UK Fuggles
German Tettnan
English ale yeast

Batch size: 5.5 US gal

Boil length: 60 min

Mash: 156°F, 60 min

Fermentation: 67–69°F

COURTESY OF RANGER CREEK BREWING & DISTILLING IN SAN ANTONIO

RANGER CREEK OPA HOMEBREW RECIPE

Ranger Creek's OPA is an American pale ale with oats.

OG 1.054–1.057

FG 1.010–1.012

IBU 35

SRM 9

> *2 Row: 77%*
> *Crystal 60 L: 7%*
> *Oat malt: 16%*
> *Centennial hops*
> *Citra hops*
> *English ale yeast*

Batch size: 5.5 US gal

Boil length: 60 min

Mash: 152°F, 60 min

Fermentation: 68°F

COURTESY OF RANGER CREEK BREWING & DISTILLING IN SAN ANTONIO

BELGIAN WHITE BEER

This is take on a traditional Belgian-style white beer for all grain brewing.

OG 1.056

FG 1.010

IBU 9

SRM 3.6

> *2 Row: 77%*
> *Crystal 60 L: 7%*
> *Oat malt: 16%*
> *Centennial hops*
> *Citra hops*
> *English ale yeast*

Batch size: 5 US gal

Boil length: 60 min

Mash: 155°F, 60 min

Fermentation: 68°F

COURTESY OF FORREST ROGNESS OF ROGNESS BREWING COMPANY IN AUSTIN

BLACK SKY STOUT PORTER

This beer is in the style of a historical strong porter.

35 IBUs, 6% ABV

27 lbs Rahr Pale Ale Malt
13 lbs Gambrinus Munich 10 L
5 lbs 4 oz Briess Special Roast
3 lbs Briess Cara 60 L
2 lbs 4 oz Weyermann CaraFa Special II
12 oz Castle Special B
12 oz crisp roasted barley
7 lbs 8 oz flaked or rolled oats
3 lbs blackstrap molasses
45 AAU German Magnum
21 AAU UK Goldings
English ale yeast (preferably White Labs 007)

Batch size: 31 US gal

Mash for 60 minutes at 154°F.

Bring to a boil and add the Magnum hops.

Forty minutes later add UK Goldings and molasses, and add kettle finings and yeast nutrient of your choice.

After another 20 minutes turn off the heat and cool wort.

Once transferred for fermentation, add yeast.

Start fermentation at 66°F, and 2–3 days after fermentation starts let the temperature rise to 72 degrees; five days later cool down to 30–40 degrees. If bottling, do so in one more week; if kegging, wait two weeks.

COURTESY OF ANDREW HUERTER OF BRAINDEAD BREWING IN DALLAS

BRIGHTSIDE BELGIAN WHITE

This beer is in the style of a traditional Belgian-style white ale.

10 IBUs, 4.8% ABV

25 lbs Rahr Premium Pilsner Malt
10 lbs raw soft red wheat
6 lbs 5 oz Rahr White Wheat Malt
2 lbs flaked or rolled oats

13.4 AAU German Magnum @ 60 minutes
6 oz dried orange peel
3 oz coarsely ground coriander
1.5 oz chopped candied ginger

White Labs 530 & 500 or Wyeast 1214 & 3787

Batch size: 31 US gal

Boil the raw wheat for about 20 minutes, then add to the mash with the rest of the grains for a target temperature of 152°F for 60 minutes.

Once the wort is collected, bring to a boil and add the Magnum hops.

After boiling for 40 minutes, add a yeast nutrient of your choice.

Twenty minutes later add the orange peel, coriander, and ginger. Turn off the heat and cool the wort.

Add either yeast blend in a 1:1 ratio and begin fermentation at about 66°F. Two days after fermentation starts, let the temperature rise to 76 degrees. Five days later cool to 40 degrees. After another seven days, keg or bottle.

COURTESY OF ANDREW HUERTER OF BRAINDEAD BREWING IN DALLAS

In the Kitchen

For a long time people usually only thought of cooking and pairing foods with wine, but beer can be used the same way. Forget about the snobbery that can sometimes come with wine and food. At the end of the day, any dish can pair with whatever you like. Beer is also a great cooking ingredient, and here are just a few examples of some great dishes you can make with beer. I encourage you to explore using different styles of beer in dishes and see what you can come up with.

Food Recipes

SHINER CHILI CHEESE BREAD

There is nothing better on a cold day in Texas than chili, and this Shiner Chili Cheese Bread is a great complement to a hot bowl or just great for a cheese snack.

> *3 cups flour*
> *3 teaspoons baking powder*
> *1 teaspoon salt*
> *¼ teaspoon sugar*
> *1 teaspoon dried chili flakes (more if you like it really spicy)*
> *1 cup shredded cheddar cheese (less 3 tablespoons to sprinkle on top of loaf)*
> *12 oz bottle of Shiner (or your favorite Texas beer)*
> *½ cup melted butter*

Preheat oven to 375°F. In a large mixing bowl, sift all the dry ingredients. Then add chili flakes and cheese. Then stir in the beer and butter.

Combine until all is incorporated. Batter will be slightly lumpy and sticky. Pour all the batter into a parchment-lined loaf pan.

Sprinkle the 3 reserved tablespoons of cheese on top of loaf.

Bake for 45 minutes to 1 hour.

When a toothpick inserted comes out dry, the loaf is done.

Let cool. Slice and slather with some good butter or better yet make yourself a pot of Texas chili to dunk a slice in.

COURTESY OF KRISTINA WOLTER, FOUNDER OF GIRL GONE GRITS BLOG IN AUSTIN

HOT STOUT MEXICAN

This is a delicious and decadent chocolate cake that is brewed with a chocolate stout and topped with an espresso cream. Pair this great dessert with a bottle of Guadalupe Brewing's Chocolate Stout to really complete the experience.

The Cake

- 1½ cups unsweetened cocoa powder plus more for dusting
- 2 cups Guadalupe Chocolate Stout
- 2 cups (32 tablespoons) Kerrygold unsalted butter (NOTE: the brand of butter DOES significantly affect taste & texture . . . substitute at your own risk.)
- 4 cups flour (50/50 whole wheat/all purpose works great)
- 4 cups sugar
- 3 teaspoons baking soda
- 1½ teaspoons salt
- 4 large eggs
- 1⅓ cups sour cream

Preheat oven to 350°F. Grease four 9-inch round cake pans with coconut oil spray, and dust them with cocoa powder. (A tall, beautiful cake only requires 3 layers, but it's great to have the extra handy in case mistakes happen: mistakes like dropping a hot pan of cake coming out of the oven after one has polished off the bomber while baking.)

In a large saucepan, bring the stout and the butter to a simmer over medium heat. Add the measured cocoa powder and whisk until smooth. Set the mixture aside, whisking occasionally as the rest of the cake batter is prepared.

In a large bowl, whisk the flour, sugar, baking soda, and salt to combine. In a separate bowl, beat the eggs and sour cream with a handheld mixer. Add the cooled cocoa mixture to the egg mixture; beat to combine. At slow mixer speed, add in increments of the flour mixture until combined.

Fill cake pans approximately ¾ full. Bake until toothpick comes out clean, approximately 23–25 minutes. Cool slightly in the pans, level off the tops with a long knife, then remove to parchment-covered wire racks to cool completely.

The Topping
>   ½ cup water
>   4 tablespoons superfinely ground espresso
>   2 cups cold heavy cream
>   ⅔ cup sugar

Boil the water. Whisk in espresso. Set aside.

Beat cream and sugar at high speed with handheld mixer until stiff peaks form. Fold the steeped espresso into the whipped cream. Refrigerate until ready to assemble the layers of cake.

The Garnish
>   4–6 oz baking chocolate (Trader Joe's Bittersweet with Almonds is a great choice—
>   shave it on the large gauge side of a box grater.)
>   3–4 tablespoons ground cinnamon
>   1–2 cups chopped pecans, if desired

Spread a generous amount of whipped coffee topping on top of the base layer of cake. Sprinkle with chocolate and cinnamon. Stack a second layer of cake upon the base; repeat the whipped cream, chocolate, and cinnamon. Add the crown layer of cake; spread with whipped cream. Smooth remainder of the whipped coffee cream around the sides of the cake; top with remaining chocolate, cinnamon, and pecans (if desired).

COURTESY OF CHRISTINE MOORE, SAN ANTONIO

PINE BELT PALE ALE DOUGHNUTS WITH CHOCOLATE STOUT GLAZE

While doughnuts are already delicious, these treats are souped up with Pine Belt Pale Ale and the glaze gets a boozy boost from Buried Hatchet Stout.

Doughnuts

1 cup sugar
4 teaspoons baking powder
1½ teaspoons salt
½ teaspoon nutmeg
⅛ teaspoon ground cloves
½ teaspoon ground cinnamon
2 eggs
¾ cup Southern Star Pine Belt Pale Ale
¼ cup unsalted butter, melted
4 cups flour (plus a little more if dough is sticky)
Oil (for frying)
Chopped walnuts (optional)

1. Using a stand mixer, mix the sugar, baking powder, salt and spices

2. Add eggs, beer, and melted butter; beat on medium until incorporated.

3. Stop mixer, add 3 cups of flour and beat until blended, only speeding up when most of the flour is incorporated. Add last cup of flour and beat until incorporated. The dough should be soft and sticky but firm enough to handle. If necessary, add 1 tablespoon up to ½ cup of flour to reach consistency.

4. Move from mixer bowl into an oiled bowl and cover and chill for 1 hour in the refrigerator.

5. After 1 hour, remove dough from fridge and begin heating oil to 350°F. (A deep fryer is preferred but it can be done in pan; just bring oil up to 1-inch deep.)

6. Divide dough in two, and roll first half on a floured surface to about ½-inch thick. Cut out circles using doughnut cutter or large biscuit/cookie cutter. Repeat until all dough is used. (Optional to cut out center)

7. Gently drop doughnuts in batches into the hot oil. Flip them over after 1–2 minutes or until golden brown on each side. You will notice they will puff up—a good indication to remind you to flip the doughnuts.

8. Remove from the oil and set on paper towels. Let sit for 5 minutes, then dip/dunk into the glaze and set on cooling rack to allow glaze to set; if desired, during this time, you can add walnuts while allowing doughnuts to rest.

Chocolate Stout Glaze

2 cups confectioners' sugar
¼ cup Southern Star Buried Hatchet Stout
½ teaspoon chocolate extract
½ teaspoon vanilla extract

1. Place confectioners' sugar in a small bowl, then add beer and stir until incorporated into a sticky slurry.

2. Add extracts to bowl and stir. Let sit until ready to use.

COURTESY OF JONATHAN PARKER, BRITTLE BREAKERS IN HOUSTON

BRANCHLINE EVIL OWL CROCK POT BEEF STEW

If you are looking for a delicious dish for a cold day or if you are in the mood for something hearty, this is a quick and easy recipe for beef stew made with San Antonio's own Evil Owl from Branchline Brewing Company.

1 lb beef stew chunks
Flour for coating beef
Salt
Pepper
Olive or vegetable oil for browning beef
3 parsnips (cut)
½ bag of baby carrots
1½ lb red potatoes
1 can Branchline Evil Owl Amber
2 bay leaves
Garlic powder, onion powder, and salt/pepper to taste

Prep beef chunks by coating in flour seasoned with salt and pepper (to taste). Brown in a pan on medium-high heat with a small amount of olive or vegetable oil. Combine browned beef with all ingredients in a crock pot and pour Evil Owl on top. Stir well. Cook on low setting for 6–8 hours. Serve and enjoy with a glass of Evil Owl Amber!

COURTESY OF PAUL FORD, HEAD BREWER OF BRANCHLINE BREWING COMPANY IN SAN ANTONIO

DEEP ELLUM CHERRY CHOCOLATE DOUBLE BROWN STOUT BROWNIES

This is for all of you chocoholics that want a rich and sweet treat to pair with a deli-cious velvety stout. These delectable brownies are made with Cherry Chocolate Double Brown Stout from Deep Ellum Brewing in Dallas.

1 stick unsalted butter
4 ounces semisweet chocolate
1 cup granulated sugar
2 eggs
2 egg yolks
¾ cup all-purpose flour
¼ teaspoon of salt
½ cup Deep Ellum Cherry Chocolate Double Brown Stout
¾ cup dried cherries

Preheat the oven to 325°F. Coat an 8x8 baking pan, then dust the inside with flour or line with parchment paper so the brownies won't stick to the sides.

In a large saucepan, melt the stick of butter on low heat. Add the 4 ounces of choco-late to the butter liquid, stirring often until the mixture is completely blended and creamy. Remove the saucepan from the heat and let it cool to lukewarm.

In a mixing bowl, combine sugar, eggs, yolks, and Cherry Chocolate Double Brown Stout until smooth.

In a different bowl, sift the flour with the salt.

Add the stout mixture, flour, and cherries to the saucepan, alternating each until the brownie batter is blended.

Pour the batter into the greased pan and bake for 45–50 minutes, checking with a toothpick until it comes out clean.

COURTESY OF DANIELLE GOFF, OF BEER DRINKERS SOCIETY IN FORT WORTH

BEER CHILI

This recipe is a little advanced, but if you put in the work you will get a delicious and spicy chili that will definitely light up your taste buds.

Mole ingredients:
2 garlic bulbs
1 red bell pepper
1 yellow bell pepper
1 orange bell pepper
2 poblanos
2 jalapenos
2 serranos
1 habanero
Drizzle of olive oil
¼ cup beef broth
½ bunch cilantro
5 oz sundried tomatoes

Dry Spices (to taste):
Salt
Pepper
Coriander
Chili powder

Chili ingredients:
5 lbs beef stew meat
2 large yellow onions
2 tablespoons olive oil
4 12 oz bottles/cans of your favorite craft wheat beer
32 oz can crushed tomatoes
15 oz can tomato sauce
(optional):
1 15 oz can black beans
1 15 oz can pinto beans
1 15 oz can kidney beans
32 oz beef broth

MOLE: (IDEALLY MADE THE DAY BEFORE)

Step 1. Remove excess skin from garlic bulbs, wrap in foil and place in 450°F oven (45 minutes)

Step 2. Drizzle olive oil and roast all peppers in 450-degree oven until evenly charred (may have to turn peppers over). Caution: mixture can smoke a lot if the oil burns. You can place the peppers in the oven 30 minutes after the garlic.

Step 3. Place peppers in plastic storage bag for 10 minutes or until cool enough to handle. Once cool, separate all seeds from peppers and squeeze softened garlic cloves from bulb.

Step 4. Place all peppers and garlic in blender and add ¼ cup beef broth, dry spices (to taste), half bunch cilantro, and 5 oz sundried tomatoes. Adjust broth volume until puree is achieved. Set aside in fridge (min. 2 hours, overnight is best).

CHILI:

Step 1. Cut meat into roughly ¼ inch cubes. Brown meat in saute pan and set aside.

Step 2. Chop 2 onions

Step 3. Add 2 tablespoons olive oil to pot on medium heat; add onions and saute until translucent.

Step 4. Add 4 bottles beer and reduce on low heat to half volume.

Step 5. To onion beer reduction add beef, crushed tomatoes, tomato sauce, and mole (make sure to leave room in pot for beans later, if using). On medium heat cook for 2 hours minimum.

Step 6. After 2 hours add beans and beef broth to adjust liquid; if too thick, cook another 2 hours. Cook longer if beef isn't to desired tenderness . . .

COURTESY OF SAMEER SIDDIQUI, OF RICKSHAW STOP IN SAN ANTONIO

Appendix:
Beer Lover's Pick List

Index